THE ITALIAN PANTRY

Also by Anna Del Conte

Portrait of Pasta
Italian Cookery
Pasta Perfect
Gastronomy of Italy

The

Italian Pantry

ANNA DEL CONTE

1817

HARPER & ROW, PUBLISHERS, New York

GRAND RAPIDS, PHILADELPHIA, ST. LOUIS, SAN FRANCISCO

LONDON, SINGAPORE, SYDNEY, TOKYO, TORONTO

FIRST EDITION

Designed by Barbara DuPree Knowles

LIBRARY OF CONGRESS CATALOGING-IN-PUBLICATION DATA

Del Conte, Anna.
    The Italian pantry/Anna Del Conte.—1st ed.
        p.   cm.
    Includes index.
    ISBN 0-06-016116-7
    1. Cookery, Italian.   I. Title.
TX723.D395   1990
641.5945—dc20   89-33734

90 91 92 93 94   DT/RRD   10 9 8 7 6 5 4 3 2 1

For my children
Paul, Guy and *Julia*
my sternest critics
and most faithful supporters

CONTENTS

ACKNOWLEDGMENTS

I am deeply grateful to the following persons, who in one way or another have contributed to this book: Massimo Alberini; Carlo Saverio Balsamo; Suzy Benghiat; Avvocato Giorgio Bernardini; Romana Bosco; Alberto Camisa of Fratelli Camisa; Giuseppe Corradi of Negroni; Camillo and Myriam de' Castiglioni; Ernesta Del Conte; Guido and Bianca Del Conte; Marco Del Conte; Michi di San Giuliano; Ugo Falavigna of the Pasticceria Torino in Parma; Vettor and Ferdinanda Galletti di San Cataldo; Geraldine Gartrell; David Gleaves of Wandsworth Wine Cellars; Caroline Hobhouse; Thérèse Ingram; Dottor Giuseppe Manfredi of Galbani; Lalla Morasutti; Betsy Newell; John Parmigiani of Parmigiani & Son; Savina Ruggero; Gigi and Maria Carla Sidoli; Giancarlo Spaggiani of the Italian Trade Centre; Rita Stancescu; Maurizio Vaglia of the Casa del Tartufo e del Fungo in Milan; Lella Vianelli.

My special thanks go to my editor at Harper & Row, Susan Friedland, and to Susan Derecskey, the copy editor, for her painstaking scrutiny of the manuscript. But my deepest thanks are for Oliver, my beloved husband and devoted word processor, who shared with me the pains and pleasures of writing this book.

INTRODUCTION

Some of my earliest memories are of watching our cook Maria at work in the kitchen. As she worked, Maria sang the Communist songs that were forbidden during the Fascist years, while I watched, fascinated by the speed with which she filled the ravioli or by her dexterity in flicking potato gnocchi down the tines of a fork. Listening to her discuss with my mother what to do with the mountain of porcini on the kitchen table or watching her point out how the beautiful slices of prosciutto di Parma had just the right amount of fat around them laid the foundations of my knowledge of cooking.

So when, years later, I had to cook for my family in London, I knew by instinct—or so it seemed—when to stop adding flour to the pasta, what a battuto should be like or when and how you add the stock to the rice in making a risotto. The sad part of this story is that when I arrived in London, in the early 1950s, the culinary scene was so bleak that I had little chance to practice my skills. The only vegetables in the shops were root vegetables, plus some limp lettuce, and cabbage and cabbage and cabbage. In my resolve to make the best of the situation, the basic instincts and the thriftiness of an Italian asserted themselves. I bought horsemeat from the butcher in Fulham Road, and with this I made polpette or polpettoni which I finished off in a tomato sauce or in an egg and lemon sauce like a fricassee. Lungs and hearts, which the English gave to their pets, were mixed with a few dried porcini which I brought back from Italy, and transformed into a tasty ragù. My friends, little knowing, roundly declared that they would never touch horsemeat or variety meats, and then tucked in with great enthusiasm.

Slowly through the years the gastronomic scene has improved, so that nowadays you can find everything in most British towns and it is quite easy to produce un pranzo all' Italiana. The only difficulty is finding first-class seasonal ingredients, which are, without doubt, the prime secret of an Italian kitchen.

The characteristics of Italian cooking

Italian cooking at its best is made up of traditional dishes to which a cook has given his or her own imprint. It is a cuisine of few surprises but of deep satisfaction, of few innovations but of innumerable variations. Italian cooking is basically home cooking of great simplicity, where the only important elements are good ingredients and love.

The best Italian cooking consists of dishes that enhance the flavor of the ingredients from which they are made, never swamping them with flamboyant side effects such as sauces and garnish. People sometimes comment on the lack of sauces in an Italian meal, but in fact food is usually served in the juice in which it has cooked, this being its sauce. Separate sauces are used to dress plain foods such as pasta or polenta, which in turn become an intrinsic part of the sauce. Sauces are sometimes added to give the main ingredient a different dimension, but the respect for each ingredient is always there, a respect it earns because of its excellence. Fish, for instance, is usually grilled or boiled; no need to disguise its flavor in a pool of cream sauce. A few drops of the best olive oil are all that is needed.

Fish, vegetables and cereals are the mainstays of this healthy cooking. Meat, traditionally, comes second in most regions; pork, a poor man's meat, being the most popular. The Italians have mastered the best ways of getting the most out of it by making prosciutto, sausage and salami of all kinds.

The importance of the seasons

Last year I visited the Renaissance cities of northern Italy in order to plan a gastronomic tour. On the last day I was in Mantua, and before leaving I went to the market in the Piazza delle Erbe to buy my favorite vegetables, so that I could cook them that evening when I got back to my mother's house in Milan. It was a perfect September morning, sunny and warm, yet cool enough to enjoy strolling among the vegetable stalls.

My first stop was to buy some free-range eggs from a man who was very insistent that I should also buy an anitra muta, a live Muscovy duck. We discussed its merits at length, and it seemed that the chief point in its favor was that it was just the right time of year for buying such a duck. In various cages there were small chicks, bigger chicks, chickens, guinea hens, ducks and geese, plus a lonely young white rabbit trapped in a tiny cage for whom even I, the unsentimental Latin, felt very sorry. I was reminded of the travel writer Colin Thubron who, when in a food market in Canton, was able to assuage his sorrow at the fate of the animals there by buying an owl—regarded as a delicacy and therefore commanding a high price—with the sole object of setting the poor creature free. But a tame rabbit would hardly have found its freedom in the middle of Mantua, nor could I arrive in Milan with a white rabbit for my mother. So on I went to the fruit and vegetable stalls.

There were still some pesche da vigna (literally, vine peaches), small and scented, with a beautiful greenish-pink bloom, as well as some prugne a fiaschetto (flask-shaped plums). The grapes were perfect and kept me happy during the journey back to Milan. The season's first pumpkins were on display, but a group of local women judged they were not yet ready. They decided to postpone the making of their tortelli di zucca for which, partly because of the excellence of the local pumpkins, Mantua is famous. I next bought a couple of pounds of tomatoes and of large meaty yellow peppers, both being in full season, to make a peperonata. Then, giving way to the acquisitive passion that grips me in such a market, and without really thinking, I asked a stall-holder if she had some fennel. "Finocchi?!? Ma, signora, finocchi in settembre!" and she shook her head, looking at me with a mixture of surprise and pity. For a moment I had forgotten where I was: in Italy they still have seasons!

Fruit and vegetables, fish and farm cheeses are sold when they are at their best, especially in provincial towns. I remember the Easters spent at our apartment in Venice, when I would go to the market at Rialto to buy the first small artichokes, pale green and so young that we ate them raw, dipped in oil. There were tender small peas from Torcello for the risi e bisi (rice with peas) and an incredible variety of local salads, both cultivated and wild. Even in Milan there is the joy of witnessing the first appearance of the various fruits: small fragoline di bosco (wild strawberries), cherries, Japanese medlars, followed by apricots and peaches, the real glories of full summer. I still make a wish when I eat the first fruit of the year, an old superstition. And I still use up the past year's dried beans, lentils and chickpeas to make way for the new crop, which reaches the shops at the beginning of autumn.

The use of seasonal foods, such an important element in the cooking of Italy, can—to a lesser extent—be practiced elsewhere. When November comes, for instance, forget the all-year-round oranges and buy the last grapes and the first chestnuts. Fennel can replace the tired zucchini, and it will be the perfect accompaniment to any roast. Make your dishes relate to the time and place where they are cooked.

- -

The Italian meal

At the end of many of the recipes I have added suggestions about what should precede or follow the dish. My suggestions usually assume that you will be serving a first and a second course, which is the traditional Italian meal, these two courses being equal in importance and quantity. At lunch Italians like to start with a dish of pasta or risotto, while at dinner they usually start with a soup. The secondo piatto is traditionally meat or fish, accompanied by only one vegetable and/or followed by a salad. At the end of the meal there is fruit, since puddings and cakes are only eaten on special occasions.

My suggestions are based on the Italian way of constructing a meal, in which the courses complement each other and have flavors that are in harmony. In other words, the meal is conceived as a whole. For instance, if you want fish as a second course, start with a first course that contains fish, such as the Fish Soup on page 57. A delicate soup or a light risotto should be followed by an elegant dish of veal or chicken, while an earthy stew must be preceded by a primo with a strong flavor, such as a robust dish of pasta. The best dishes in the Italian cuisine are first courses, with the magnificent array of pasta dishes, risottos, gnocchi and so on. So if, like me, you love these primi but do not always fancy a full meal, follow the primo with a vegetable dish; you will find many good recipes to choose from in this book.

Even if you have decided what your dinner is to consist of, you should be prepared to alter the menu according to what you find when you go shopping. Do not stick to your plan for sea bass if the sea bass looks tired; buy the fresher-looking sole instead. If a lovely duck takes your fancy, the menu can be changed so that it replaces the veal chops on your list. When I think about what to prepare for dinner, whether it is just for the family or for a small group of friends, my first thought is of the best vegetables in season at the time. It may be peppers for a pasta al forno or artichokes for a risotto. The vegetables are the clue to what follows, and if I am thinking of them as an accompaniment, my favorite way of cooking them determines the meat or fish I buy. I construct my meal around them. You will find shopping much more stimulating and creative when it is done on the basis of what looks good in the shops rather than from that strict disciplinarian, the shopping list.

About this book

In order to pay due respect to the fundamental importance of the ingredients in Italian cooking, I have arranged this book by ingredients. Each chapter is dedicated to an ingredient or group of related ingredients. The ones I have chosen are those which feature most prominently in Italian cooking, the ones Italians use with particular success. In each chapter you will find recipes in which the featured ingredient is either the main ingredient or the one that gives the dish its particular character. In the index at the back of the book recipes are listed in all the usual ways, so that you can easily locate the recipe you are looking for.

To allay any suspicions that the real secret of Italian cooking is to buy your ingredients in Italy, I must make it clear that in testing the recipes in this book I have always used ingredients that I have bought in England or America.

Some of the recipes are ones that I have created, some come from my family's or my friends' recipe books and others are derived from the inexhaustible store of local Italian cooking tradition. Most of the dishes are simple and unpretentious, a few are more complicated and elegant, but all of them are dishes that I associate with homes rather than restaurants. Restaurant dishes may dazzle in their theatrical presentation and puzzle by their complexity; home cooking should never do that, or it becomes vulgar. I have been aware of this difference since childhood, when my mother used to disapprove of the dinners she was served at a certain friend's house, calling them "un pranzo da ristorante."

What I hope I achieved in this book is to bring into focus the basic characteristics of Italian cooking. After that, I hope my recipes will inspire you to embellish them, following your own creativity, inspiration and palate. Once you get the feeling of what you should do to make your food taste really Italian, I'm afraid you will hardly need me any more!

THE ITALIAN PANTRY

The Italian Pantry

Sometimes, when I look into the pantry in my London home, I catch myself gazing into the past . . . into the pantry of the house we lived in, in the country in Emilia, when I was a child. Jar after jar of vegetables preserved in oil, fruits preserved in spirits, sacks of lentils and borlotti beans, flour for making pasta and, between the wire baskets that were always full of fresh eggs, prosciutto and salami hanging from the ceiling like stalactites. For, although this was during the war, we were living on the prodigal riches of the land, at a time when there was virtually no way of transporting these riches to the empty pantries in the cities.

In the darkest corner stood a few unlabeled bottles filled with the special, and illicit, grappa that had been distilled from vine tendrils by Signora Crocioni, the elderly owner of the house. But then, on one memorable occasion, the still, which was in the kitchen, blew up with a great explosion. Wilma, the maid, ran out of the house, screaming, "I Tedeschi hanno tirato una bomba!" (the Germans have thrown a bomb) while the Tedeschi themselves, who were quartered in the villa, rushed to their arms fearing a Partisan attack. Soon enough, old Signora Crocioni was found in the kitchen, together with her equally old cook, sadly contemplating the end of their clandestine activities, as a lake of the precious liquid crept slowly toward them over the stone floor.

Today's typical Italian pantry would contain pasta in five or six different shapes: spaghetti, tagliatelle, fusilli, penne, bucatini, and pastina and ditalini for soups. However, unless you eat a lot of pasta it is best to stick to fewer shapes, otherwise you will find your cupboard full of packs containing handfuls of different kinds of pasta that you cannot mix. Italian rice for risotto, coarse cornmeal for polenta, dried beans, lentils and chickpeas are also necessary standbys. I usually keep some dried fava beans, which are not so easy to come by, for my husband's favorite puree. For myself, for a quick bite, I like a salami hanging from a hook, ready at hand with no cooking to be done. Cans of peeled tomatoes and of tomato paste, of cannellini beans, tuna and anchovy fillets, a full bottle of extra-virgin olive oil and one of red wine vinegar are also essential items to have in reserve. For me, balsamic vinegar is another must.

In the refrigerator you will need a mozzarella or two (unless you have easy access to fresh), a wedge of crumbly parmesan wrapped in cheesecloth, some olives kept in a jar covered with olive oil flavored with garlic and chili, a tube of anchovy paste, a jar of capers and a few pine nuts (nuts keep longer in the fridge and longer still in the freezer) for pesto or for various stuffings. I also keep some almonds in the fridge or freezer, as they are my favorite ingredient for puddings, cakes and biscuits, as well as some candied peel, mixed with sugar, in an airtight jar.

In my freezer you will always find a few small packets of pancetta and salt pork. When I go to my favorite Italian shop I buy a pound of each and divide them up into portions suitable for one recipe, then put them in the freezer. I also keep some Italian sausage in the freezer.

Whenever I come across some really fresh ricotta I buy a pound, some to eat as it is, some to use in cooking. But I never buy more than I can use within the next 24 hours, as it very quickly acquires la punta di amaro (a touch of bitterness). And if, as I do, you like to make your own pasta, which is a totally different thing from the fresh pasta you can buy, you will also need to keep a large bag of flour in your Italian pantry.

Last, but certainly not least, an Italian fridge will contain unsalted butter, the only butter Italians use for cooking. I have, in fact, used unsalted butter in all the recipes in this book.

Basic preparations

Certain basic pantry/refrigerator ingredients you must prepare. Stock can be made whenever you have time and then stored in small quantities in the freezer. It will keep in the refrigerator for about 3 days, after which it must be brought back to the boil and boiled for at least 5 minutes. Tomato sauce (see pages 112–113) can also be made whenever convenient and stored in the freezer. The Béchamel Sauce and the Battuto must be made just before you need them, but it is likely you will have all the ingredients on hand.

Brodo di gallina o di carne
CHICKEN OR MEAT STOCK · MAKES 1½ TO 2 QUARTS

A good stock depends entirely on the quality of the meat used. Chicken stock should be light and delicate, but not bland. A fowl gives a tastier and less fatty stock, which is what you want, but fowl are hard to come by nowadays, so that you may have to buy a roasting chicken. You can also use fresh necks, backs, and wings or parts and scraps you've saved in your freezer. When I make stock, I serve the chicken or the meat itself, hot, for a family meal, surrounded by the vegetables and some potatoes which I boil separately. As dressing I use, simply, the best olive oil.

Remove and discard the fat you may find in the cavity of the chicken. Wash the chicken and put it in a large pot with a selection of vegetables—a carrot, an onion stuck with 1 or 2 cloves, a leek, 2 or 3 celery stalks, 1 ripe tomato, parsley leaves and stalks, 1 garlic clove and a bay leaf. I also add 2 whole cardamom pods which give the stock a very flowery taste. Add enough cold water to cover everything by about 2 inches and cook over very low heat until the chicken is done, skimming the foam as it rises. The surface of the liquid should just be broken by an occasional bubble. The best stock is made from liquid cooking at 185°F. It will take 1 to 1½ hours if you are cooking a roasting chicken, 2 to 2½ hours or more for a fowl. Halfway through the cooking add about 1 teaspoonful of salt. (It is always better to add very little salt to stock, in case you want to reduce it. If you add what might seem the right amount of salt in the first place, the reduced stock would be much too salty.) Remove the chicken and strain the stock. Cool and place in refrigerator or freezer.

For a good meat stock, buy about 2 pounds of a selection of beef and veal pieces and scraps, with some bones attached. You can add 2 or 3 chicken wings, if you like, or any other bits you have in the freezer, except pork or lamb. Add the vegetables and herbs (the same as for chicken stock, except for the cardamom), and simmer for at least 3 hours, as instructed in the previous paragraph. Strain, leave to cool and store in the refrigerator or freezer.

Brodo vegetale

VEGETABLE STOCK · MAKES ABOUT 1½ QUARTS

3 celery stalks
3 carrots
2 leeks, both white and green
   parts
1 onion stuck with 1 clove
2 tomatoes
1 zucchini
a handful of beet greens or
   lettuce leaves
2 garlic cloves
a large handful of fresh parsley,
   leaves and stems
a very small quantity of fresh
   herbs, whatever is available
2 bay leaves
5 to 6 peppercorns
salt

A good vegetable stock is just as useful a standby in the kitchen as meat stock. It can be used for many vegetable risottos, for stewing vegetables, for adding to soups and sauces and even for drinking on its own when you feel the need for something simple and refreshing. Once upon a time, when the seasons were observed, the vegetables used were those in season. Now that everything is "in season" all year round, use the freshest vegetables, preferably local, as they have more flavor. Do not use cabbage as that would give the stock the wrong taste. The indispensable vegetables are onion, celery, carrot and leek; I have used an orthodox selection in this recipe.

1 Peel and wash the vegetables and cut them into pieces. Put them in a large stockpot with the herbs and the peppercorns. Cover with 2 quarts cold water, add half a tablespoon of salt and bring to the boil.

2 Simmer slowly for at least 2 hours. Strain and leave to cool, then place in the refrigerator or freezer.

Salsa besciamella

BECHAMEL SAUCE · MAKES ABOUT 1¾ CUPS

Béchamel is out of favor at present, but it can never be banned from the kitchen because it is the basis of so many other sauces. For this reason it is important to be able to make a good smooth béchamel. I find it best to cook béchamel for at least fifteen minutes so as to kill the bitter, metallic taste of uncooked flour.

The density of béchamel can vary according to its use. I prefer to make a thin sauce when I use the béchamel in combination with pasta. A thick sauce is needed whenever it is to be used as a binder for stuffings. I like to change the flavoring according to what I want to use the sauce with. For a plain pasta with béchamel I infuse two garlic cloves in the milk. If I want the béchamel as a base sauce for fish, for instance, I would put a bay leaf in the milk.

2¼ cups milk
4 tablespoons unsalted butter
⅓ cup flour
salt
freshly grated nutmeg

1 Heat the milk until it just begins to bubble at the edge.

2 Meanwhile melt the butter in a heavy saucepan over low heat. Blend in the flour, stirring vigorously. Remove the pan from the heat and add the hot milk, a few tablespoons at a time. You must let the flour mixture absorb each addition thoroughly before going on to the next.

3 When all the milk has been absorbed and the sauce is lovely and smooth, return the pan to the heat. Add salt to taste and bring to the boil. Cook over the gentlest heat for 20 minutes, stirring frequently. I prefer to use a flame disperser or to put the saucepan in a larger saucepan containing 2 inches or so of simmering water. Now add a grating of nutmeg, which is the most usual flavoring.

BATTUTO and SOFFRITTO

In a culinary context, battuto, literally "beaten," means chopped so fine as to appear pounded. It is the starting point for most Italian recipes for sauces, meat dishes and soups. A battuto consists traditionally of ingredients found in an Italian pantry—chopped pork fat and/or pancetta, onion, garlic, parsley, celery and carrot. The traditional lardo (pork fat) is now often replaced by lighter types of fat, oil being the most popular. The battuto is used crudo (raw) in some dishes, in a bean soup, for instance. It gives a fresher, less rich flavor to the dish and is certainly a healthier method. Usually, however, the battuto becomes a soffritto, by being sautéed in some kind of fat.

Soffritto means underfried: the battuto is subjected to a slow, careful sautéing, as a result of which "a cook achieves part of that unmistakable taste which can be identified as Italian," as Marcella Hazan so aptly puts it.

There are three secrets of a good soffritto. First, the battuto should be extremely finely chopped. Second, the soffritto should cook very gently, while being watched carefully, with a hand ready to stir whenever any of the ingredients begin to stick to the bottom. The third secret is that when the first ingredient to be sautéed is onion, you should add a pinch of salt to it at the beginning. The salt releases the water in the onion, thus preventing it from frying too quickly.

Pasta

Spaghettini alla puré di olive
SPAGHETTINI WITH OLIVE PUREE,
ANCHOVIES AND CAPERS

Spaghettini e cozze in cartoccio
SPAGHETTINI AND MUSSELS EN PAPILLOTE

Sugo di pomodoro crudo
UNCOOKED TOMATO SAUCE

Tagliatelle al mascarpone
TAGLIATELLE WITH MASCARPONE

It is, I am sure, not necessary to introduce pasta as if it were some novel foodstuff, yet its relative novelty has allowed one or two popular misconceptions to go unchallenged. One concerns the difference between fresh pasta and dried pasta and has arisen partly from the use of those words "fresh" and "dried." Since by implication that which is not fresh is stale, or is second best in some way, the phrase "fresh pasta" implies that the other kind is not all that it might be, is even a bit off. This is simply not so. There is no doubt in my mind that good brands of dried pasta are better than much of the fresh pasta sold in shops. Fresh pasta has become something of a fad, and yet in Italy—undeniably the home of pasta—most people eat dried pasta most of the time. My advice is that you should either make your own, a quick-and-easy job with the cheap hand-cranked machine, or buy good-quality dried pasta.

Another misconception is that pasta should be well drained. It is a great mistake to drain pasta too much; as soon as it is al dente you should tip it all into a large colander, give the colander a couple of shakes and—while the pasta is still wet and slippery—quickly turn it into a heated dish or into the frying pan with the sauce. In Naples, in fact, long pasta is lifted from the water with a long wooden fork instead of being drained in a colander, and a long-handled wicker strainer is used for draining short pasta. They say, "gli spaghetti devono avere la goccia," meaning that the spaghetti should still be thoroughly wet when it goes into the dish. When serving some types of pasta dressed in a thick and creamy sauce, Neapolitans fill an earthenware jug with the water in which the pasta has cooked, for pouring on the pasta at the table if required.

Another rule is summed up in the saying, "gli spaghetti amano la compagnia" (spaghetti loves company). You need to stay around while it is cooking, unless, that is, you prefer to use the method I learned from Vincenzo Agnesi, the Ligurian pasta manufacturer, a method suitable only for dried pasta. When I went to see him in 1974 for my first book, *Portrait of Pasta*, he was the fittest octogenarian I had ever met, "due," he said, "to eating 100 grams [about a quarter of a pound] of pasta every day of my life." He told me how he cooks his pasta, the advantage of his method being that the goodness is not boiled out of the pasta. This is the Agnesi method. Bring a large saucepan of water to the boil, add salt to taste and then add the pasta and stir vigorously. When the water has come back to the boil cook for two minutes, stirring frequently. Turn off the heat, put a Turkish towel over the pan and close with a tight-fitting lid. Leave for the same length of time that the pasta would take to cook by the normal method, that is, if it were still boiling. When the time is up, drain the pasta. The water will be much clearer than usual, and you will have a dish of pasta that has retained the characteristic flavor of semolina. The other advantage is that it does not become overcooked if you leave it one minute too long in the pot.

The cooking time for pasta is, to a certain extent, a matter of taste. A dish of pasta in Naples might seem undercooked to a traditional northern palate. I was amused to see this piece of advice in a 1900 edition of *Baedeker:* "The Maccaroni of Naples is much esteemed, but is generally hard, and should therefore be ordered *ben cotti.*"

My last piece of advice, or should I say commandment, is to dress the pasta immediately after you drain it. If, by an error in timing, the sauce is not ready, toss the pasta with some butter or oil; never leave any kind of pasta sitting undressed in a colander or a bowl.

Pasta

PASTA • MAKES ENOUGH FOR 3 SERVINGS TAGLIATELLE OR 4 SERVINGS STUFFED PASTA

Having experimented with various combinations of flours, plus eggs, water, oil, etc., I went back to the original recipe for la vera sfoglia Emiliana, the authentic dough of Emilia—plain flour and eggs. The flour used in Italy is doppio zero, oo grade, a soft flour with a low gluten content, easy to stretch and roll out thin. I use unbleached flour. After trying various electric machines I came to the conclusion that the most useful machine for a family is the hand-cranked one, which is silent and quick to clean. The following recipe makes about 10 ounces of pasta dough.

1⅓ cups unbleached flour, about
    3 tablespoons more if using a
    hand-cranked machine
  2 large eggs
generous pinch of salt

1 Pile the flour on a work surface, make a well in the center, break in the eggs and add the salt. Using a fork or your fingers, draw the flour gradually into the eggs. Knead to form a ball, adding a little more flour if necessary. Clean your hands and wipe the work surface.

2 If you are using the machine, knead for 5 minutes and then allow the dough to rest for about 30 minutes, wrapped in plastic. Divide the dough into 4 parts and work on one part at a time, keeping the rest covered by a bowl or between

2 soup plates. Knead and roll out the dough, following the manufacturer's instructions. For tagliatelle and fettuccine, stop at the next-to-the-last notch, for stuffed pasta stop at the last notch.

3 If you are rolling out the dough by hand, dust the work surface and your hands with flour and knead for 5 minutes more, by which time the dough should be compact, smooth and elastic. Let the dough rest, wrapped in plastic or a kitchen towel.

4 Dust the work surface and the rolling pin with flour and stretch and roll the dough, working away from you. Rotate the circle of dough regularly and evenly so that it remains circular. Ideally you should roll out the sfoglia or sheet of dough to a thickness of a little under $\frac{1}{16}$ inch for stuffed pasta, $\frac{1}{16}$ inch for flat pasta.

5 Whether you have used the machine or the rolling pin, you can go on to the next stage more or less straight away if the pasta is going to be stuffed or if you are making lasagne or pappardelle (see page 10). But for tagliatelle and fettuccine you must leave the sfoglia to dry on a clean kitchen towel for about 30 minutes, or it will stick. Put the circle of sfoglia or the strips on kitchen towels and let the pasta hang over the edge of the work surface, turning it around, and over, to allow it to dry evenly. The length of time needed depends on the humidity and heat of your kitchen.

6 If you are making the pasta by hand, roll the sfoglia up very loosely and cut into the desired width with a broad knife. Open out the rolls of noodles, which are now ready to be cooked.

HOW TO COOK PASTA. Dried and fresh pasta are cooked in the same way (unless, of course, you are using the Agnesi method, as described on page 8). The only difference is in the length of time they take to cook, since fresh pasta only needs two to three minutes.

The general rule for the amount of water needed is one quart to each four ounces of pasta. Use a large saucepan, add salt in the proportion of one teaspoon per quart, and bring to the boil. Add the pasta and stir with a wooden spoon. Cook until al dente.

When you are cooking fresh pasta, pour a cupful of cold water into the pan before you drain it, to stop the pasta from cooking any further. Stir well and then drain. Remember also that fresh tagliatelle will absorb more of the sauce. For this reason never overdrain tagliatelle and always keep a cupful of the cooking water in case the pasta is too dry.

CHOOSING THE RIGHT SAUCE. There are some general rules that govern the choice of sauce with which to dress the various shapes.

Long thin dried pasta should be dressed with light oil-based sauces, which allow the strands to remain separate and slippery. Long pasta that is thicker, such as bucatini or tagliatelle, is best with sauces based on cream, cheese or eggs, or on meat. Medium tubular pasta goes well with vegetable sauces, while large short pasta like penne or rigatoni is suitable for rich sauces and ragù, or for baked dishes. These rich sauces are also perfect with tagliatelle or fettuccine.

PAPPARDELLE

Of all homemade pasta, pappardelle is my favorite. For one thing, the strips are large, so that you can really feel them between your teeth. Pappardelle has another advantage over the other long shapes of homemade pasta: living in a country where the humidity is high, as it is in England and much of America, I find that the sheets of pasta you lay out to dry can take much too long before they are ready to be cut into tagliatelle. You have to hang about, feel, wait, feel again and even then, out of impatience, you begin to put them through the machine when they are still damp. Next, unless you cook the tagliatelle straight away, another problem arises. How can you spread the strips out so that they won't touch each other? You need lots of space. And if you roll them in pretty nests you are likely to finish with soggy bundles that look most unappealing.

As for hanging tagliatelle over the backs of chairs, it might look very decorative and impart a highly festive air to the occasion, but it is not practical. Because of their weight, the strips may well break when they are dry, or even while they are drying.

With pappardelle, none of these problems arises. To make pappardelle roll each sheet of pasta to the same thickness as for tagliatelle. Wait 10 minutes and then cut it into ribbons about 5 to 6 inches long and ¾ inch wide, using a pastry wheel. Lay the ribbons, not touching each other, on a clean cloth. You can cook them straight away or leave them until you are ready.

Pappardelle con le fave
PAPPARDELLE WITH FAVA BEANS • SERVES 3 OR 4

Pappardelle is one of the few shapes of pasta traditionally made in Tuscany. Here pappardelle is combined with another Tuscan favorite, fava beans. The dish is much improved if you peel the beans.

PAPPARDELLE

1⅓ **cups unbleached flour**
   2 **eggs**
pinch of salt

1 Make the pasta dough as directed on page 8 and then cut your pappardelle.

2 Plunge the beans into a saucepan of boiling water for about 3 minutes and then drain them. Peel them and set aside.

3 Make a little battuto with the onion and the pancetta. I do this in the food processor, pulsing the machine so that the mixture is chopped evenly. Heat the mixture with half the oil in a pan, preferably earthenware. Sauté for 1 minute or so, sprinkle with a little salt and add a couple of tablespoons of the stock. Cover the pan and cook gently for 10 minutes, adding a little more stock if necessary. Stir frequently.

4 Add the fava beans, the parsley, half the remaining stock, salt and plenty of pepper. Cook very slowly in a covered pan until the beans are tender, about 10 minutes. Keep a watch on the pan and add a little stock if the beans get too dry. There should be some liquid left in the pan when the beans are cooked. Taste and check the seasoning.

5 Cook the pasta in plenty of salted water. Remember that since the pappardelle is fresh it will cook in 1½ to 2 minutes.

6 When the pasta is ready, lift it out of the water and transfer straight into the pan with the beans, using a spaghetti lifter or a long wooden fork. If you prefer you can drain the pasta in a colander, but remember to reserve a cupful of the water for later.

7 Stir-fry for a minute, lifting the pasta up high as you do so. Add a little of the reserved water if the pasta appears too dry. Remove the pan from the heat and pour the remaining oil over the pasta. Mix well and serve at once straight from the pan, or, if you wish, transfer to a bowl.

✄ This country pasta dish can be followed by Chicken Braised with Vinegar and Herbs (page 219) or, for a vegetarian meal, by Artichokes Stuffed with Mint and Parsley (page 88) or Eggplant Parmigiana (page 99).

2 **pounds fava beans, shelled (2 cups)**
2 **shallots** *or* 1 **small onion**
¼ **pound pancetta**
4 **tablespoons extra-virgin olive oil**
salt
⅔ **cup vegetable stock (see page 4)**
2 **tablespoons chopped fresh parsley**
pepper

Tagliatelle col sugo di cipolla
TAGLIATELLE WITH ONION SAUCE • SERVES 4

There are many versions of this traditional sauce from Emilia-Romagna; this is mine.

¾ **pound red or other sweet onions, very finely sliced**

1 **teaspoon sugar**

6 **tablespoons unsalted butter**

1 **teaspoon flour**

4 **tablespoons strong meat stock (see page 3)**

4 **tablespoons dry white wine**

salt

pepper

——————

TAGLIATELLE

2¼ **cups unbleached flour**

3 **eggs**

1 **teaspoon salt**

——————

freshly grated parmesan

NOTE: If you do not wish to make your own tagliatelle, you may substitute 1 pound store-bought fresh tagliatelle or ¾ pound dried egg tagliatelle.

1 Prepare the tagliatelle following the instructions on page 8.

2 Cook the onions with the sugar in half the butter over medium heat until they turn gold, about 10 minutes. Stir occasionally.

3 Turn the heat down, blend in the flour and cook for 1 minute. Add the meat stock and cook for 2 minutes, then add the wine. When the liquid is boiling, season to taste with salt and pepper and cover the pan. Cook over very gentle heat until the onion is very soft and nearly reduced to a puree, about 30 minutes. Add a couple of tablespoons of boiling water if the sauce gets too dry.

4 Cook the tagliatelle in plenty of salted water. When ready, scoop out 1 cupful of the water in which the pasta has been cooking. Lift the tagliatelle out of the water with a spaghetti lifter or a long fork and transfer to a heated bowl. Toss with the remaining butter and then spoon over the sauce. If the pasta appears too dry, add a couple of tablespoons of the reserved water. Serve with freshly grated parmesan.

To serve as a primo, choose a veal dish as a secondo, Veal Scaloppine with Basil and Lemon (page 210), or chicken, Chicken with Orange (page 176). For a vegetarian meal I would serve Stuffed Zucchini, Mantua Style (page 156), making the dinner a tribute as well to the great cooking of Mantua.

Tagliolini e merluzzo in salsa
TAGLIOLINI AND HADDOCK IN TOMATO SAUCE • SERVES 4

The ideal pasta for this dish is homemade tagliolini, a sort of thin tagliatelle. It is a simple dish that can be prepared with many different kinds of fish—haddock, hake, cod, halibut or monkfish—but not with bluefish which is too strong and oily. The cooking time of the fish would vary, but the basic method would be the same. You can also vary the tomato sauce, or serve the fish with boiled potatoes or boiled rice instead of tagliolini.

1 First make the pasta dough as directed on page 8. Roll it out up to the second-to-last notch on the machine or as thin as you can if you are rolling by hand. Allow the pasta to dry and then put it through the narrow grooves of the cutting roller of the machine; if you are cutting the pasta by hand, cut it a little over ⅛ inch wide.

2 Skin the fish fillets and cut into bite-size chunks, removing any bones. Dry with paper towels.

3 Chop the garlic, chili and parsley together and, in a sauté pan, sauté in half the oil until you can smell the garlic. Add the fish, salt and pepper, cover the pan and cook for 10 minutes. Keep an eye on the fish and turn it over once during the cooking.

4 While the fish is cooking, cut the tomatoes in half, squeeze out the seeds and some of the juice and cut into cubes. Add them to the fish and continue cooking for 5 minutes.

5 Meanwhile cook the tagliolini in salted water. Drain and return it to the cooking pot and dress immediately with the remaining oil.

6 Put the fish with all the sauce in the center of a round dish and surround it with the pasta. If you use an oval dish, make a bed of spaghetti and place the fish on top.

✘This can be a primo, followed either by a salad or by Braised Broccoli (page 201) or Lemon-flavored Eggplant (page 94). For a meal based on one kind of ingredient, fish in this case, you could start with Stuffed Onion Cups (page 84) or Broiled Eggplant Stuffed with Tuna and Anchovies (page 98).

TAGLIOLINI
- 1⅓ cups unbleached flour
- 2 eggs
- pinch of salt

- 1 pound haddock fillets
- 1 garlic clove, peeled
- ½ dried chili, seeded
- 3 tablespoons chopped fresh parsley
- scant ½ cup extra-virgin olive oil
- salt
- pepper
- ¾ pound ripe tomatoes, peeled

Tonnarelli alla polpa di granchio
TONNARELLI WITH CRAB SAUCE • SERVES 4 TO 6

This is one of the best dishes served at the Ristorante Ciccio in Bocca di Magra, a seaside resort at the southern extremity of Liguria, from which one looks across the plain of the Magra to the magnificent Apuan Alps. These are the mountains where Carrara marble is quarried. Because of the huge quarries, the mountainsides change color with the changing light of day, varying from deep greeny-blue in morning to the most delicate pink in evening.

We first went to Ciccio 30 years ago when it had just been opened and Bocca di Magra was a delightfully sleepy little village with one pensione and one restaurant, Ciccio. Now there are several hotels and scores of yachts in a newly built harbor, but Ciccio is still most pleasant and offers some very good dishes. When we were there in the spring of 1988 there was a big lunch party to celebrate a golden wedding anniversary. La sposa d'oro (the golden bride) and her 40 guests managed to eat their way through seven mixed antipasti, a seafood risotto, tonnarelli with crab (as in this recipe), porgies in a salt crust, fritto misto, salads of arugula, wild plants and tomatoes, fruit salad with ice cream, the wedding cake (a millefeuille with whipped cream) and coffee. My husband and I felt ashamed to be able to manage only a two-course meal, after which we withdrew for a siesta. When we walked back past the restaurant at half past four, the adults were still sitting round the table in a somewhat dazed condition, while the children were careening around the tables, free at last from parental discipline.

PREPARING A FRESH CRAB. If you cannot find a live crab, make sure that the one you buy has been freshly boiled. In this case the fishmonger will open it for you and discard the inedible part. If you manage to obtain a live creature, put it in a sink or a bowl and pour over it enough boiling water to cover. When no more bubbles float to the surface—it takes no longer than 5 minutes—the crab is ready to be prepared.

Twist off the legs and claws. Scrub the body and legs with a hard brush. Crack the claws and the legs with a hammer or a nutcracker, trying not to mash the meat. Scoop out the meat. Hold the crab with the underside up and pull it away from the body by lifting the flap and pulling hard; this will also remove the intestine. Now tear away the inner rim and then pick out the meat using the pointed handle of a teaspoon. Discard the gray sac of the stomach, the mouth and the gills. The female crab, recognizable by a wider flap, may also contain the coral, which, with the creamy tomalley, is the best part.

When you have picked out as much meat as you can, put the carcass in a pan, cover with water and boil for 15 minutes. Remove from the water and pick out the remaining meat which you could not detach when the crab was uncooked. Keep the cooked meat apart from the raw meat. Now the hard work is done, and the sauce is quick and easy.

Tonnarelli are square spaghetti made with an egg dough; they have the perfect firmness for this sauce.

1 First prepare the tonnarelli following the instructions on page 8. Make the pasta dough as usual, knead it and roll it out through the machine, stopping at the second-to-last notch. The strips of pasta should be as thick as the width of the narrowest groove on the machine's cutting roller. (If you are making the pasta by hand, roll it ⅛ inch thick. Let it sit until just dry to the touch. Roll loosely, as for a jelly roll, and cut in strips ⅛ inch wide.)

2 Prepare the fresh crab, as described in the introduction to this recipe.

3 Put the oil and the garlic in a saucepan over low heat and when the garlic begins to become golden, remove and discard. Add the shallots with some salt, cover the pan and cook over very low heat until soft. Do not let the shallots brown; if necessary add a tablespoon or so of crab or vegetable stock.

4 Add the tomato paste and cook for 1 minute, stirring constantly. Pour in about 6 tablespoons of the stock and bring to the boil. Simmer for 10 minutes, then add the cream and bring to the boil. Add the raw or frozen crabmeat and cook for 2 minutes. If you are using a fresh crab, mix in the cooked meat at the very end. Remove from the heat and process the sauce to a smooth thin puree. Return the sauce to the pan. Add cayenne pepper to taste and check salt. The sauce is now made and can be warmed up in a bain-marie or double boiler when you are ready to dress the pasta.

5 Cook the pasta in plenty of salted water. Scoop out a mug of the cooking water; you will need it for thinning out the sauce. Drain the pasta, but do not overdrain, and turn it into a heated bowl. Toss immediately with the butter and then mix in the sauce very thoroughly. Add 3 or 4 tablespoons of the reserved water. The pasta should be well coated with the sauce, but not thickly coated. Bring to the table together with the mug of cooking water, in case the sauce becomes too thick as it cools. I do not serve parmesan with this dish because its taste is too strong for the delicate flavor of the crab sauce.

✘ This is the kind of dish one makes only for a special occasion. Served as a first course it makes a magnificent

TONNARELLI

2¼ cups unbleached flour
3 eggs
pinch of salt

———

1 crab, about 1 pound, *or* ½ pound frozen crabmeat, thawed
4 tablespoons extra-virgin olive oil
2 garlic cloves, peeled
2 shallots *or* ½ onion, very finely chopped
salt
1 tablespoon tomato paste
stock from the crab's shell *or* vegetable stock
1 cup heavy cream
cayenne pepper
2 tablespoons unsalted butter

NOTE: You may substitute 1 pound of fresh spaghetti or ¾ pound dried egg tagliatelle for the tonnarelli.

(*continued*)

opening to a meal. After that, if you are giving a formal dinner party, you might serve a light dish of meat or poultry such as Chicken with Orange (page 176) or Cold Roast Veal with Herbs (page 206), which you can prepare totally beforehand. Personally, on a less formal level, I find that a vegetable dish is just right as a secondo. My choice would be Lemon-flavored Eggplant (page 94) or Fennel and Orange Salad (page 119) or one or more stuffed vegetables—zucchini (page 156), eggplants (pages 96–98) and/or onions (page 84).

Timballo di pesce
FISH TIMBALE • SERVES 6 AS A PRIMO OR 4 AS A SECONDO

For years I made a very good pasticcio di pesce, a baked dish of lasagne layered with fish, béchamel and a creamy pink sauce. Then, thanks to Suzy Benghiat, I came across a recipe for a fish timbale by Fulvia Sesani, who runs a cooking school in Venice. Judging by the recipe, it seemed this unmolded dish of tagliatelle would be as pretty as it would be delicious; it was too seductive not to give it a try. So I turned my pasticcio di pesce into a timballo di pesce. The final result is this dish, not to be attempted by a beginner, yet not too difficult for anyone who likes to try something a bit more enterprising.

The dish is so good that if you can you should spare the time to make your own lasagne. The kinds of fish I use vary depending on what I find fresh. A halibut steak or a piece of hake or haddock are all suitable, as are turbot and sea bass. Buy some fish with their heads on, lemon sole, for instance, to give more flavor. Try to buy three different kinds of fish. They should be poached in a court bouillon. I often have some fish fumet in the freezer, a fumet being a court bouillon in which fish or fish heads have already been cooked, and I use it with a little water added if necessary.

You can prepare the whole dish in advance, even the day before, and chill it. I expect you can even freeze it, although personally I find that frozen pasta becomes heavier in taste. If you freeze it, bring it back to room temperature before heating it in the oven.

1 Put the onion, celery, bay leaf, herbs and salt in a large saucepan, add a generous quart of cold water and bring to the boil. Simmer, covered, for 10 minutes, add the wine and the peppercorns and continue to simmer for 20 minutes or so. The court bouillon is now ready.

2 Add all the fish to the pan and bring back to the boil. Turn off the heat and let the fish cool in the liquid.

3 Now make the lasagne following the instructions on page 8. Roll out the dough as thin as you can if you are doing it by hand or put it through a hand-cranked machine up to the second-to-last notch.

4 Cut the pasta strips into 8-inch lengths, leaving them the width they are when they come out of the machine, about 4 inches wide.

5 The best pot to use for cooking lasagne is a large, deep one. Fill it with 4 quarts of water and bring to the boil. Meanwhile place a large bowl of cold water next to the pan, and lay 2 clean kitchen towels on the work surface.

6 When the water is boiling, add 1 tablespoon coarse salt and 1 tablespoon oil and slide in 3 or 4 strips of pasta. Cook for 2 minutes, then retrieve the strips and plunge them in the bowl of cold water. Give each strip a gentle rub, as you would a delicate piece of fabric, and lay it on the kitchen towel. Repeat with the remaining strips, 3 or 4 at a time. Lay the strips so that they do not touch, otherwise they will stick together. When you have cooked, rinsed and spread out all the strips, pat them dry with paper towels.

7 Lift the fish out of the court bouillon and strain the liquid. Measure 1 cup of the liquid, add the same amount of milk and make a thickish béchamel as directed on page 4, using the milk and fish liquor mixture in place of the milk.

8 While the béchamel is cooking, remove the head, bones and every bit of skin from the fish. Put the fish in a food processor and, while the machine is working, add the eggs one at a time. Transfer to a bowl and add the béchamel and the parmesan. Mix very well and check seasoning.

9 Grease a 6-cup metal loaf pan with half the butter. Line the mold with pasta strips, overlapping them as little as possible. Leave about 2 inches hanging over the edge all round. (It is easier to cut the strips with scissors than with a knife.) Spread about 3 or 4 tablespoons of the fish and béchamel mixture and then cover with a strip of pasta, cutting it to the right size if necessary. Continue alternating these 2 layers, finishing with the fish mixture. Fold the hanging-over pasta over the last layer of fish and place the last strip of pasta over the top, tucking it in all around the edges.

10 Preheat the oven to 400°F.

11 Melt the remaining butter, brush it over the top and cover with a piece of foil. The dish is now ready to be finished off in the oven. It is cooked in a bain-marie. The

COURT BOUILLON

- 1 onion, peeled and sliced
- 1 celery stalk, coarsely chopped
- 1 bay leaf

a few fresh parsley sprigs, some fennel and thyme *or* other herbs, depending on the season

salt

1¼ cups dry white wine

a few peppercorns

———

1½ pounds assorted white fish

LASAGNE

1⅓ cups unbleached flour

2 eggs

pinch of salt

1 teaspoon olive oil

———

coarse salt

vegetable oil

BECHAMEL SAUCE

- 1 cup fish stock
- 1 cup milk
- 4 tablespoons unsalted butter
- 6 tablespoons flour
- 2 eggs
- ½ cup freshly grated parmesan
- 2 tablespoons unsalted butter

NOTE: You may substitute ¾ pound store-bought fresh lasagne or ½ pound dried lasagne for the home-made.

(*continued*)

FISH TIMBALE
(*continued*)

SHRIMP SAUCE

- 4 tablespoons olive oil
- 2 garlic cloves, peeled and bruised
- 1 dried chili
- 2 tablespoons tomato paste
- ½ cup dry white wine
- ¾ pound shrimp, cooked
- 1 cup heavy cream

salt

pepper

timing varies: if the dish was cold, it will need about 1 hour; if you have just made it, 30 minutes will do. However, it will not spoil if you leave it in the oven for a little longer.

12 To make the shrimp sauce, heat the olive oil with the garlic and the chili in a very heavy saucepan. When the garlic begins to give off its characteristic aroma, remove and discard it. Remove and discard the chili as well.

13 Add the tomato paste to the sizzling oil and cook, stirring constantly for 1 minute. I find that the rather unpleasant concentrated taste of tomato paste disappears more quickly if the puree is cooked by itself to begin with. Now add the wine slowly and bring to the boil. Let the sauce simmer very gently for 15 minutes.

14 Meanwhile put aside a few of the best shrimp for decoration. Peel the others. Put the shells in a piece of cheesecloth. Make a little bag and place it in a mortar. Crush the bag with the pestle so as to release all the juices. Squeeze the bag over the pan; the juice that will come out gives the sauce a more marked flavor. Mix well, then add the cream, the peeled shrimp and salt and pepper to taste. Cook slowly until the sauce begins to boil. Simmer for a couple of minutes and then transfer to a food processor. Process until smooth and homogenous. Return to the pan and keep warm in a bain-marie or double boiler.

15 When the timbale is ready, run a metal spatula round the edges to release it from the pan then place an oval dish over it. Turn upside-down to unmold and lift the pan away. Spoon some of the sauce around the timbale and pour the rest of the sauce into a bowl or a sauceboat. Remove the shells from the shrimp you have set aside and decorate the timbale.

✷ In a very non-Italian way I serve this timballo as a main course, by itself, followed by a salad. To start the meal, make an easy soup with which you are familiar, or start with an antipasto of prosciutto and melon.

✷ If you want to be really à la mode, prepare a "pink dinner." Start with a tomato soup, then the timballo, and finish with a raspberry mousse or sherbet or strawberry ice cream. Make everything harmonize in flavor as well as in color. The tomato soup should be delicate, not a gazpacho, for instance.

Pasta e broccoli

PASTA WITH BROCCOLI • SERVES 4

The combination of vegetables and pasta has its origins in southern Italy. In Apulia this broccoli sauce is always served with orecchiette or little ears, so-called because of their hollow shape. Orecchiette are made at home there, with semolina, flour and water. They are now produced commercially by the best Italian pasta manufacturers and are generally available both in Italy and elsewhere. I find that this sauce besides being good with orecchiette is also one of the few that can stand up to the nutty flavor of brown pasta made with whole wheat flour (a flavor which, like most Italians, I do not particularly like). Whole wheat pasta is made in a number of shapes; spaghetti is by far the most successful.

- **1 pound broccoli**
- **coarse salt**
- **3/4 pound orecchiette or other medium pasta *or* whole wheat spaghetti**
- **2 garlic cloves, peeled**
- **1 dried chili, seeded**
- **3 salted anchovies, boned and washed, *or* 6 anchovy fillets**
- **5 tablespoons extra-virgin olive oil**
- **4 tablespoons freshly grated pecorino romano**
- **freshly grated parmesan (optional)**

1 Trim and wash the broccoli, then divide into small florets and cut the stalks into 1-inch rounds.

2 Bring a large saucepan full of water to the boil, add about 1½ tablespoons coarse salt and then slide in the broccoli. Stir well and cook for 5 minutes after the water has come back to the boil. Retrieve the broccoli pieces from the water with a slotted spoon and lay them on paper towels. Pat dry and set aside.

3 Bring the broccoli water back to the boil and add the pasta. Cook until very al dente.

4 While the pasta is cooking, chop the garlic, chili and anchovies and sauté them for 2 minutes in half the oil, using a large frying pan. Add the broccoli and sauté for 5 minutes.

5 When the pasta is done, drain and turn it quickly into the frying pan. Stir-fry for a minute or so, then taste and check the seasoning.

6 Before you serve the pasta, pour over the rest of the olive oil and mix in the romano. If you like you can serve a bowl of freshly grated parmesan on the side, although I find that the romano gives the dish enough of a cheesy taste.

I always like to serve pasta as a primo; it should be eaten as soon as it is drained. I would follow this dish with Hake in a Milky Sauce with Rosemary (page 54) or with Broiled Eggplants with Pizza Topping (page 95).

Pasta e peperoni al forno

BAKED PASTA AND GRILLED PEPPERS • SERVES 4

This robust dish epitomizes the taste and aroma of southern Italian cooking. The recipe is from Basilicata, where chili is a favorite spice. Buy very fresh, meaty peppers—the heavier they are the more pulp they have—and use the best extra-virgin olive oil. The grilling and peeling of the peppers is rather laborious, but quite necessary to release their flavor and rid them of the skin. Use dry pasta, not fresh, preferably a medium tubular shape such as penne.

1½ pounds yellow, red and green bell peppers

2 teaspoons dried oregano

salt

freshly ground black pepper

6 tablespoons extra-virgin olive oil

1 or 2 garlic cloves, peeled and finely sliced

2 tablespoons dried breadcrumbs

2 tablespoons chopped fresh parsley

a few fresh basil leaves, if available, torn

½ dried chili or 1 fresh chili, seeded and chopped

12 black olives, pitted and cut into strips

1 teaspoon anchovy paste

10 ounces penne

1 Wash and dry the peppers. Grill them under a preheated broiler or on a wire rack directly over a gas flame. (I find the latter method easier.) Cook them, turning from time to time, until the skin is black and charred on all sides, as well as the top and bottom. Allow the peppers to cool. I find there is no need to put them in bags while they are cooling, as is sometimes recommended; the skin is very easily removed if properly charred.

2 Peel the peppers with the help of paper towels and a small knife if necessary. Do not wash them, as the lovely taste will wash away too. Cut in half, discard the seeds and remove the white ribs. Cut into strips about ½ inch wide. Place the strips in a bowl and sprinkle with the oregano and some salt and pepper. You can do this the day before; then keep the peppers, covered, in the refrigerator.

3 Now put a large pot with 4 quarts of water on to boil; meanwhile prepare the sauce.

4 Heat 2 tablespoons of the oil in a small frying pan and then add the garlic, breadcrumbs, parsley, basil, chili, olives and anchovy paste. Cook, stirring constantly, for about 2 minutes. Taste and check the salt.

5 Preheat the oven to 400°F.

6 When the water for the pasta is boiling fast, add about 1½ tablespoons salt. Bring the water back to a fast boil and then add the pasta. Stir and cook for about 6 minutes after the water has come back to the boil. Scoop about half a mug of boiling water out of the pan and reserve. Drain the pasta and return it to the pan. Toss with half the remaining oil and add 2 or 3 tablespoons of the reserved water and the breadcumb mixture. Mix thoroughly. If the pasta seems too dry, add a little more reserved water.

7 Grease a deep 2-quart ovenproof dish and put about half the pasta into it.

8 Cover with half the peppers, then with the rest of the pasta; top with the remaining pepper strips, taking care that all the pasta is covered by the peppers. Pour over the remaining oil in a thin stream. Place the dish in the oven for about 15 minutes. Allow to stand out of the oven for at least 5 minutes before serving. This dish can be prepared a few hours in advance. To reheat, place in the oven for about 30 minutes so that it heats through.

✕ This earthy pasta dish can be served as a primo, followed by Red Mullet en Papillote (page 60) or Stewed Octopus (page 65). If you prefer to serve pasta as the main course, start the dinner with Broiled Radicchio with Parmesan (page 87) or Frittata Strips in Tomato Sauce (page 114).

Reginette imbottite

STUFFED REGINETTE • SERVES 4 OR 5

This dish is derived from a recipe from Emilia-Romagna called rotelle imbottite (stuffed wheels), in which it is made with homemade pasta ribbons. In my version, you do not have to make your own pasta, and the end result is stuffed little crowns instead of stuffed wheels. You simply go to a good supermarket or an Italian shop and buy reginette (literally, little queens), which are wide ribbons of dried pasta with one ruffled edge. For this dish I prefer to cook the pasta by the Agnesi method (see page 8) as it is less likely to break. If you cannot find reginette, you can make lasagne instead (see page 8), cutting the ribbons with a pastry wheel, 1½ inches wide, with one straight edge and one ruffled edge.

(*continued*)

STUFFED REGINETTE
(*continued*)

HAM AND SPINACH STUFFING

scant ½ cup chopped ham
½ cup cooked or frozen spinach, thawed
½ cup ricotta
1 egg
3 tablespoons freshly grated parmesan
¼ teaspoon freshly grated nutmeg
salt
pepper

½ pound reginette
butter for greasing

CHEESE SAUCE

2 cups milk
2 tablespoons unsalted butter
½ tablespoon flour
3 ounces gruyère, coarsely grated (about 1 cup)

NOTE: You can cook and stuff the reginette in advance.

1 First make the stuffing. Put the ham in a food processor with the spinach and ricotta. Process for 10 seconds, then add the egg and the parmesan. Process to a smooth puree and transfer to a bowl. Add the grated nutmeg and season to taste with salt and pepper.

2 Cook the pasta either in the orthodox way or following the Agnesi method as described on page 8. Be very gentle when you put the pasta in and when you first stir it with a wooden fork. Drain when very al dente and lay each ribbon on lengths of paper towel or on clean kitchen towels.

3 Butter a small shallow oven dish very generously. It should be just large enough for the reginette rolls to stand up close to one another. Cut each pasta ribbon in half, to a length of about 5 inches. Spread some of the stuffing all over the ribbon pieces and roll them up neatly. Do not worry if a few reginette are slightly torn; they will stay together once they are stuffed and rolled. Stand the rolls in the dish with their ruffled edges up.

4 For the sauce, heat the milk. Melt the butter in a heavy saucepan. Stir in the flour and cook for 1 minute, stirring the whole time. Remove the pan from the heat and gradually add the hot milk while beating constantly, until it has been completely incorporated. Return to the heat and bring to the boil. Simmer very slowly for about 10 minutes, stirring often. The heat must be very low indeed: use a flame-disperser or cook the sauce in a bain-marie or double boiler.

5 Preheat the oven to 350°F.

6 Add the gruyère to the sauce together with salt and pepper to taste. Stir well until the cheese has melted.

7 Spoon the sauce over the pasta rolls. Cover the dish with foil and place it in the oven. Bake until hot, about 20 minutes. Serve immediately.

This is a very good dish, which happens to be extremely attractive to look at as well. To follow it, my choice would be something not too heavy or time consuming, for instance Veal Scaloppine with Basil and Lemon (page 210) or Red Mullet en Papillote (page 60).

Rice, Polenta and Beans

POLENTA

Polenta alla griglia e polenta fritta
GRILLED POLENTA AND FRIED POLENTA

Polenta alla pizzaiola
POLENTA WITH PIZZA TOPPING

Polenta pasticciata alla piemontese
BAKED POLENTA WITH PORCINI

RICE

Risotto in bianco
RISOTTO WITH PARMESAN

Risotto al limone
RISOTTO WITH LEMON

Risotto alla marinara
RISOTTO WITH SHELLFISH

Risotto alla milanese
RISOTTO WITH SAFFRON

Risotto con gli asparagi
RISOTTO WITH ASPARAGUS

BEANS

Anatra alla pavese
DUCKLING WITH LENTILS

Fagioli all'uccelletto
DRIED BEANS WITH SAGE

Ceci e rucola
CHICKPEAS AND ARUGULA

SEE ALSO

Pomodori ripieni di riso e olive nere
TOMATOES FILLED WITH RICE AND BLACK
OLIVES

Risotto alle ortiche
RISOTTO WITH NETTLES

Risotto coi carciofi
RISOTTO WITH ARTICHOKES

Trevisana coi borlotti
RADICCHIO WITH CRANBERRY BEANS

Rice

Thomas Jefferson loved Italian rice so much that in contravention of a local law he smuggled two sacks out of Piedmont so that he could plant the rice on his estate in Virginia. By the time Jefferson tasted it, rice was already quite popular in northern Italy, thanks primarily to the Sforza, the Dukes of Milan, who had succeeded in developing an excellent variety from the rice first brought to southern Italy by the Aragonese in the fifteenth century. Rice found the ideal climatic conditions in northern Italy, and it became the staple food of northern Italians just as pasta was in the South.

Italian rice is not long-grained, but it has the property of absorbing the liquid in which it cooks. From this rice was created one of the most successful dishes in the Italian culinary repertoire, risotto. Rice is also used in Italy to thicken vegetable soups and as a stuffing, but never as an accompaniment to meat or fish, as is done in other cuisines.

Although it is a peasant dish in origin, risotto is not a dish that can easily be mastered. I was weaned on it, and yet it was a long time before I dared cook a risotto for my mother or my critical brothers. The standard I had to reach represented quite a challenge, since I have tasted few risottos better than my mother's.

The first thing to remember is that risotto is prepared according to a well-defined method. It is not just a mixture of rice and other ingredients, and it is certainly not a dish that Italians make from an assortment of leftovers. Rice is often the only ingredient apart from flavorings. When there are other ingredients, they are almost always cooked with the rice, so that the flavors fuse together. Although there are certain rules that must be observed, the feel of making a good risotto can only be achieved with practice.

Rule number one is that the rice must be medium-grain white rice, which absorbs the liquid in which it cooks and which swells up without breaking or becoming mushy. There are four types of rice: superfino, fino, semifino and ordinario, of which only the first two can be used for making risotto. Arborio is a popular rice of the superfino type, easily available outside Italy because it is very widely produced. It has large plump grains with a delicious nutty taste when cooked. Other superfino varieties are Roma, Maratelli and Carnaroli. A good rice of the fino type is Vialone, a little shorter than Arborio, but still suitable for risotto. The semifino and ordinario types of rice are used for soups, salads, torte di riso (rice cakes), pies and puddings.

Secondly, the choice of saucepan is crucial to the success of the dish. I use a saucepan that is stainless steel on the inside and outside of the pan with an alloy in between; it has a heavy base containing a layer of copper. A heavy copper pan or an enameled cast-iron one would also be ideal. The pan must be large enough to contain the rice when it has finished cooking, by which time it will have nearly tripled in volume. Ideally it should also be round-bottomed to prevent the rice from sticking in the corners, and have a capacity of about three quarts.

Thirdly, risotto requires a generous amount of butter and, usually, cheese. It is the butter and the parmesan that give the risotto that lovely creamy consistency. I allow at least two ounces (four tablespoons) of butter to ten ounces (a scant cup and a half) of rice, which is the right amount for four people.

Another important factor is the quality of the stock. It should be a good, but light, meat stock (see page 3), made with a piece of veal, beef, a chicken part and very few bones, all flavored with vegetables, herbs and seasonings. Pork and lamb are too strong for this kind of stock. Vegetable stock (see page 4) is also very suitable for a vegetable or fish risotto. If you have not got any stock already prepared, use good quality canned broth.

Finally, the mantecatura. This happens at the very end when the risotto is taken off the heat. A knob of butter (preferably unsalted) and, when required, a few tablespoons of grated parmesan are added. The lid is put firmly on, and as soon as the butter has melted the risotto is stirred vigorously so that it becomes well mantecato, which means beaten to a creamy consistency.

A risotto should always be made just before being served. However if you have guests and you do not want to spend the last half an hour in the kitchen, you can try this method:

✂ Prepare the soffritto, sauté the rice and add about one cup of stock. As soon as the stock is boiling again, turn off the heat and leave the pot with a lid firmly on. When you go back to finish the dish you will find that the rice has absorbed all the stock and is half done. Add a knob of butter and proceed with the cooking, which will now take only ten minutes or so.

There are as many different kinds of risotto as there are ways of dressing pasta. The number of dishes that can be produced from these two basic ingredients has been greatly increased by the creativity of the new generation of chefs, who have combined unlikely flavors and textures in a risotto or in a pasta sauce. We have seen risottos with radicchio (perfect), with lobster (very chic), with champagne (strictly for weddings), with lemon (see page 27) or with rosemary.

All the traditional risottos are from northern Italy, which is where the rice grows. Lombardy, Piedmont and Veneto compete in offering magnificent risottos. The one that wins the prize, at least for me, is the risotto with truffles made in southern Piedmont. It is a plain risotto in bianco (page 26) with the local truffles grated over it at the table. From Venice come the risottos with fish and seafood, some of which are difficult to reproduce because of the difference in the fish available here. And Milan offers the best-known risotto, the risotto giallo, with saffron. It is one of the few Italian dishes to have been described in lyrical terms by a Frenchman. Edouard de Pomiane wrote, "On vous apporte une préparation que le soir, à la tombée du jour, vous paraîtra composée de grains d'or. Une bonne odeur vous énivre petit à petit et on se délecte déjà, rien qu'à regarder ce riz aux grains bien séparés et bien dorés." (They bring you a dish which, at the end of the day, will seem to you to be made of grains of gold. Little by little a good aroma intoxicates you, and you get pleasure just by looking at these beautifully golden, perfectly separated grains of rice.)

Risotto in bianco

RISOTTO WITH PARMESAN • SERVES 4

This is the basic risotto and as such the purest of any. It is the one which during the truffle season is crowned with slivers of white truffle. I prefer to serve this risotto, rather than the milanese, with both Osso Buco, Milanese Style (page 170) and Veal Chops, Milanese Style (page 50).

4 to 5 cups light meat stock
   (see page 3)
2 shallots *or* 1 small onion
4 tablespoons unsalted butter
1½ cups Arborio rice
scant ½ cup freshly grated
   parmesan

NOTE: This dish can successfully be made in advance, in which case serve in ramekins, which should be placed in a bain-marie of boiling water shortly before serving and heated in the oven until the risotto is hot through.

1 Bring the stock to a gentle simmer.

2 Meanwhile chop the shallots very finely and put them in a heavy saucepan with half the butter. Sauté until translucent and soft.

3 Add the rice and stir until well coated with the butter. Sauté, stirring constantly with a wooden spoon, until the grains become translucent and the rice begins to stick to the bottom of the pan.

4 Now pour over about ⅔ cup of stock. Let the rice absorb it and then add another ladleful. Continue to add stock gradually, and in small quantities, so that the rice always cooks in liquid but is never drowned by it. Stir constantly at first; after that you need to stir frequently but not all the time. In Milan we say that a good risotto should just catch at the bottom. The heat should be moderate, so as to keep the rice at a lively simmer.

5 When the rice is cooked (good Arborio rice takes about 25 minutes), remove the pan from the heat, add the rest of the butter, cut into small pieces, and the parmesan and put the lid firmly on the pan. Leave for 1 minute, until the butter and the parmesan have melted, then give the risotto a vigorous stir. This is to mantecare (cream) the risotto. Serve at once, with more parmesan passed separately.

✂ This risotto can easily become a risotto with dried porcini. Pour boiling water over 1 ounce of dried porcini. Leave them for 15 minutes, then lift them out and rinse under cold water. Chop them finely and add them to the softened shallots or onion. Sauté them for 1 minute before you add the rice, then proceed with the recipe. Strain the liquid in which the porcini soaked and add it to the rice while it is cooking.

✂ An attractive and convenient way to serve this risotto is to put it into ramekins, to be unmolded onto individual plates. Generously butter four 1-cup ramekins and sprinkle with dried breadcrumbs. Shake off excess crumbs and then fill the ramekins with the risotto, pressing down to get rid of any air bubbles. Put in a hot oven for 5 minutes or so, then unmold onto the plates. The timbales are delicious surrounded by Braised Mushrooms (page 131).

Risotto al limone

RISOTTO WITH LEMON • SERVES 4

For this excellent recipe I am indebted to my friend Romana Bosco, a talented cook who runs a cooking school in Turin. She, for her part, owes it to Giovanni Goria, a member of the Accademia Italiana della Cucina. The first time I made it, my husband looked very dubious at the idea of a risotto with lemon. He thought it sounded "rather white and insipid." From the first mouthful, however, he was a convert, and later he declared it his favorite risotto. It is indeed delicious—creamy and yet so light.

1 Heat the stock and keep it simmering all through the preparation of the dish.

2 Heat half the butter with the oil, the shallots and the celery in a heavy saucepan and cook until the soffritto of shallots and celery is done, about 7 minutes. Mix in the rice and continue cooking and stirring until the rice is well coated with fat and partly translucent.

3 Pour in about ⅔ cup of stock. Stir very thoroughly and cook until the rice has absorbed most of the stock. Add another small ladleful of simmering stock, and continue in this manner until the rice is ready. You may not need all the stock. Good quality Italian rice for risotto takes about 25 minutes to cook.

4 Meanwhile chop together the rind of half the lemon and the herbs, and mix them into the rice halfway through the cooking.

5 Combine the egg yolk, parmesan, the juice of half the lemon, the cream and a very generous grinding of black pepper in a small bowl. Mix well with a fork.

6 When the risotto is al dente remove the pan from the heat and stir in the egg and cream mixture and the remaining butter. Cover the pan and leave to rest for 2 minutes or so.

4 cups homemade light meat stock *or* vegetable stock (see pages 3–4)
4 tablespoons unsalted butter
1 tablespoon olive oil
2 shallots, very finely chopped
1 celery stalk, very finely chopped
1½ cups Italian rice, such as Arborio
1 lemon, very thoroughly scrubbed and washed
5 or 6 fresh sage leaves *or* 1 teaspoon dried sage
2 mint leaves
1 sprig celery leaves
1 small fresh rosemary sprig *or* 1 teaspoon dried rosemary
1 egg yolk
4 tablespoons freshly grated parmesan
4 tablespoons heavy cream
freshly ground black pepper

NOTE: Risotto should be prepared at the last minute, but if you cannot do this, read my note on page 25.

(*continued*)

RISOTTO WITH LEMON (*continued*)

Then give the risotto an energetic stir, transfer to a heated dish or bowl and serve at once, with more grated parmesan in a little bowl if you wish.

I find that this risotto goes very well as an accompaniment to some meat dishes, for instance Veal Chops, Milanese Style (page 50). I also like it with one of my family's chicken dishes: a cut-up chicken sautéed in butter and cooked in a covered casserole in a 375-degree oven with 1 cup heavy cream poured over—an old Milanese recipe.

Risotto alla marinara

RISOTTO WITH SHELLFISH • SERVES 6

This delicious risotto, originally from Venice, should contain a good selection of shellfish which can be varied according to what you find on the market. Whatever shellfish you pick, buy only the freshest and, if possible, avoid frozen shellfish. Freezing destroys much of the delicate flavor, and the final result will not be the same.

- **1 pound mussels, in the shell**
- **1 pound littleneck or cherrystone clams, in the shell**
- **5 garlic cloves, peeled**
- **1 lemon**
- **1 pound squid**
- **½ pound large shrimp, in the shell**
- **2 tablespoons white wine vinegar**
- **6 cups vegetable *or* fish stock *or* water**
- **½ cup olive oil**
- **1 shallot *or* ½ small onion, very finely chopped**
- **2 tablespoons chopped fresh parsley, preferably flat-leaf**
- **1 garlic clove, peeled and chopped**
- **2 scant cups Arborio rice**
- **½ cup dry white wine**
- **3 large sea scallops**
- **salt**
- **freshly ground black pepper**

1 Clean and prepare the mussels and clams with the garlic and lemon as described on page 66. Strain the liquid left at the bottom of the pan through a sieve lined with a piece of cheesecloth; set aside.

2 Clean and prepare the squid as described on page 62. Cut the squid into very small pieces. Set aside.

3 Wash the shrimp. Bring about 1½ quarts of water to the boil, add the vinegar and the shrimp. Cook for about 2 minutes after the water has come back to the boil. Drain the shrimp, cool slightly and then peel and cut into ¼- to ½-inch rounds. Set aside.

4 Put the shrimp shells in a piece of damp cheesecloth and, with your hands, squeeze out all the juices into the liquid reserved from the mussels and clams. You may find it easier to put the little bag in a mortar, bash it with the pestle a few times and then squeeze out all the juices. These juices and the liquid from the mussels and clams give the risotto a delicious fish flavor.

5 Bring the stock slowly to a simmer.

6 Reserve 2 tablespoons of the oil and heat the rest with the shallot or onion in a heavy saucepan and sauté gently until it is soft but not brown. Stir in half the parsley and the chopped garlic and sauté for about 1 minute. Add the squid and cook for 5 minutes, stirring very frequently. The squid will change from translucent to opaque and white.

7 Add the rice and stir well for about 1 minute. Turn the heat up to high and pour over the wine. Boil for about 1 minute to reduce, stirring the whole time.

8 Turn the heat down to medium and add about ¾ cup of simmering stock to the rice. Cook, stirring constantly, until nearly all the stock has been absorbed, then add another ½ cup of stock. Continue adding small amounts of simmering stock as soon as the rice absorbs the previous amount. You may not need all of the stock. The rice needs to be stirred every now and then, but not the whole time, so that you can do something else in the kitchen while the rice is cooking.

9 Halfway through the cooking (Arborio rice takes about 25 minutes to cook) wash and dry the scallops, and slice into 2 or 3 rounds. Add to the rice with the reserved liquid from the mussels and clams.

10 Five minutes before the risotto is ready, add the mussels, clams and shrimp. Stir well and add salt and pepper to taste.

11 Remove the pan from the heat and stir in the reserved 2 tablespoons of olive oil and the remaining parsley. Mix well, transfer to a warm dish and serve immediately.

This risotto could be followed by Porgy en Papillote (page 55), Sole with Artichoke Puree (page 91) or, indeed, any other fish. As this is a rich and very nourishing dish, you may like only to serve a vegetable dish to follow. I would choose Lemon-flavored Eggplant (page 94) or Wine-dressed Green Beans and Tomato Salad (page 120).

Risotto alla milanese

RISOTTO WITH SAFFRON •

SERVES 4 AS A FIRST COURSE OR 6 AS AN ACCOMPANIMENT

Risottos are usually served as first courses. However, risotto alla milanese is also the traditional accompaniment to Osso Buco (page 170) and Veal Chops, Milanese Style (page 50). If you cannot find beef marrow use unsmoked pancetta. In traditional Milanese households red wine is used instead of the more usual white; it gives a stronger flavor and a deeper color.

4 cups light meat stock (page 3)

1 small onion, very finely chopped

2 ounces beef marrow, chopped

5 tablespoons unsalted butter

1½ cups Arborio rice

⅔ cup dry red wine

½ teaspoon powdered saffron *or* about ½ teaspoon saffron threads crushed to a powder

salt

freshly ground black pepper (optional)

⅔ cup freshly grated parmesan

1 Bring the stock to a gentle simmer.

2 Put the onion, beef marrow and 4 tablespoons of the butter in a saucepan, sauté until soft and translucent, and then add the rice and stir until well coated with fat. Pour in the wine, boil for 1 minute, stirring constantly, and then pour in 1 cup of the stock. Cook until nearly all the stock has been absorbed and then add another cup of the simmering stock. Continue cooking and adding small quantities of stock. The risotto should cook at a steady lively simmer.

3 About halfway through the cooking (risotto takes about 25 minutes to cook) add the saffron dissolved in a little stock. When the rice is ready—it should be soft and creamy, not mushy or runny—taste and adjust the seasoning.

4 Remove from the heat and mix in the rest of the butter and half the parmesan. Put the lid on and leave for 1 minute. When the butter and the parmesan have melted give the risotto a vigorous stir and transfer to a heated dish. Serve immediately, with the rest of the cheese passed separately.

Risotto con gli asparagi

RISOTTO WITH ASPARAGUS • SERVES 4

This is a good vegetable risotto, to be made in the spring when local asparagus are on the market. If you haven't got any stock, use good quality canned broth instead.

1 Scrape the asparagus and wash thoroughly. Cut or snap off the hard bottom part of the stalks and put them in a

saucepan with the stock and boil for 15 minutes to extract the flavor. Lift them out with a slotted spoon and discard.

2 Cut off about 1 inch of the tender tips of the spears. Add the tips to the simmering stock and cook until al dente. Lift them out and set aside for decoration. Cut the rest of the spears into short lengths and put them in the boiling stock. Cook until tender. Lift out with a slotted spoon, place on a board and chop coarsely.

3 Put three-quarters of the butter and the onion in a heavy saucepan. Sauté very gently, adding a pinch or two of salt to release the liquid from the onion and prevent it from getting brown.

4 When the onion is soft, add the rice and cook it in the butter, turning it over and over until the grains become translucent.

5 Pour in a ladleful of simmering stock and let the rice absorb it while you stir it a few times. Risotto should be stirred frequently, but not the whole time. When all the stock in the pan has been absorbed, add another ladleful. Continue adding stock and letting the rice absorb it until the rice is al dente. You may not need to add all the stock. Halfway through the cooking, about 10 minutes after the rice has been added, stir in the chopped asparagus.

6 Remove the saucepan from the heat and add the remaining butter and half the cheese. Put the lid on, wait a couple of minutes and then give the risotto an energetic stir. Transfer to a heated dish, scatter the reserved asparagus tips over the top and serve at once, passing the remaining parmesan in a little bowl on the side.

✄ This delicate primo can be followed by either a fish, a meat or a poultry dish, as long as it is not too strongly flavored. Porgy en Papillote (page 55), Chicken with Orange (page 176) or Cold Roast Veal with Herbs (page 206) would all be good.

1 pound asparagus
7 to 8 cups vegetable stock *or* light meat stock (see pages 3–4)
5 tablespoons unsalted butter
1 small onion *or* a shallote, finely chopped
salt
1½ scant cups Arborio rice
½ cup freshly grated parmesan
pepper

LEFTOVER RISOTTO

There are two good ways of using left-over risotto, both better than just heating it up, or putting it in a soup with the result that it becomes overcooked. One is tortino di riso (rice cake), the other is risotto balls, which originated in Sicily. They are called arancini and are now also popular in the North. Traditionally arancini are stuffed with a meat ragù, a chicken-liver ragù or tomato and mozzarella. I prefer to stuff them only with mozzarella because I like my risotto so much that I do not want its flavor to be adulterated by the taste of tomatoes. Since some of my family like to combine the tastes, I serve a bowl of tomato sauce separately. All the vegetable risottos in this book make lovely mozzarella arancini.

✖ If you have 1½ cups of risotto left over, you can make 6 arancini the size of tangerines, enough for 3 people. You will need 4 ounces of mozzarella, 2 eggs, about ¼ cup of grated parmesan and some dried breadcrumbs. Cut the mozzarella into small pieces. Mix 1 egg and the parmesan into the risotto. Shape the risotto into balls. (If you moisten your hands the risotto won't stick to them.) Make a hole in each ball and push an equal amount of mozzarella into each one. Close the hole, dip the ball in the remaining egg, lightly beaten with a little salt and pepper, and then coat with the breadcrumbs, pressing the crumbs in with your hands.

If you have time, put the balls in the refrigerator; they fry better when chilled. About 10 to 15 minutes before dinnertime deep-fry the balls in hot (350°F.) vegetable oil. Fry them over medium-to-high heat for the first 5 minutes, then reduce the heat and fry for 5 minutes more, so that the mozzarella inside melts.

These arancini are an ideal dish for vegetarians. They make a lovely first course as well as a good accompaniment to steaks or roast chicken. They are also excellent cold.

✖ For a tortino di riso (rice cake) for 3 or 4 people, mix 2 eggs and 6 tablespoons grated parmesan into 1¼ to 1¾ cups of risotto. Add ¼ cup heavy cream and mix well. Put a knob of butter (1 tablespoon) in a nonstick frying pan and add the risotto mixture. Press it down neatly into a cake shape. Cook over very low heat for 7 minutes or so and then slide it under a preheated broiler until the top is crusty. Run a spatula around the edge of the pan and turn the tortino over onto a round dish. This is an excellent family first course or light lunch dish.

Polenta

The classic polenta is a mixture of cornmeal and water, although in some areas of northern Lombardy buckwheat flour is also included. In antiquity, however, polenta—puls or pulmentum in Latin—was made from spelt, a kind of wheat, and other cereals, while in the Middle Ages and the Renaissance, millet, chestnuts and even acorns provided the flour from which polenta was made. Corn was introduced to Europe by Columbus, who wrote in the diary he kept after landing in the New World: "Corn has a pleasant flavor and all the people of this country live on it." Within Europe corn was first cultivated in Spain, and the Spanish began to enjoy it so much that Charles V, who thought that wheat was the right food for Christians, promoted the cultivation of wheat rather than corn by means of various incentives to farmers. From Spain, corn reached Italy, arriving first in Venice at the Rialto market. The bridge was not yet built, but the market was there as it is now, and it was there that goods from abroad were unloaded.

This yellow grain was soon christened granoturco (Turkish grain), but why it was given this name is still the subject of dispute. Was it called granoturco because of the similarity between the silk of the cob and the beard of a Turk? Or was it, as Pianigiani wrote in his eighteenth-century *Etymological Dictionary,* "because of a mistake in the translation of the name the English gave to the cereal—turkey wheat—that is to say food for the turkey, a bird so called because of a certain likeness between the bird's neck and the Turkish turban"? To my mind the only credible explanation of the name is that in the sixteenth century so many things of foreign origin came (or were thought to come) from Turkey that turco became synonymous with foreign.

In Italy, granoturco was first cultivated in the Polesine, an area of marshy land between Padua and Ferrara around the Po delta. It was soon found to grow well where no other plant would grow, in hot and very humid places similar to its native land. For this reason granoturco became a very popular crop, and from it the first yellow polenta was made. This polenta had a far more pleasant taste than those made from other cereals, and before long, in northern Italy it became the staple food of the poor. Indeed, so good was this new polenta that in 1556 an aristocrat from Cremona sent a bag of seeds to Duke Ferdinando de' Medici in Florence, explaining to him that "it makes very good polenta." From the tables of the poor, polenta had reached the tables of the rich.

Here a sad episode in the history of polenta has to be recorded. By the early eighteenth century a strange new disease began to be noticed and written about. Characterized by red skin lesions, digestive disturbances, weakness and even mental and physical degeneration, the disease acquired the name of pellagra, from pelle agra, meaning rough skin. The symptoms occurred in the spring of each year, after a winter of eating little but polenta. In 1786, Goethe wrote in his *Italian Journey,* "Their features spoke of misery and their children looked just as pitiful . . . I believe the unhealthy condition is due to their constant diet of corn and buckwheat or, as they call

them, yellow and black polenta." Not unnaturally, polenta was blamed, and before long its consumption was forbidden by law. There followed widespread suffering as a result of malnutrition and hunger: in a few years the food that had been the main nourishment of many thousands of people had been taken away and declared fit only for animals.

It was not until early in this century when vitamins were discovered that the truth emerged. Pellagra was not due to any substance contained in the corn, but rather to a serious deficiency of protein and vitamins that occurs when corn is the only source of nourishment.

Polenta has been acclaimed, written and sung about and altogether celebrated more than any other Italian food. Societies were formed in Italy and abroad, some of which concealed political movements behind the pretense of discussions on the merits of a dish of polenta. The most famous society was the Ordine dei Polentoni, formed in Paris in the second half of the last century. The order numbered many well-known people among its members, including the painter De Nittis, Emile Zola, Edmond de Goncourt and the musician and librettist Arrigo Boito, who wrote a long poem in Venetian dialect on the art of stirring polenta. Polenta also inspired artists such as Magnasco and Longhi who, when representing a country interior, both showed golden polenta being poured out of a copper paiolo onto a white tablecloth as the centerpiece of their paintings. A paiolo is the vessel in which, traditionally, polenta is made. It has the shape of a wide, round-bottomed bucket, with a bucket handle, and it is made of unlined copper.

The actual making of polenta is a ritual, described by Giovanni Arpino, a twentieth-century writer, in nostalgic mood: "Between the stirring of the paiolo, the eating and the next unavoidable hunger, you had to devote a day to it. In the slower world, in the world that ignored frenzies, polenta acted as a clock. Can you seek, or find, these virtues in a lobster or a soufflé or even a raviolo? It is the unique, golden, refuge-food." And Alessandro Manzoni, in *I Promessi sposi,* wrote that when polenta was turned out onto the board it "looked like a harvest moon in a large circle of mist."

This golden moon is a very versatile food; it is so ready to be matched with others that in the province of Cuneo in Piedmont they call it La Traviata! It goes with butter and cheeses, with rich stews, with game and with salt cod. Left over, polenta makes rich layered dishes—polenta pasticciata—or it is fried or grilled to accompany many meat and fish dishes. The simplest of all polenta dishes, which used to be our Sunday supper when my children were young, is polenta with egg and bacon, a dish they used to compare to themselves—half Italian, half English and wholly remarkable! Cook your polenta in the usual way (try the pressure-cooker method on page 34). Mix in a good lump of butter and serve topped with fried eggs and surrounded by bacon, crisply fried.

Polenta is to an alpine Italian what pasta is to the southerner. Sadly it has lost ground to the all-conquering pasta, and this is partly because, for all its virtues, polenta is certainly not fast food.

HOW TO MAKE POLENTA. First you will need the ground corn, of which there are two kinds: finely ground for a soft, thin polenta, and coarsely ground cornmeal, for a harder and tastier polenta. The disadvantage of the latter is that it needs a longer cooking time to break down the harder outside casing of the grain. Then, as you are unlikely to have a paiolo hanging in your fireplace, you will need a large saucepan, a long and stout wooden spoon, a strong arm and some 30 to 45 minutes (depending on the coarseness of the meal) at your disposal (which explains why, in Italy, you can now buy a gadget that you plug in and set to stir for the prescribed time).

To remove the polenta that sticks to the bottom of the pan, never an easy job, fill the pan with enough water to cover the polenta that is sticking and leave it for up to 24 hours, after which it should come away easily. In the country of my youth this polenta from the bottom of the pan was given to the chickens. I now give it to my dog, Pippo, who loves it.

✄ To serve 4 to 6 people, fill a large saucepan with 6 to 7 cups of water and bring to the boil. Add 2 teaspoons coarse salt and turn the heat down. The water should only be simmering when you add the 1½ cups of cornmeal—a very important point, this—otherwise lumps will form very readily. For the same reason you should add the cornmeal in a very thin stream. The best way to do this is to pick up a fistful of meal and let it run through your closed fist. Meanwhile stir constantly with the wooden spoon. Continue stirring for at least 10 minutes after all the meal has been added. After that you can attend to other little jobs in the kitchen, as it is enough if you give the polenta a strong, hard stir every minute or so. You should let it cook for 30 to 45 minutes.

When the polenta is done, turn it out onto a wooden board on which you have laid a large white napkin. The polenta is now ready to be served with the dish of your choice or left to cool before being cooked again to make other dishes.

What I have just described is the traditional, time-honored method of making polenta. There is, however, another method which I first saw described in a recently published book, *Polenta, piatto da re,* by Maria Zaniboni Rivieccio. It is easy, quick and quite satisfactory, especially if you are going to give your polenta a second cooking, by frying it, making gnocchi or baking it in layers for a polenta pasticciata. This new method consists simply of making polenta in a pressure cooker, and I hope I will be forgiven for promulgating such a heresy.

✄ Put 6 cups of water and 1 tablespoon coarse salt in the pressure cooker and bring to the boil. Turn the heat down until the water is just simmering. Add 2 cups cornmeal in a very thin stream, letting it run through your clenched fist, while with the other hand you stir rapidly with a long wooden spoon, always in the same direction. When you have added all the cornmeal, turn the heat up and bring to the boil, stirring constantly. Fit the lid on the pressure cooker and bring to pressure. Put the weight in position and cook for 20 minutes. The polenta is now ready.

Polenta alla griglia e polenta fritta
GRILLED POLENTA AND FRIED POLENTA

Grilling and frying are the two most usual ways of using leftover polenta in northern Italy. Polenta alla griglia and polenta fritta are used as accompaniments to many dishes, including game, fritto misto and fried fish.

If you prefer to grill it, cut the cold polenta into slices ½ to ¾ inch thick and place them on the broiler pan. Brush each slice with olive oil and pass under the preheated broiler until a crust forms.

Leftover polenta, cut as above, can also be fried in a little butter or oil in a very heavy pan. Fry the slices on one side until a light crust forms, then turn them over and fry the other side.

Polenta alla pizzaiola
POLENTA WITH PIZZA TOPPING

This is another excellent way to use leftover polenta.

Cut the cold polenta into 2-inch squares. (Make smaller squares to serve with drinks; they are good either hot or at room temperature.) Drizzle a little olive oil over each square, cover with a slice of mozzarella and top that with a dollop of well-drained peeled and chopped tomatoes. Sprinkle some oregano and a pinch of salt over the pizzette, add plenty of pepper and dribble some more olive oil on top. Bake in a hot (375°F.) oven until the cheese has melted, about 5 minutes.

Polenta pasticciata alla piemontese
BAKED POLENTA WITH PORCINI · SERVES 4 TO 6

In Italy this dish is usually made with leftover polenta. The cold polenta is cut into slices and layered (pasticciata) with other ingredients. This can be done either by layering the polenta with a bolognese ragù and béchamel sauce, as with lasagne, or in the way described in this recipe. To my mind, and palate, the latter gives a more pleasing and harmonious result. This same sauce can also be used in layers with lasagne.

An optional ingredient here is the white truffle which, along with Barolo, is the gastronomic jewel of Piedmont. Nowadays white truffles are too precious to be cooked, but there is an excellent white truffle paste which gives the dish a delicious truffle flavor.

cooked polenta (page 34)
1½ ounces dried porcini
3 cups milk
4 tablespoons unsalted butter
⅓ cup flour
salt
pepper
1 tablespoon truffle paste (optional)
¼ pound Italian fontina, cut into thin slices
¼ pound gruyère, cut into thin slices
½ cup freshly grated parmesan

NOTE: The dish can be prepared totally in advance, even the day before. Bake it for a little longer so that it can heat through.

1 Make the polenta as described on page 34 at least 2 hours—or, if you like, 1 or 2 days—in advance, as it must be cold before you can prepare the dish. Pour the polenta onto a board and shape it into a rectangle that is about 2 inches thick, or pour it into a rectangular dish previously rinsed with cold water. Allow to cool.

2 Soak the dried porcini in a small bowl of warm water. I find that the recommended 30 minutes is often not enough to reconstitute them fully, and I prefer to leave them for 1 hour. Lift them out gently, rinse under cold water and dry very thoroughly. Chop the porcini coarsely.

3 Strain the liquid of the porcini through a sieve lined with a piece of cheesecloth or some paper towels. Pour gently and you'll find that any sand or grit will be left at the bottom of the bowl.

4 Preheat the oven to 425°F. Heat the milk until simmering. Melt the butter in a heavy saucepan, add the chopped porcini and sauté them gently for 10 minutes, adding a couple of tablespoons of their liquid during the cooking whenever necessary.

5 Stir in the flour and cook for 1 minute, stirring the whole time. Remove from the heat and incorporate the milk gradually, as you do for a béchamel. Add salt and pepper. Return the pan to the heat and bring to the simmer. Transfer to a double boiler or put a flame disperser under the pan and continue cooking the sauce for at least 15 minutes. I find that this slow cooking is essential for a delicate and well-blended sauce. At the end mix in the truffle paste. Check seasonings.

6 Cut the cold polenta vertically into slices just under ½ inch wide. Lightly butter a 10 x 6-inch ovenproof dish or

lasagne pan. Spread 2 tablespoons of the mushroom sauce over the bottom. Cover with a layer of polenta slices and then place some cheese slices here and there. Sprinkle with some parmesan and with a grinding of pepper. Spread some sauce over the cheese and then cover with another layer of polenta. Repeat these layers until you have used up all the ingredients, finishing with the sauce.

7 Bake in the preheated oven for 10 to 15 minutes. Let stand for 5 minutes before serving.

✄ This nourishing, warming dish can be followed by Red Mullet en Papillote (page 60) or Chicken with Orange (page 176).

Beans

Chickpeas and certain beans were everyday food in Roman times. Horace, in one of his Odes, talks of going home to his supper of lasagne and chickpeas—ciceri in Latin. Indeed, one of Cicero's ancestors is said to have acquired the name because he had a wart on his nose that looked like a chickpea. In the Middle Ages, beans were valued highly enough to be accepted as currency in the payment of taxes or alimony. By the Renaissance, however, beans had fallen out of favor. In 1589 a doctor from Bologna, Baldassare Pisanelli, wrote that beans were "food for peasants, not suitable for refined people." Worst of all, lentils "are harmful to melancholy people, make one have horrible dreams, fatten the blood so that it cannot run in the veins . . . induce leprosy, cancer and other melancholy infirmities."

All this reads very strangely nowadays, when beans are considered among the healthiest of foods and their popularity is so widespread. It is a well-deserved popularity, as they are quite delicious whether on their own, in combination with other ingredients or mixed together in salads dressed with olive oil and generously flavored with herbs.

The beans that feature most often in Italian cooking are various varieties of the common bean, favas, lentils and chickpeas. The common bean (Phaseolus vulgaris), which reached Italy from the New World, quickly became a great favorite. It began to be successfully cultivated in Veneto early in the sixteenth century. It is said that Charles V gave a sack of these beans to Pope Clement VII, who in turn presented them to one Piero Valeriano, a tutor at the court of the Medicis. Valeriano distributed the beans among the country people of Lamon, not far from his native Belluno, and when they planted some of these foreign beans an excellent crop resulted. Thus were born the fagioli di Lamon, which are large, with a very tender skin and a full flavor.

Different varieties were successfully developed from the fagioli di Lamon, of which the borlotti are perhaps the most popular. It is in northern Italian recipes that borlotti have come into their own, while Tuscany has given us the best ways to use the white cannellini. These include ribollita, which is a soup based on cannellini and Tuscan black cabbage, and Dried Beans with Sage (page 40). Just as remarkable are the various versions of pasta e fagioli from Veneto.

The motherland of fava beans is Apulia, where they are staple fare all year round. There, favas are mostly eaten dried, as in the excellent dish we had when we visited a farmhouse near Cisternino in Apulia. The first thing we noticed when Maria, the farmer's wife, showed us around was that although there was only one very small sitting room totally dedicated to a leather suite and a massive television set, there were no less than three kitchens, "one for everyday use, one for making pasta and the third for visitors," Maria explained. It was fairly late in the evening as we sat in the visitors' kitchen drinking the strong local wine, but nonetheless a large bowl full of a puree of dried beans was placed in the middle of the table. Called 'ncapriata, it was a soft creamy mixture of pureed dried fava beans and boiled turnip greens, flavored with garlic and generously dressed with thick local oil. Even after a good dinner, this simple dish was memorable.

The lentils of Italy are the brown variety, which keep their shape when cooked. The best ones are from Castelluccio, a town in Umbria. They are small and dark brown, with a full, sweet flavor, and they cook in only 20 minutes.

Chickpeas, like fava beans, are more popular in the South, where they are cooked very simply and are often mixed with pasta. Perhaps their popularity is due to their reputation as an aphrodisiac; they are one of the few peasant foods for which this claim is made.

The most important thing when buying beans is to go to a supplier who has a quick turnover. All dried beans must be eaten within twelve months of being harvested—from one summer to the next—otherwise they stay hard however long you soak them, and they lose their flavor. Have a good look at them. They should have a fresh look, without wrinkles.

HOW TO SOAK AND COOK BEANS. Lentils can be cooked without being soaked, a great advantage if like me, you never plan a meal until you have come home from the shops. Chickpeas and dried fava beans, on the other hand, need long soaking, sometimes as long as 24 hours, but certainly overnight.

Cover chickpeas with cold water. Make a thin paste with 1 teaspoon baking soda, 1 tablespoon flour and 1 tablespoon salt. Stir this mixture into the chickpeas and leave overnight. When they are ready, drain and rinse them, and cook them in unsalted water. Do not lift the lid of the saucepan for the first 1 to 1½ hours, or the chickpeas may harden. They can take as long as 4 hours to cook, longer than any other bean.

In general, the soaking of common beans is a subject that always causes great argument among cooks and gastronomes. When, as often happens, I have forgotten to put my beans in to soak for the recommended four to six hours, I fall back on the excellent method of boiling them for two or three minutes, draining and rinsing them and then cooking them in fresh water until soft. They usually need just 1 to 1½ hours. This method makes the beans more digestible.

Cook beans in an earthenware pot if possible. Add vegetables and herbs to the pot, but do not add salt until the very end, about ten minutes before the beans are ready. Harold MacGee, in his *On Food and Cooking,* suggests cooking beans in a small quantity of water, since "the less cooking water, the fewer carbohydrates are leached out. . . . So give the seeds enough water both to soak up *and* cook in (many a pan bottom has been charred because the cook forgot that beans imbibe), but don't drown them."

Anatra alla pavese
DUCKLING WITH LENTILS • SERVES 4

Lentils are very successfully combined with duck in this recipe from Pavia, one of my favorite provincial cities in Lombardy. The lentils, partly cooked, are added to the seared duck pieces for a final braising. The lentils absorb some of the fat from the duck, thus becoming rich and tasty.

1 Wash the duckling inside and out, put it on a slanting board and leave to drain for 10 minutes or longer. Cut into pieces and pat dry with paper towels.

2 Put the back, wings and neck of the duck in a stockpot. Add the onion, celery, bay leaves, parsley, garlic, peppercorns and salt, cover with water and bring to the boil. Skim the foam that rises at the beginning. Turn the heat down very low—just enough for a bubble to break the surface of the liquid every now and then. Cook for 2 hours. Strain into a clean saucepan and reduce the stock until full of the flavor of the duck, to about 1 cup. Allow to cool and skim off the fat. If you prepare the stock a day in advance, you can easily remove the fat from the cold stock.

3 To prepare the lentils, put them in a sieve and rinse under cold water, picking out any small stones or bits of grit. Then put them in a saucepan, cover with cold water, add the oil, onion, celery and a little salt and bring slowly to the boil. Simmer gently, covered, until the lentils are just beginning to get soft. It is difficult to give an exact time since this depends on the quality and freshness of the lentils. The tiny delicious lentils of Umbria, for instance, only need a blanching.

4 Choose a heavy deep frying pan and lay the pieces of the duck in it, skin side down. Cook the breast for 5 minutes and the legs for about 10 minutes, moving the pieces a little at the beginning to prevent the skin from sticking to the bottom of the pan. Transfer the duck to a casserole. Drain off most of the fat (keep it for roast or sautéed potatoes).

5 Add the shallot, celery and a bit of salt to the pan and sauté until the vegetables are tender. Scoop them out and add to the casserole.

6 Pour the grappa over the duck and flame it. When the flame has died out, add the wine and about ½ cup of the duck stock. Bring to the boil. Drain the lentils and add them. Season with a little salt and a good deal of pepper. Cover the casserole and simmer gently until both the lentils and the duck are tender, about 20 to 30 minutes.

7 Mix the cornstarch with a couple of tablespoons of the stock and stir into the sauce. Let the sauce bubble for 5 minutes and then check the seasoning. Serve directly from the casserole or, for a more formal occasion, lay a bed of lentils on a platter and place the duck on top.

1 duckling, 4½ to 5 pounds

STOCK

1 onion, stuck with a clove
1 celery stalk, with its green leaves if possible
2 bay leaves
4 fresh parsley sprigs
1 garlic clove, peeled
5 peppercorns, lightly bruised
salt

LENTILS

½ pound brown lentils (1 cup)
1 tablespoon olive oil
1 onion, cut in half
1 celery stalk, cut in half
salt

_____

3 shallots *or* 1 onion, very finely chopped
a handful of celery leaves *or* 1 small celery stalk, very finely chopped
salt
2 tablespoons grappa *or* marc
⅔ cup dry white wine
freshly ground black pepper
1 teaspoon cornstarch *or* arrowroot

NOTE: This dish can be prepared in advance and slowly reheated.

(*continued*)

✖ Do not serve any other vegetables with this dish, just a fresh salad afterward. For a primo I have served penne with ricotta salata in a tomato sauce, or, for less hearty eaters, Lemon-flavored Eggplant (page 94).

Fagioli all'uccelletto
DRIED BEANS WITH SAGE • SERVES 4

This characteristic dish from Tuscany is made in many ways. I give here my two favorite versions, which I first had in Chianti some years ago when we had a farmhouse near Gaiole. I prefer the version without tomato, fagioli all'uccelletto in bianco, because the sweet earthy taste of the beans comes through without being dominated by the tomato sauce.

Fagioli all'uccelletto means, literally, beans made the little bird's way. In fact the name must have come about because beans prepared like this are the traditional accompaniment to uccelletti (little birds), of which the Tuscans are inordinately greedy. This explanation is also given by Lynda Brown in Number 24 of the *Petits propos culinaires,* where she describes another version of the beans without tomato sauce which she had in Radda, north of Gaiole. In her version the beans are added to a sautéed onion, another good alternative.

NOTE: I hesitate to suggest the use of canned beans for this recipe because they often lack flavor and tend to become mushy. You might end up with a dish far removed from the real fagioli all'uccelletto.

NOTE: You can serve the dish with braised or grilled meat, although I like to serve these beans on their own.

For 4 people you will need 2½ to 3 cups of cooked and drained beans. Put 3 tablespoons of extra-virgin olive oil in a sauté pan with a beautiful sprig of fresh sage and 2 garlic cloves, peeled and bruised. Sauté until the sage begins to sizzle and the garlic aroma rises. At that point remove and discard the garlic. If you want your fagioli red, add 2 tablespoons of tomato paste at this point; stir for a minute or so to allow the paste to cook through and lose its metallic flavor. Add the beans and flavor them in the oil, with or without the tomato paste. Pour in just enough water or stock to cover the bottom of the pan, about a couple of tablespoons. Season with a little salt and a lot of pepper and cook until most of the liquid has been absorbed, about 10 minutes. Transfer the beans to a dish or bowl and let them cool: they should be eaten just warm. Pour over a couple of

tablespoons of extra-virgin olive oil before serving—this is
the touch that makes all the difference!

Ceci e rucola

CHICKPEAS AND ARUGULA • SERVES 4

I love the look of this salad, with the many-pointed green leaves of
the arugula mixed in with the simple roundness of the chick peas. I
have used canned chickpeas for this dish and they were perfectly all
right, although I missed the fuller flavor of the dried ones. If you
want to use dried chickpeas, see the instructions on page 38 for
soaking and cooking them. This is my husband's favorite dish when
he is alone; he opens a can from the pantry and collects the arugula
from the garden. Easy, nourishing and really excellent.

1 Drain the chickpeas and rinse quickly under cold
water. Now, if you have time, squeeze the skin off the
chickpeas one by one. This is much easier than it sounds and
quite quick, and it makes a big difference in the final dish.
Apart from avoiding pieces of skin between the teeth, it
allows the oil to penetrate the chickpeas much better.

2 Heat half the oil and the garlic in a sauté pan. When
the aroma of the garlic rises, remove and discard it. Add the
chickpeas and heat until hot. Turn off the heat and leave the
chickpeas to cool.

3 Remove the stalks from the arugula and wash and dry
the leaves.

4 Transfer the chickpeas to a salad bowl and add the
arugula. Dress with the remaining oil, with salt to taste and
plenty of pepper.

3 cups cooked or canned
  chickpeas
⅔ cup extra-virgin olive oil
2 garlic cloves, peeled
about ¼ pound arugula
salt
pepper

NOTE: This recipe is good using lentils instead of chickpeas.

✕ This is a cheerful and informal first course,
particularly good at lunch. It can also serve as a nourishing
yet fresh second course for vegetarians.

Bread

Pancotto
BREAD SOUP

Canederli
BREAD GNOCCHI

Tortino di zucchine
BAKED ZUCCHINI IN TOMATO SAUCE

Cavolfiore strascinato con la mollica
CAULIFLOWER AND BREADCRUMBS WITH
ANCHOVIES, CAPERS AND OLIVES

Torta di Pane
BREAD CAKE

Passatelli
PASSATELLI

Costolette alla milanese
VEAL CHOPS, MILANESE STYLE

SEE ALSO

Funghi al forno
BAKED MUSHROOMS WITH ANCHOVIES AND
CAPERS

La cotoletta a la lavandera
BREADED VEAL CHOPS IN A SWEET-AND-SOUR
SAUCE

La mia mozzarella in carrozza
FRIED MOZZARELLA AND SALAMI
SANDWICHES

La panzanella a modo mio
PANZANELLA

Bread is one of the essential ingredients for making many Italian dishes. It is used as a thickener, as in salsa verde; in soups, both to thicken and to make the soup more filling; and in stuffings to add a neutral element as well as for economic reasons. Torta di pane—literally, bread cake—is made everywhere in Italy, always slightly differently, and is usually as good as the best bread-and-butter pudding, its northern European counterpart.

The Italians are said to eat more bread than any other nation in the world. They like their bread fresh, which often means bread baked the same day, yet their education, culture and natural thrift would never allow bread to be thrown away. So once the animals were fed with the stale bread, other ways of using what was still left had to be found. Thus some of the best recipes of the cucina povera were created, cucina povera meaning not poor cooking but cooking as done by the poor. It is in fact a cooking rich in flavor, originality and local aromas. Try the Bread Soup (page 43), one of the innumerable versions of this soup made up and down the country, and you will see what I mean. The bread used is usually white, but it is thick, coarse country bread, not the light airy rolls usually eaten at the table.

I keep a loaf of bakery white bread, cut in half, in the freezer for the many times I need bread in my recipes. Whole wheat bread, which I prefer for the table, has a nutty taste that would often interfere with the dish I want to make.

Pancotto

BREAD SOUP • SERVES 4

Every region, town, village and family in Italy has a favorite pancotto, and here is mine. It is the best way to use up good leftover bakery white bread.

- **½ pound good-quality white bread, crust removed**
- **4 tablespoons extra-virgin olive oil**
- **1 dried chili, or more according to taste, crumbled**
- **3 garlic cloves, peeled and chopped**
- **3 tablespoons chopped fresh parsley**
- **6 cups vegetable stock *or* light meat stock (pages 3–4)**
- **salt**
- **freshly ground black pepper**
- **freshly grated pecorino romano or parmesan**

1 Break up the bread into pieces and process for a few seconds or chop coarsely by hand.

2 Put half the oil, the chili, garlic and parsley in a heavy stockpot (earthenware is best) and sauté for 1 minute or so, stirring constantly. Add the bread and stir it in the oil for about 5 minutes, until it begins to become golden.

3 Pour the stock over the bread and simmer, uncovered, for 35 to 40 minutes. Taste and adjust seasonings.

4 Ladle the soup into individual bowls and divide the rest of the oil between each bowl. Serve with the cheese passed separately in a bowl.

I prefer this soup at room temperature, especially in the summer.

Canederli

BREAD GNOCCHI •
SERVES 4 AS A PRIMO OR 6 AS AN ACCOMPANIMENT TO A STEW

1¼ to 1½ cups milk

about ¾ pound whole wheat
    bread and good-quality
    white bread

½ pound thick-sliced bacon

5 tablespoons unsalted butter

1 medium onion, very finely
    chopped

3 tablespoons chopped fresh
    parsley

½ cup freshly grated parmesan

2 eggs

pinch of grated nutmeg

salt

freshly ground black pepper

flour

12 cups meat *or* vegetable stock

1 teaspoon rosemary

4 or 5 fresh sage leaves *or* 2 or 3
    dried leaves

NOTE: When you serve these gnocchi
with meat, make them larger—the
size of a tangerine. They go better and
it takes less time.

NOTE: You can prepare the gnocchi
in advance through Step 8 and then
heat them in the oven, covered with
foil, for 20 minutes or so.

These gnocchi are, as their name suggests, the Italian version of the
Austrian knödel. They can be made with whole wheat, rye or coarse
white bread—any bread, in fact, as long as it is good—and they can
be as large as oranges or as small as walnuts. When they are big they
are best served with goulash, which is the traditional way, or with
other meat stews. I prefer small canederli dressed with butter melted
until it becomes just lightly nutty, and flavored with a little sprig of
rosemary and a few fresh sage leaves. I use stale leftover bakery
whole wheat and white bread mixed together, with the crust left on.
It is one of the most successful dishes one can make from the old
pieces of bread at the bottom of the bread box.

The canederli are boiled in stock. If I haven't got enough
meat or chicken stock ready, I prepare a vegetable stock with an
onion stuck with a clove, a carrot, a couple of celery stalks, some
parsley stems, a leek, a garlic clove and a tomato. If you are in a
hurry, boil the canederli in canned chicken broth or canned beef
broth and a little soy sauce.

You can make bread gnocchi di magro for vegetarians by
leaving out the bacon and putting in more onion, parsley and
parmesan.

1 Heat the milk. Break the bread into small pieces and
put in a bowl. Pour over enough hot milk to cover and leave
for about 3 hours. You might have to add a little more milk
after a while; it is difficult to be exact, but what you should
have at the end is a moist yet solid mixture. Break it up very
thoroughly with a fork. It is important to incorporate as
much air as you can while breaking it up, and for this reason
you should not use a food processor, which would mash the
mixture. After you have broken up the larger lumps of bread,
however, you can use an electric beater. The mixture should
not be pureed but should look like wet cracked wheat.

2 Fry the bacon in a frying pan until it changes color
and part of the fat has run out; don't brown the bacon, just
soften it. Cut it into tiny cubes and add to the bread mixture.

3 Pour off the bacon fat from the frying pan and put in
2 tablespoons butter and the onion. Sauté very gently for 5
minutes, stirring very frequently, and then add the parsley.
Continue to cook for another minute. Mix in 3 tablespoons of
the parmesan and add the contents of the pan to the bread
mixture.

4 Lightly beat the eggs and add to the bread mixture together with the nutmeg and salt and pepper to taste. Now mix everything together very thoroughly, lifting the mixture lightly, using a large metal spoon.

5 Before you make the gnocchi, shape one dumpling about the size of a small walnut and slide it into a small saucepan of boiling water. If it holds its shape, proceed to make all the dumplings; if it breaks apart, add a little flour to the mixture and test once more.

6 Put some flour on the work surface. Pluck out small spoonfuls of the mixture, shape them into ovals or balls and coat them lightly in the flour. This sticky job is much easier to do with moist hands: I keep a damp kitchen towel nearby and wipe my hands with it after every four or five shapes.

7 Put the gnocchi on a tray lined with a clean kitchen towel and put the tray (or trays) in the refrigerator for at least 30 minutes. It does not matter if you leave them longer.

8 Bring the stock to the boil. Taste and adjust salt and then gently drop in the gnocchi. When the stock comes back to the boil, regulate the heat so that it will keep a lively simmer. Do not let the stock boil vigorously, or the gnocchi will break up. Let them simmer for 20 minutes and then take them out with a slotted spoon and put them on a board lined with paper to drain. Keep the stock for a soup, it is even tastier than it was before you started the dish!

9 Preheat the oven to 400°F.

10 Transfer the gnocchi to a buttered ovenproof dish that is large enough for the gnocchi to fit more or less in a single layer. Heat the rest of the butter with the rosemary and the sage in a small pan until the butter turns a deep gold. Remove and discard the herbs, pour the butter over the gnocchi and sprinkle with a little of the cheese. Put the dish in the oven for a few minutes, just until the cheese melts, and then serve, with the rest of the cheese on the side.

These gnocchi are also very good dressed with a tomato sauce, as is done in Trentino. If you serve them as a first course, any meat, fish or vegetable dish can follow. I would choose Rabbit with Herbs and Dried Porcini (page 132) or Tuna Baked with Tomatoes, Capers, Black Olives and Chilies (page 59). They can also be served as an accompaniment to any rich stew, such as Sweet-and-sour Shoulder of Lamb (page 223) or Beef Stewed in Barbera Wine (page 215).

DRIED BREADCRUMBS

In every Italian kitchen there is a jar or a tin full of dried breadcrumbs, an essential ingredient in many dishes. Breadcrumbs are used to thicken sauces, as in salsa verde, and they are sprinkled on gratin dishes to form a thin crust, and into buttered pans to prevent food from sticking. There are also some dried breadcrumbs in most stuffed dishes, while in southern Italy they are used instead of grated cheese in many pasta dishes.

Dried breadcrumbs should be made with good quality white bread that is coarse in texture. You can use a mixture of white and whole wheat bread, but breadcrumbs should be tasteless as they are used as a background to other ingredients. Do not make them only from dark bread as they will then have a noticeable taste. To make the breadcrumbs, break the bread into small pieces and toast them in the oven. Process the pieces until they are crumbs. The breadcrumbs should be stored in the refrigerator in an airtight container, but they should not be kept for longer than two months. I always make a lot of breadcrumbs, and put one jar in the fridge and another in the freezer, where the crumbs will keep for several months.

COSTOLETTA AND COTOLETTA. In northern Italy the main function of dried breadcrumbs is to give that delicious outside coating to food that is fried in butter. This method of cooking is typical of Lombardy, where butter plays such an important part. The best known dish is costoletta alla milanese, which consists of a veal chop, lightly pounded, coated in eggs, breaded and fried in butter. It is a mouth-watering dish, though not so easy to make perfectly as you might think. The outside crust must be beautifully golden, with no black specks of burnt crumbs, while the veal inside must be cooked à point, i.e., no longer pink but still succulent. Co-tolette, veal scaloppine cooked in the same way, are easier to make. The scaloppine, being sliced thin, need very little cooking, and there is thus less danger of burning the crust. Both costolette and cotolette can also be eaten cold; they make excellent picnic food.

I still remember the grand picnics we used to have every summer before the war, on our way to Forte dei Marmi in Tuscany for our seaside holidays. We went with our cousins, a caravan of three cars loaded with children, nannies, trunks, suitcases and dogs. The road over the Apennines was long and twisting—no Parma–La Spezia highway then—and it took the whole day to get there. This was partly because we stopped high up on the Cisa pass to have our elaborate picnic lunch. White tablecloths were spread out on the emerald green pasture, the hampers came out of the vast car trunks and the food boxes were opened. I was the youngest of the cousins and I had to fight to get my costoletta, my favorite food, so delicious, and so perfect to eat with its bone serving as a handle. The grown-ups often had cotolette instead, which they ate with a touch of mayonnaise. (French dishes and customs had become part of the Lombard cuisine during the nineteenth century).

Pork, chicken breast, liver, brains and sweetbreads can be cooked a cotoletta (breaded and fried) as, of course, can fish steaks or fillets of fish. Slices of eggplant are delicious prepared in this way. Meat cotolette can also form part of more elaborate dishes. You can put a slice of gruyère over each cotoletta, place the cotolette in an ovenproof dish, spoon over some béchamel and bake in the oven for ten to fifteen minutes. Another way to serve cotolette is to place a slice of mozzarella over the meat, cover with a spoonful of tomato sauce, sprinkle with a little oregano and then bake until the cheese has melted. Breaded pork chops can be served with a sweet-and-sour sauce. An advantage of all these dishes over plain costolette is that the meat can be fried in advance.

Tortino di zucchine

BAKED ZUCCHINI IN TOMATO SAUCE • SERVES 4 TO 6

A tortino is a baked vegetable dish of any sort. It is usually baked without a pastry case; with pastry it becomes a torta. It is the sort of dish that I like best: easy, uncomplicated and with as many variations as you care to make. The crust here is made with a mixture of breadcrumbs and parmesan; whole wheat breadcrumbs are perfect in this dish.

1½ pounds zucchini
salt
2 tablespoons unsalted butter
4 tablespoons olive oil
2 onions, finely sliced
2 garlic cloves, peeled and finely sliced
1 tablespoon chopped fresh parsley, preferably flat-leaf
½ pound fresh ripe tomatoes, peeled, seeded and coarsely chopped, *or* 1½ cups coarsely chopped canned plum tomatoes
1 teaspoon oregano
freshly ground black pepper
3 tablespoons fresh soft brown breadcrumbs, very lightly toasted
3 tablespoons freshly grated parmesan

1 Gently scrub the zucchini under cold water. Unless the zucchini are very small, remove the more protruding ribs with a potato peeler.

2 Cut the zucchini into ¼-inch rounds, put them in a colander, sprinkle generously with salt and mix well with your hands. Let drain while you prepare the tomato sauce.

3 Heat the butter and half the oil in a medium sauté pan and, as soon as the butter is melted, add the onion and a pinch of salt (this will make the onions wilt without browning). Sauté over low heat until soft and then add the garlic and the parsley. Fry gently for 1 minute, stirring constantly.

4 Turn the heat up to medium and add the chopped tomatoes with their juice. Bring to the boil, turn the heat down to low and simmer for 10 minutes, stirring frequently.

5 Preheat the oven to 375°F.

6 Rinse the zucchini under cold water and dry thoroughly with a cloth or with plenty of paper towels.

7 Add the zucchini to the tomatoes and cook, uncovered, for about 15 minutes. They should be tender but still firm. The timing depends on the freshness and size of the zucchini. Stir every so often, using a fork rather than a spoon, as this is less likely to break them. Add the oregano and the pepper, taste and check salt.

8 Grease a shallow ovenproof dish with a little of the remaining oil.

9 Mix the breadcrumbs with the cheese in a bowl. Spoon the zucchini into the oiled dish and sprinkle the breadcrumb mixture on top. Pour over the rest of the oil in a thin stream and bake for about 15 minutes, until the crumbs have turned brown. Allow the dish to stand for a few minutes out of the oven before serving.

NOTE: You can prepare the dish in advance through Step 7. Heat the zucchini with the tomato sauce on top of the stove before putting them in the oven dish.

✂ This tortino can be served as a primo, as a secondo

(*continued*)

or as an accompaniment to plain roast or grilled meat or poultry. Like any good Italian, I like to start my meal with a nourishing dish, so I prefer to serve the tortino as a light second course after a fairly substantial primo, such as Bread Gnocchi (page 44) or Risotto with Luganega (page 73). If you want to serve it as a first course, you can follow it with Braised Shoulder of Pork with Herbs and Garlic (page 203) or with Porgy en Papillote (page 55). In fact any other meat or fish dish will go well, as long as it does not contain tomatoes and is robust enough to hold its own after this Mediterranean overture.

Cavolfiore strascinato con la mollica

CAULIFLOWER AND BREADCRUMBS WITH ANCHOVIES, CAPERS AND OLIVES • SERVES 4

Whole wheat breadcrumbs are better than white for this tasty dish from southern Italy. I make my soft crumbs in a food processor, a very quick job. You can use broccoli instead of cauliflower.

1 head of cauliflower, about 1 pound

6 tablespoons extra-virgin olive oil

1 cup soft breadcrumbs

3 salted anchovies, boned and washed, *or* 6 anchovy fillets

1 or 2 dried chilies, according to taste, seeded

2 garlic cloves, peeled

1½ tablespoons capers, rinsed and dried

12 black olives, pitted and cut into strips

salt

pepper

1 Divide the cauliflower into small florets and cut the tender stalks into small pieces. Wash carefully. Blanch in boiling salted water for 5 minutes and then drain and dry with paper towels.

2 Heat the oil and then add the breadcrumbs. Cook for 3 minutes, stirring to coat them with the oil.

3 Add the cauliflower florets and stalks, and cook until tender but still crunchy, stirring very frequently. Use a fork rather than a spoon, as this helps to keep the florets whole.

4 Meanwhile chop the anchovies, chilies, garlic and capers and add them to the cauliflower and bread mixture. Add the olives and cook for another minute or so. Stir well. Taste and add salt and pepper as necessary.

Torta di pane
BREAD • SERVES 8

This dessert, made from stale bread, is like a cake, since it is unmolded and served cold. There are as many different versions as there are regions of Italy, and a few more. You can use bits of chocolate or almonds and other nuts in place of the candied peel. In fact, you can vary it as you like, according to what you have in your cupboard. You could also use less cream and more milk, or vice versa, to suit your taste, your diet or your health worries. I think my recipe is a reasonable compromise.

I try to keep a small jar of raisins steeped in rum ready for use; being already soaked, and in rum rather than in water, they come in very handy. You can soak them in marc or in brandy and simply add them with the spirit to your dessert. Scrub the lemon very thoroughly before you grate it to get rid of the pesticides.

1 Preheat the oven to 375°F.

2 Remove the crust from the bread, cut it roughly and toast it in the oven for 5 minutes. Put the bread in a bowl and add the butter.

3 Bring the milk and the cream to the boil and pour it over the bread and butter. Beat well and leave to cool.

4 Meanwhile soak the raisins in the rum for 15 minutes.

5 When the bread mixture is cool, beat it with a fork until soft and mushy. Add the sugar, the raisins and rum, the lemon rind, cinnamon, cloves, ginger, saffron, candied peel and pine nuts and mix very well.

6 Lightly beat the egg yolks and add to the bread mixture. Whip the egg whites until they form stiff but not dry peaks, and fold them gently into the mixture.

7 Line a buttered 8-inch cake pan with parchment paper, butter the paper and spoon the mixture into the pan. Bake for about 1 hour, turn the oven down to 300°F. and bake for 20 minutes more, or until a skewer inserted into the middle of the cake comes out dry.

8 Allow to cool in the pan and then unmold and peel off the paper. Put the cake on a pretty dish and sprinkle lavishly with confectioners' sugar.

✖ If you are a cream fan, you may like to pass around some heavy cream in a pitcher, although I find the cake is excellent without it.

about ¼ **pound one-day-old, good-quality white bread**
5 **tablespoons unsalted butter**
1 **cup milk**
1¼ **cups light cream**
¼ **cup golden raisins**
3 **tablespoons rum**
⅔ **cup sugar**
grated rind of 1 lemon
½ **teaspoon ground cinnamon**
pinch of ground cloves
pinch of ginger
pinch of powdered saffron
2 **tablespoons chopped candied peel**
2 **tablespoons pine nuts**
3 **eggs, separated**
confectioners' sugar

NOTE: This cake is better made a day in advance, to allow all the flavors to blend together.

Passatelli

PASSATELLI • SERVES 4

This delicate soup from Romagna is made with breadcrumbs, eggs, veal marrow and parmesan. The stock must be of good quality, delicate yet full of flavor. To make it easier to get the marrow from the bone, ask your butcher to split the bone lengthwise. Scoop the marrow out with a teaspoon. You can freeze the marrow you don't use for this soup; it's perfect in a soffritto for risotto or in stuffing for ravioli.

6 cups homemade meat stock (page 3)

⅓ cup freshly grated parmesan

6 tablespoons fine dried breadcrumbs

2 tablespoons veal marrow

1 egg

freshly grated nutmeg

1 Heat the stock and bring to the boil.

2 Meanwhile mix the parmesan and the breadcrumbs together in a bowl. Crumble in the marrow, break in the egg, add a generous amount of nutmeg and knead everything together. The mixture should have the consistency of couscous.

3 Fit the disk with the largest holes into your food mill. When the stock is boiling, press the mixture through the food mill straight into the simmering stock. Simmer for a couple of minutes and then remove from the heat. Allow to stand for a few minutes before ladling the soup into individual bowls.

Costolette alla milanese

VEAL CHOPS, MILANESE STYLE • SERVES 4

This is by far the best way to prepare veal chops. It is not easy, but if you buy the right meat and follow the method carefully, you will be amply rewarded by the result. When you buy veal chops for this dish, check that the meat is very pale pink and the fat milky white. Ask the butcher to pound the chops to a thickness of half an inch. Ask him also to knock off the corner where the rib joins the backbone and to trim off the tail end of the chop. (You can use these trimmings for stock or for a ragù).

I fry my costolette, and any other breaded food, by putting them with the butter in a *cold* pan, a method I learned from the gastronome and cook, Livio Cerini di Castegnate. In this way the butter does not become too dark, and the chops cook through while remaining golden on the outside.

1 Beat the eggs lightly in a soup plate with a little salt and the nutmeg. Spread out the breadcrumbs in a dish.

2 Dip the chops in the egg, coating both sides, then let the excess egg fall back into the plate. Coat the chops with the crumbs, pressing them into the meat with your hands.

3 Choose a heavy large frying pan into which the chops will fit easily in a single layer. If you do not have a large enough pan, use two smaller ones and increase the amount of butter by 1 tablespoon. Butter the bottom of the pan very generously and put little pieces of butter here and there. Only use about three-quarters of the butter. Lay the chops in the buttered pan and put on a low-to-moderate heat. Move the chops around all the time to prevent them from sticking. Cook for about 4 minutes on one side, then turn them over and fry the other side. Add the rest of the butter in small pieces, placing them here and there between the chops. Continue cooking gently and moving the chops around for another 3 minutes. The timing depends on the thickness of the chop. The meat should be cooked through to the bone, but still moist and succulent.

4 When done, transfer the chops to a heated dish, pour over the sizzling butter and serve at once.

2 eggs
salt
freshly grated nutmeg
4 veal rib chops
⅓ cup dried breadcrumbs
5 tablespoons unsalted butter

✂ Veal Chops, Milanese Style are one of the very few dishes traditionally served with Risotto with Saffron (page 30). Just this once I do not uphold tradition; I prefer to serve them with Risotto with Parmesan (page 26) or with sautéed potatoes. A little green salad afterwards is de rigueur at a Milanese table.

✂ Costolette are also excellent al cartoccio (wrapped in parchment paper) with a few sautéed mushrooms and a little prosciutto, and then finished off in the oven.

Fish and Shellfish

FISH

Trancie di nasello al rosmarino
HAKE IN A MILKY SAUCE WITH ROSEMARY

Fragolino al cartoccio
PORGY EN PAPILLOTE

Coda di rospo e cozze in salsa gialla
MONKFISH AND MUSSELS IN A SAFFRON
SAUCE

Zuppetta di pesce
FISH SOUP

Tonno alla calabrese
TUNA BAKED WITH TOMATOES, CAPERS,
BLACK OLIVES AND CHILIES

Spaghetti al tonno
SPAGHETTI WITH TUNA AND TOMATO SAUCE

Triglie al cartoccio
RED MULLET EN PAPILLOTE

SHELLFISH

Calamari ripieni
STUFFED SQUID

Spaghetti coi calamari
SPAGHETTI WITH SQUID STEW

Polpo in umido
STEWED OCTOPUS

Spaghettini e cozze in cartoccio
SPAGHETTINI AND MUSSELS EN PAPILLOTE

Spaghetti alle vongole in bianco
SPAGHETTI WITH CLAMS

Fish

The Italians' love of fish is reflected in every fishmonger's shop up and down the country. An amazing assortment of fish, nestling in crushed ice, is arranged with precision on scrubbed Carrara marble. These shops are a joy to look at, a temple of cleanliness dedicated to the gifts of the waters. I often find myself staring at the display in just such a fishmonger's in Corso Buenos Aires in Milan, only to have one of the assistants come up and ask what I would like. "Oh nothing," I say, "I was just admiring your fish."

In the front row are the anchovies and sardines in their shiny silvery-blue livery. Although these used to be fish for the poor, they are now exhibited with pride, since, alas, they are rare in the Mediterranean, their numbers having been decimated in the interests of the canners. Behind the blue fish are the mussels, clams, sea urchins, canestrelli (small scallops) and date-shells, all shut tight waiting to finish their days in a soup, in a sauce for pasta or in a salad. Next to them are the large and small crustaceans, crawling sleepily over each other in a last attempt to survive. The delicious moleche (soft crabs from the Venetian lagoon) look naked and vulnerable next to the gray cicale (small flat lobsters). Cuttlefish, octopus and squid come in all sizes from the tiny ones no longer than two inches to big monsters who stare at you with their vacant deep blue eyes. The large fish, the sea bass, turbot and porgies, are displayed at the back of the shop for the buyers who can afford to serve them at the dinner party they are giving that evening. Unfortunately, many of these fish are unavailable in the United States and all too few fishmongers can offer such profusion or such quality.

When you are buying fish, do not even bother to go into a fish store if there is an unpleasant smell emanating from it. Fresh fish straight from the sea has no "fishy" smell; it smells only of the sea. When you are in the shop, look at the fish's body—it should be stiff with a shiny skin, and its eyes should be bright. Large fish last longer than small fish; sole, turbot or sea bass, for instance, do not go off as quickly as, say, sardines or mackerel. One last piece of advice: when you want fillets of small fish such as sole, buy the whole fish and have it filleted. It is usually fresher than the fillets, and the heads and bones you take home will make an excellent fish stock.

- -

Trancie di nasello al rosmarino
HAKE IN A MILKY SAUCE WITH ROSEMARY • SERVES 4

I owe this simple but excellent recipe to Romana Bosco, who runs a cooking school called Il Melagrano in Turin.

1 cup milk
1 tablespoon flour
3 garlic cloves, peeled
4 scallions
2 sprigs of fresh rosemary, chopped, *or* 2 teaspoons dried rosemary
2 tablespoons unsalted butter
⅔ cup light meat stock (page 3)
4 hake steaks, ½ to ¾ inch thick (about 1½ pounds)
salt
pepper
1½ pounds boiled or steamed potatoes (optional)

1 Blend the milk with the flour. Add the garlic and bring to the boil over low heat, stirring constantly. Simmer for 10 minutes, stirring very frequently to prevent the mixture from forming lumps.

2 Meanwhile, chop the white part of the scallions with half the rosemary and heat it with the butter. Cook very gently in a covered sauté pan. The scallions must cook without getting brown. Add a couple of tablespoons of the stock to keep the scallions moist.

3 Dry the fish steaks with paper towels and add to the scallions. Still keeping the heat low, cook for 1 minute on each side and then add the milk mixture, half the remaining stock and salt and pepper to taste. Cover the pan and continue cooking until the fish is done, about 10 minutes. Keep a watch and add more stock during the cooking if the fish gets too dry. Add the remaining rosemary, taste and check seasoning. Remove and discard the garlic.

4 If you are using the potatoes, cut them into slices and add to the pan about 2 or 3 minutes before serving to heat and to absorb the milky fish sauce. Add a little more stock if necessary. The potatoes become quite delicious when finished with the hake in this way.

Fragolino al cartoccio

PORGY EN PAPILLOTE • SERVES 4

Because they have a delicate flesh porgy are particularly suited to being prepared in cartoccio with a simple herb-flavored salsina (little sauce). You can choose any herbs, which should be fresh for this recipe, but either fennel or fennel tops should be included.

I prefer the traditional way of wrapping the fish, in parchment paper rather than in foil. I've found the fish cooks better in paper than in foil, and it certainly looks better when brought to the table.

1 Ask the fishmonger to scale and clean the fish thoroughly, leaving the heads and tails on. Before cooking the fish, wash well and let drain on a sloping board while you prepare the sauce.

2 Preheat the oven to 400°F.

3 Chop all the herbs and the garlic. You can use a food processor, but do not reduce to a mush. Transfer to a bowl, add salt and pepper to taste and the lemon juice and then gradually add the oil, while beating with a fork to thicken the sauce.

4 Cut 2 squares of parchment paper (or foil) large enough to wrap around the fish and to fold together at the top and sides. Brush with a little oil. Lay a fish on each square and spoon a little of the sauce inside the fish and a little around it. Wrap the fish up by twisting the edge of the paper or foil all around.

5 Put the packets in a baking dish and cook in the oven 25 to 30 minutes. This timing is just enough to cook the fish through without drying it, so that it will be moist and succulent from its own juices.

6 Place the packets on a serving dish and open them by cutting off the twisted edges. Spoon the cooking juices over each portion.

✗ I find it is best not to serve any accompaniment with fish en papillote, but you might like to serve a few steamed potatoes. Plenty of crusty white bread is all serve, with a salad afterwards. A salad I like very much is one made with boiled vegetables, and in this case my favorite would be Wine-dressed Green Bean and Tomato Salad (page 120) or Fennel and Orange Salad (page 119).

2 porgies, about 1 pound each

3 tablespoons mixed fresh herbs, such as parsley, a small sprig of rosemary, 2 sage leaves, 1 sprig of thyme, 2 sprigs of marjoram, a few basil leaves and a full sprig of fennel or fennel tops

½ garlic clove, peeled

salt

pepper

juice of ½ small lemon

3 tablespoons extra-virgin olive oil

Coda di rospo e cozze in salsa gialla

MONKFISH AND MUSSELS IN A SAFFRON SAUCE • SERVES 4

I had this very good dish at the home of one of our Venetian friends. It was a pleasant change from the usual grilled monkfish one so often eats in restaurants in Venice.

- **1 pound mussels**
- **¼ teaspoon powdered saffron *or* saffron strands**
- **1¾ pounds monkfish**
- **½ pound ripe tomatoes, peeled and seeded and coarsely chopped, *or* 1 cup canned plum tomatoes, without their juice**
- **2 shallots *or* ½ onion, finely chopped**
- **1 tablespoon unsalted butter**
- **3 tablespoons olive oil**
- **2 garlic cloves, peeled and chopped**
- **½ small dried chili, seeded and crushed**
- **4 tablespoons chopped fresh parsley, preferably flat-leaf**
- **½ cup dry white wine**
- **salt**
- **pepper**

1 Clean and prepare the mussels following the instructions on page 66. Put the shelled mussels in a bowl and strain the liquid into a small bowl through a sieve lined with cheesecloth. Add the saffron to the liquid and stir well. Set aside.

2 Remove the dark skin from the monkfish, if still on, and remove the thin transparent skin, as this would cause the fish to shrink when cooking. Wash and dry the fish, and cut into small chunks.

3 Put the tomatoes in a small saucepan and cook over low heat for 10 minutes, stirring frequently, until they have become mushy.

4 Sauté the shallots or onion gently in the butter and oil until soft. Add the garlic, the dried chili and about 2 tablespoons of the parsley and sauté for another minute or so. Press this soffritto down against the bottom of the pan with a spoon to release the shallot liquid.

5 Add the monkfish and sauté for 3 minutes, turning it over and over. Splash with the wine and let it bubble away until there is only a little left.

6 Add the tomatoes and the saffron and mussel liquid, season with salt and pepper and continue cooking until the fish is done. This will take from 7 to 10 minutes depending on how big the pieces are. If there is too much liquid, remove the fish to a heated dish and reduce until the liquid becomes rich and tasty. Add the shelled mussels. Turn off the heat immediately as the mussels do not need to cook, only to heat through. Taste and check the seasoning. Transfer to a heated dish, sprinkle with the remaining parsley.

Serve the monkfish and mussels surrounded by some spaghettini tossed in a little extra-virgin olive oil or boiled rice. No other accompaniment is needed, only a salad afterward. You can start the meal with Grilled Peppers (page 105) or Stuffed Onion Cups (page 84). If you want yellow to be your theme color, use only yellow peppers to start with, and end the meal with Almond and Orange Cake (page 191), served with an orange salad.

Zuppetta di pesce

FISH SOUP • SERVES 4

In keeping with the fashion for lighter dishes, this zuppa di pesce has replaced the heavy cacciucco, brodetto and burrida of former days. I am not a champion of the nuova cucina, but I find this fresh, light zuppa quite delicious and full of traditional Italian flavors. It is also less demanding to make than the heavier soups. Another advantage is that it does not depend so much on local fish, which means that it can be made with the more restricted selection of fish available outside Italy. A fish head is quite necessary to give the soup flavor and body. Buy uncooked shrimp; if they are frozen, defrost them completely before using them.

½	pound mussels
1	pound shrimp
1	pound monkfish
5	tablespoons extra-virgin olive oil
1	garlic clove, peeled and thickly sliced
2	tablespoons chopped fresh parsley, preferably flat-leaf
1	dried chili
4	fresh plum tomatoes, peeled and seeded, *or* canned plum tomatoes, coarsely chopped
1	fish head, cod or hake or other large white fish, not salmon
½	cup dry white wine
4	cups boiling water
salt	
8	slices French bread, toasted

1 First clean the mussels following the instructions on page 66, but do not cook them.

2 Peel the shrimp and devein if necessary. Wipe and skin the monkfish and cut into bite-size pieces.

3 Heat half the oil in a pot, preferably a flameproof earthenware one, with the garlic, half the parsley and the chili. Sauté until the garlic begins to change color and then add the chopped tomatoes and the fish head. Splash with the wine and, as soon as it has nearly all evaporated, add about 3 to 4 cups boiling water. Season with salt and cook for about 20 minutes.

4 Add the monkfish and the mussels and cook for 3 minutes. Add the shrimp and cook for another 2 minutes.

5 Lift the fish head out of the broth and discard it (I add the cheeks to the soup). Dress the soup with the rest of the oil and the rest of the parsley. Taste and check seasoning.

6 Put 2 slices of toasted French bread into each soup bowl and ladle the soup over it.

✖ I recommend a fish dish to follow this fish soup, in the Italian manner. Stuffed Squid (page 62) or Hake in a Milky Sauce with Rosemary (page 54) would be perfect. If you prefer to follow with meat, choose Pork Tenderloin with Berries, Almonds and Balsamic Vinegar (page 227) or Ham in Onion Sauce (page 79).

TUNA

"Tonno is a fish of exceptional proportions," said Platina, the fifteenth-century writer, in his *De Honesta voluptate et valetudine*. It can in fact be as long as six-and-one-half feet. It swims at amazing speed, its beautiful dark blue body looking like a torpedo flashing through the water. Tuna migrate towards the shore, and even up the mouths of rivers, to spawn early in the summer; at that stage they are known as tonni di corso, and when they return in late summer they are called tonni di ritorno. Their migratory movements, however, are something of a mystery. Alan Davidson, in his invaluable *Mediterranean Seafood,* suggests that they "might be mainly governed by water temperatures and by the movements of other fish on which the tunny feed."

It is when the tuna are on the move, to spawn, that the Sicilian mattanza del tonno—the slaughter of the tuna—takes place. The mattanza has always been a ritualistic occasion much enjoyed by the Sicilian fishermen. Apparently the method of catching and killing the fish was learned from the Phoenicians, and it has changed very little since then. Patrick Brydone, in one of his letters from Sicily written in 1770, describes how this was (and still is) done. "These fish do not make their appearance in the Sicilian seas till towards the latter end of May; at which time the *tonnaros,* as they call them, are prepared for their reception. This is a kind of aquatic castle, formed, at great expense, of strong nets, fastened to the bottom of the sea by anchors and heavy leaden weights. These *tonnaros* are erected in the passages amongst the rocks and islands that are most frequented by the tunny-fish. They take care to shut up with nets the entry into these passages, all but one little opening, which is called the outward gate of the *tonnaro*." Brydone then describes how the fish are driven from the "hall" to the "antechamber" by the fishermen making a noise on the surface of the water, their escape being cut off by a net that is let down to shut them in. After the antechamber comes the

"*Camera della Morte,* The Chamber of Death: this is composed of stronger nets and heavier anchors than the others. As soon as they have collected a sufficient number of tunny-fish, they are driven from all the other apartments into the chamber of death, when the slaughter begins. The fishermen, and often the gentlemen too, armed with a kind of spear or harpoon, attack the poor defenceless animals on all sides; which now giving themselves up to despair, dash about with great force and agility, throwing the water over all the boats; and tearing the nets to pieces, they often knock out their brains against the rocks or anchors, and sometimes even against the boats of their enemies."

Tuna is an excellent fish, and it is now easily available. The flesh is rather dense and dry, and I find that it is improved by being marinated in a mixture of vinegar and water, as suggested by the Sicilian writer Alberto Denti di Pirajno in his fascinating book, *Il Gastronomo educato*. Tuna has been popular since Roman times. Apicius wrote recipes in which the tuna is boiled—a favorite cooking method of the Romans for both fish and meat—and then dressed with a sweet-and-sour sauce containing oil and garum. The combination of tuna with a sweet-and-sour sauce is still popular, together with the classic Mediterranean method of cooking it with tomatoes, as in the recipe on page 59.

A very important use of tuna is its preservation in olive oil or brine. In the old days it used to be preserved in barrels covered with olive oil, tonno sott'olio, the best part being the tender, juicy belly of the fish, called ventresca. You can buy tins of ventresca in some specialty delicatessens in Italy, as well as tuna preserved in barrels and sold by weight. Preserved tuna is used quite extensively in Italian cooking: some hors d'oeuvres are made with it; vegetables are stuffed with it (see the recipe on page 98); and it is used in many pasta sauces.

Possibly the best-known dish made with tuna is the Tuscan insalata di fagioli e tonno (bean and tuna salad), which is found on the menu of most Italian restaurants outside Italy. The basic recipe is very simple, the principal ingredients being canned tuna, cannellini beans, usually canned, and onions. I add a few touches which I think make it prettier and better. I start with dried cannellini, which are better than the canned ones; first I soak and cook them. Then I use red onions, which are sweeter than white ones or scallions, and I marinate them in lemon juice for about 2 hours. I spoon the beans over a bed of radicchio, which adds a touch of color, a slightly bitter edge and a crunchy texture. The flaked tuna comes next and the red onion is scattered on top. The dressing is the best olive oil and lots of black pepper.

Tonno alla calabrese

BAKED TUNA WITH TOMATOES, CAPERS, BLACK OLIVES AND CHILIES • SERVES 4

Try to buy steaks from the belly of the fish, which is more delicate in taste and softer in texture. If the steaks are too large for one portion, cut them in half.

4 tuna steaks, about ½ inch thick (about 1½ pounds)
salt
pepper
4 tablespoons olive oil
2 tablespoons wine vinegar
4 bay leaves
4 ripe tomatoes
2 tablespoons dried breadcrumbs
3 tablespoons capers, rinsed and dried
12 black olives
2 dried chilies
12 fresh basil leaves, coarsely torn

1 Remove the tough skin from the fish if it is still on and rub salt and pepper into both sides of the steaks. Lay the steaks in an ovenproof dish and pour over half the oil and all the vinegar. Place a bay leaf on each steak and let marinate for 1 hour, turning them over once.

2 Preheat the oven to 400°F.

3 Blanch and skin the tomatoes. Cut them in half and squeeze out the seeds, then chop them coarsely and spread on the steaks. Sprinkle with the breadcrumbs, scatter with the capers and olives and add the chilies. Drizzle with the remaining oil. Cover the dish with foil and bake until the fish is cooked through; this will take about 20 minutes, depending on the thickness of the steaks.

4 Transfer the fish to a heated dish. Remove and discard the bay leaves and the chilies. Add salt and pepper to the cooking liquid if necessary, then spoon it over the fish, sprinkle with the basil, and serve.

I like to place some grilled polenta fingers around the fish, thus matching a dish from the deep South with the very northern Italian polenta. Start the meal with Risotto with Shellfish (page 28) or with an earthy minestrone (page 209). A bowl of green salad is ideal to cleanse the palate after the fish.

Spaghetti al tonno

SPAGHETTI WITH TUNA AND TOMATO SAUCE • SERVES 4

This recipe differs from the usual one for a sauce with tuna, in that here the tuna is not cooked. As a result the taste of the tuna comes through more clearly and is more pleasing.

1 or 2 garlic cloves, according to taste

5 tablespoons extra-virgin olive oil

4 peeled ripe tomatoes, coarsely chopped

10 black olives, pitted and cut into strips

1 tablespoon capers, rinsed and dried

12 fresh basil leaves, torn

salt

10 ounces spaghetti

1 can (7 ounces) tuna packed in olive oil

pepper

1 Peel and cut the garlic into thick slices. Put it in a small saucepan with half the oil, the tomatoes, olives and capers. Bring to the boil and then add the basil and cook for 5 minutes. Add salt if necessary.

2 Cook the pasta as usual in boiling salted water.

3 Meanwhile drain the tuna, flake it and put into a serving bowl. Mix in the remaining oil and plenty of pepper.

4 When the spaghetti is done, lift it out of the water with a wooden fork or a spaghetti lifter or drain it in a colander and transfer to the bowl with the tuna. If you use a colander, reserve a cup of the water in which the pasta cooked. Mix in the tomato sauce and toss very thoroughly. If the dish seems too dry, add a little of the reserved water.

✄ After this tasty opening you must serve an equally strong secondo. I would choose the lovely Red Mullet en Papillote (page 60). If you want to serve the pasta as a main course, start with Fish Soup (page 57) or Eggplant Stuffed with Luganega, Pine Nuts and Raisins (page 96).

RED MULLET

Red mullet is one of the best Mediterranean fish and one that, in Italy, has been highly prized since Roman times. It is found mainly in the Ligurian and Tyrrhenian seas, where it lives in the deep rocky waters. In this country, you can successfully substitute pompano or butterfish.

Triglie al cartoccio

RED MULLET EN PAPILLOTE • SERVES 4

Being so pretty and so tasty, red mullet is particularly suited to cooking al cartoccio. I have always liked to cook fish in this way, the main advantage being that the flavor of the fish is sealed in, and a secondary one that there is no saucepan to wash up. In Italy this method of cooking has been used for centuries, and it is now a favorite with both hostesses and restaurateurs. Unlike many restaurant dishes, it is very suitable for entertaining at home—having prepared the fish, all beautifully wrapped up, you can forget about it until fifteen minutes before serving.

You can cook many things al cartoccio. My favorite is fish, as you can see from this book, but meat too is good done this way. Try pork fillets with mushrooms, a few dried porcini and a little vermouth, or the recipe for spaghetti on page 66. One warning: make sure you add the right amount of flavorings and seasonings. The food, once wrapped, stays that way until it reaches the table. When you cook fish al cartoccio you must be doubly sure that it is fresh, because, with its juices sealed in the paper packets, the flavor becomes concentrated.

In this recipe I add an exotic touch to the characteristic Mediterranean ingredients, a little chopped ginger which, as the Chinese have taught us, goes so well with fish and garlic. You can use foil instead of parchment paper, although personally I prefer to do it in the traditional way, with paper.

1 Ask the fishmonger to scale and clean the fish properly, but to make only a short slit underneath rather than a cut from the anal aperture to the head, a gash that ruins the look of the fish. Naturally, head and tail must be left on too. Cut off a little of the tail, preserving its original shape, and wash the fish thoroughly. Dry it and then leave it on a slanted board to drain.

2 Heat the oven to 400°F. Do not put the fish in the oven until you are sure it has reached the right temperature.

3 Cut the tomatoes in half, squeeze out the seeds and juice, cut into small cubes and put in a small bowl. Chop the basil leaves, garlic and ginger and add to the bowl. Stir in the oil, mixing everything together.

4 Cut 4 squares of parchment paper large enough to wrap around the fish and to fold together at the top and sides. Brush with a little oil.

5 Sprinkle the fish with salt and pepper inside and out. Put a little of the tomato mixture on each square of paper, lay the fish over it and cover with another knob of the mixture. Now fold the paper over in tiny pleats all around the fish. Seal well and put the packets in an ovenproof dish. Cook in the hot oven for 15 minutes. Cook larger fish longer.

6 Place the packets on individual plates and open by cutting off the folded edges. Bring the plates to the table and let your guests eat from the paper dishes.

4 **pompano, butterfish or other firm, white-fleshed saltwater fish (2½ pounds total cleaned weight, heads and tails intact)**

4 **small tomatoes, ripe but firm, peeled**

⅔ **cup fresh basil leaves**

1 **garlic clove, peeled**

½-inch **piece of gingerroot, peeled**

4 **tablespoons extra-virgin olive oil**

salt

freshly ground black pepper

NOTE: I sometimes add a few cubes of parboiled waxy potatoes to the packets. The potatoes finish cooking in the tomato and fish juices, and the final result is your fish already accompanied by tasty potatoes. Bread is essential, as is a green salad afterward.

The Cephalopods

This small group of aquatic creatures comprises cuttlefish, squid and octopus, none of them very attractive except when presented in the pot. Then their taste is so delicious that you are unlikely to be put off by their looks. Like all fish, they should be fresh, but nowadays they are more often frozen. On being thawed after freezing their flesh is relaxed, making them cook more quickly. They are, however, less tasty. If you are at the seaside and lucky enough to have the chance to buy some squid or cuttlefish that have just been caught, you must leave them in the fridge for about two days to relax their flesh before you cook them. Italians love to eat these strange-looking fish and have created many recipes around them.

SQUID

I cut large squid into strips and stew them or I boil them and use them in a seafood salad. I like to stuff the smaller ones in any one of a number of different ways. Basically the stuffing is made with the chopped tentacles, parsley and garlic, plus breadcrumbs or rice to give body. Tomato may go in the stuffing or in the cooking liquid with some wine. You may find it fun to experiment with different stuffings.

It is not easy to cook squid—or the other cephalopods—properly. They should either be boiled very briefly, deep-fried in fat as the Chinese do, or stewed at length over very low heat in the Italian manner. In Italy the small calamaretti are fried, usually as part of a dish of fritto misto di mare. They are tiny, no longer than two inches, and are lightly coated in flour then fried in hot oil. They are utterly delicious. Larger squid can be deep-fried too, but they must first be cut into rings.

HOW TO CLEAN SQUID. Squid are quick and easy to clean. Hold the body in one hand and with the other pull off the tentacles. As you do this the viscera will come out too. Cut the tentacles above the eyes and squeeze out the small bony beak in the center of the tentacles. Peel off the mottled skin, holding the squid body under running water. Feel inside the body and remove the transparent backbone and any bits left inside. Rinse the bodies and the tentacles thoroughly under running water. Place in a colander to drain. The squid are now ready. Dry them thoroughly with paper towels before you cook them.

Calamari ripieni
STUFFED SQUID • SERVES 4

This recipe combines two of the pillars of Italian fish cookery, calamari and preserved tuna. The recipe was created by Francesco Leonardi, a gifted Neapolitan chef of the eighteenth century who finished his successful career by becoming chef to Catherine the Great. But he became homesick, as all southern Italians do, and went back to Naples, and there he wrote his *Apicio moderno,* a vast book of 3,000 recipes, arranged more like an encyclopedia than a cookbook. In it, he often adapted foreign ideas and recipes to his Italian taste.

1 Prepare the calamari according to the instructions on page 62. Remove the triangular flap from the body. Leave the bodies whole and cut the tentacles and the flaps into small pieces.

2 Put the shallots or onion and 2 tablespoons of the oil in a sauté or frying pan, add a little salt and sauté very gently for 10 minutes until soft. Add the garlic, parsley and chili and sauté for another 2 minutes, stirring frequently. Add the cut-up tentacles and flaps and the anchovy to the frying pan and sauté gently until the liquid runs out of the tentacles, 2 or 3 minutes.

3 Preheat the oven to 325°F.

4 Crumble the bread by hand or in a food processor and add to the pan. Fry on a slightly higher heat for 3 to 4 minutes, stirring very frequently and letting the bread absorb the liquid. Sprinkle with 2 tablespoons of the wine and cook for 5 minutes more. Remove from the heat.

5 Flake the tuna and chop fine. Mix it into the breadcrumb mixture and add salt and pepper to taste. Mix everything together very thoroughly.

6 Fill the bodies with the stuffing, leaving about a quarter of each empty. This is because squid shrinks as it cooks, and if the body were too full it would crack or burst open. Stitch the openings closed with toothpicks.

7 Grease an ovenproof dish with 1 tablespoon of the remaining oil and lay the calamari close to each other in a single layer in the dish. Boil the remaining wine for 30 seconds and pour it over with the rest of the oil. Cover tightly with foil and cook in the oven for 1 hour. Baste occasionally during the cooking and turn the squid over 2 or 3 times.

8 When the squid feel very tender when pricked with a fork, they are done. If the juices are too thin, pour them into a small saucepan and reduce over high heat until tasty and syrupy. Taste and adjust seasonings. When the squid are cool, remove the toothpicks and carve into rounds. Serve with the sauce spooned around them.

✖ This dish can be a primo or a secondo, when it can be accompanied by some steamed new potatoes, or boiled rice, tossed with a little olive oil and sprinkled with parsley. A fresh green salad served afterward is very welcome.

2 pounds calamari, with bodies about 4 to 5 inches long

2 shallots or 1 small onion, very finely chopped

5 tablespoons olive oil

salt

1 garlic clove, peeled and finely chopped

2 tablespoons chopped fresh parsley, preferably flat-leaf

1 dried chili, seeded and crumbled

1 salted anchovy, washed and chopped, or 2 anchovy fillets, chopped

2 slices good-quality white bread, with the crust removed

5 tablespoons dry white wine

1 can (3½ ounces) tuna packed in olive oil

freshly ground black pepper

NOTE: Serve these squid at room temperature; they are much nicer than when they are hot.

Spaghetti coi calamari

SPAGHETTI WITH SQUID STEW • SERVES 4

You can prepare the squid stew entirely in advance and keep it in the refrigerator for up to two days.

1½ **pounds squid**

5 **tablespoons olive oil**

1 **medium onion, very finely chopped**

salt

2 **garlic cloves, peeled and finely chopped**

2 **tablespoons fresh parsley, finely chopped**

1 **small dried chili, seeded and chopped**

1½ **cups canned plum tomatoes**

⅔ **cup dry white wine**

freshly ground black pepper

¾ **pound spaghetti**

1 First clean the squid as directed on page 62.

2 Put 4 tablespoons of the oil, the onion and the salt in a heavy-based saucepan and cook, covered, over gentle heat for about 5 minutes, stirring frequently. Salt added at this stage releases the onion's moisture and thus helps it to cook without browning.

3 Stir in the garlic, the parsley and the chili and continue cooking for another minute. Turn the heat up to medium and add the tomatoes. Cook for 10 minutes at a lively simmer, then pour in the wine and boil for 5 minutes.

4 While the sauce is cooking, cut the squid bodies and flaps in narrow strips and the tentacles in bite-size pieces. Add them to the sauce with a generous grinding of pepper. Reduce the heat to very low and cook, uncovered, until the squid are tender when pricked with a fork. (Cooking time depends entirely on the size of the squid, but it will take at least 20 minutes.) You might have to add a couple of tablespoons of hot water if the sauce gets too dry, although it should be quite dense by the end of the cooking and not at all watery.

5 When the squid is ready, drop the spaghetti into salted boiling water and cook until al dente. Drain and turn the pasta into a deep heated dish. Toss with the rest of the oil and a few tablespoons of the sauce. Toss well and then spoon the rest of the sauce with the squid around the pasta.

✘ This is a robust one-course meal which should be followed only by a green salad.

OCTOPUS

There are two kinds of octopus; the best, the polpo verace or true octopus, has two rows of suckers on each of its eight tentacles. The other kind, called moscardino or sinisco in Naples, is tougher and less sweet. However the small moscardini of the Ligurian sea are excellent stewed with porcini in tomato sauce, flavored with the wonderfully aromatic local basil; it is a traditional Genoese dish.

In Italy, along the quays around the Mediterranean, you can often see fishermen banging a large octopus on the ground to relax its flesh and make it tender. Octopus are usually sold ready to cook, although I would recommend beating the tentacles where they are thicker with a mallet or meat pounder before cooking. Octopus are stewed in earthenware pots, often with tomatoes, sometimes with wine. The cooking must be very slow and lengthy or the flesh will harden. My favorite way to eat fresh octopus is boiled and dressed with the best olive oil.

In Lerici, at the restaurant Le Due Corone, we were recently served the best octopus I can remember. There was only one tentacle, tender and sweet, which had been boiled in sea water—as indeed it should be—and it was served with a hot boiled potato. Just as memorable as the octopus was the potato, a yellow new potato of the sort that makes perfect gnocchi. I realized that I had forgotten what a good potato tastes like. I have been told that the deterioration in the quality of potatoes is due to the fact that they are planted too near the surface in order that they can be more easily harvested by machines, and also that they are dug out before they are ready, so that they will keep longer without sprouting.

- -

Polpo in umido
STEWED OCTOPUS • SERVES 4 OR 5

The simplicity of this dish adds to its attractiveness. If the octopus is too big, ask your fishmonger to cut off the amount you need.

1 Put the octopus in a basin of cold water and leave it there for about 30 minutes to get rid of the sand from the suckers. Examine the suckers and squeeze out any remaining sand. Beat the thick part of the tentacles with a mallet or meat pounder. Drain thoroughly.

2 Choose a flameproof earthenware pot, as this will keep the liquid simmering at a very low heat. Put the oil, the tomatoes, half the parsley and 3 garlic cloves in the pot and lay the octopus on top. Season with lots of pepper, but do not put in any salt at this stage as the octopus may be salty enough. Bring to the simmer and then cover the pot with foil and with a tight-fitting lid. Turn the heat down and let the octopus bubble away until tender, about 1½ hours. When done, the prongs of a fork should easily penetrate the thicker part of the tentacles.

3 Chop the remaining garlic and add to the pot with the remaining parsley. Mix well, taste and add salt if necessary.

4 Lift the octopus out of the pot and transfer to a platter. Keep it warm in a very low oven with the door ajar.

3 **pounds octopus**
6 **tablespoons olive oil**
3 **canned tomatoes, coarsely chopped**
5 **tablespoons fresh parsley, preferably flat-leaf**
4 **garlic cloves, peeled**
pepper
salt

NOTE: If you have any octopus left over, cut it into small pieces and use it to dress some spaghettini, previously tossed with a couple of tablespoons of extra-virgin olive oil.

(*continued*)

5 In cooking, the octopus will have released a lot of liquid, which you must now reduce fiercely. When it is rich and syrupy, return the octopus to the pot and serve from the pot, cutting the octopus into portions.

✖ I like to serve this octopus with polenta, which is very unorthodox since it involves matching a Neapolitan dish with a northern accompaniment. Boiled new potatoes are good too, or boiled rice. A salad to follow is all that is needed. This rich dish can be preceded by Lemon-flavored Eggplant (page 94) or Baked Mushrooms with Anchovies and Capers (page 134).

Mollusks

Many years ago I went on a seaside vacation with my family in England. As soon as we arrived, we rushed down to the sea, and there two things immediately caught my attention: the rocks towering over the beach at low tide were covered with lovely large mussels and nobody was collecting them. We soon set to, and back in our rented cottage we began the long but happy process of soaking and scrubbing them. We had them with spaghetti and in salads, we made soup out of them and we stuffed them. Why no one else took advantage of the God-given bounty was always a mystery to me.

HOW TO CLEAN MOLLUSKS. Put the mussels or clams in a basin of cold water. Leave the clams in the water for some time so that they disgorge the sand. Scrub the shells hard with a stiff brush. Some clams and farm mussels are quite clean; other mussels are often covered with barnacles, though these are easy to knock off. Also tug off the beards. Wash thoroughly in several changes of cold water. Drain and throw away any mussel or clam that remains open when tapped on a hard surface; it is dead and must not be eaten.

When I cook mollusks in order to open them, I put eight or ten garlic cloves and one or two lemons cut into quarters at the bottom of a large pan. The lemons help to destroy any bacteria in the mollusks, and they make the liquor left at the bottom of the pan after the mollusks have opened tastier. Discard any mollusk that remains tightly shut after heating.

Spaghettini e cozze in cartoccio
SPAGHETTINI AND MUSSELS EN PAPILLOTE • SERVES 4

I cannot think of two more typically Italian ingredients than spaghetti and mussels. In this recipe they are combined in small paper packets. One reason I like this dish is purely social, a cartoccio always being fun and a talking point. My other reason is practical: you do not have to hurry your guests to the table because the spaghettini is getting cold. As it is wrapped up in parchment paper, it keeps beautifully hot.

1 First make the Quick Tomato Sauce as directed on page 113.

2 Clean and heat the mussels with lemon and garlic, as directed on page 66.

3 While the mussels are cooking, cut four 10-inch squares of parchment paper.

4 Take the mussels out of their shells and discard the shells. Do this over the pan in which the mussels have cooked, so that the juice is collected in the pan. Now discard the lemons and all but one of the garlic cloves and filter the juice through a sieve lined with paper towels into a small bowl.

5 Drop the spaghettini into salted boiling water and bring back to the boil.

6 Heat the oven to 350°F.

7 Chop about a third of the mussels, the reserved garlic clove and the parsley and heat this mixture with the oil in a large frying pan for about 1 minute.

8 Drain the pasta when still slightly undercooked and turn it into the frying pan. Add the unchopped mussels, 3 or 4 tablespoons of the reserved mussel liquid and a good deal of pepper and turn the pasta over to flavor it in the sauce for 30 seconds.

9 Divide the pasta into 4 portions and place each portion on a square of parchment paper. Put a tablespoon or so of the tomato sauce in the middle of each portion. Fold the edges together by twisting them over tightly, starting from the corners and meeting at the top. Put the packet in a roasting pan and cook in the oven for 10 minutes.

10 Place the packets on 4 plates and cut them open below the folded edge. Serve in the opened packets.

✕ A lovely second course would be Stuffed Squid (page 62). But if you are not a devotee of fish, serve Braised Shoulder of Pork with Herbs and Garlic (page 203) or Cold Roast Veal with Herbs (page 206). In fact, most meat or fish dishes are suitable as long as they have enough flavor to stand on their own after this positive primo.

4 tablespoons Quick Tomato Sauce (page 113)
2 pounds mussels
12 garlic cloves, peeled and bruised
2 lemons, quartered
salt
10 ounces spaghettini
⅔ cup fresh parsley leaves
4 tablespoons extra-virgin olive oil
freshly ground black pepper

NOTE: Use parchment paper, not foil, for this cartoccio.

Spaghetti alle vongole in bianco

SPAGHETTI WITH CLAMS • SERVES 4

The sauce in this recipe is the pasta dressing that used to be made by Neapolitan fishermen on board their boats. Unlike the usual clam sauce, it does not contain tomatoes and as a result the taste of the clams comes through in a way that is fresher and more fragrant. Mussels, too, are excellent served in this way with spaghetti. Scrub the lemon hard with salt and water before you use it to get rid of the pesticides.

- **2 pounds clams *or* mussels**
- **4 tablespoons dry white wine**
- **¾ pound spaghetti *or* spaghettini**
- **⅓ cup olive oil**
- **3 garlic cloves, peeled and finely chopped**
- **3 tablespoons chopped fresh parsley, preferably flat-leaf**
- **rind of ½ lemon, with no white pith, grated**
- **½ dried chili, crumbled and seeded**
- **freshly ground black pepper**
- **salt**

1 Prepare the clams or mussels following the instructions on page 66.

2 Put the wine in a large frying or sauté pan, add the cleaned clams or mussels and cook, covered, over lively heat, until they are open. Shake the pan frequently.

3 Remove the meat from the shells and discard the shells.

4 Strain the liquor through a sieve lined with cheesecloth into a small saucepan. Reduce it over high heat until only about half remains.

5 Bring a large saucepan of salted water to the boil. Drop the pasta into the water and cook until the spaghetti is nearly, but not completely, done.

6 While the pasta is cooking, put the oil, garlic, half the parsley, the lemon rind and the chili in a large sauté pan and sauté over medium heat until the garlic begins to color.

7 Drain the pasta and add to the sauce.

8 Mix in the clams or mussels and the liquor and stir-fry for 1 minute, lifting up the spaghetti, and the sauce, as you stir. Remember that the clams or mussels should only heat through, not cook. Season with pepper, and with salt if necessary.

9 Serve immediately straight from the pan or transfer to a heated bowl.

This is a robust dish that can be followed by Stuffed Squid (page 62) or Hake in a Milky Sauce with Rosemary (page 54).

Sausage, Salami and Ham

Cotechino in camicia
COTECHINO WRAPPED IN PROSCIUTTO AND
STEAK

Riso e luganeghin
RISOTTO WITH LUGANEGA

Luganega e peperoni in salsa
LUGANEGA AND PEPPERS IN TOMATO SAUCE

Tortino di puré di patate
MASHED POTATOES BAKED WITH SALAMI AND
MOZZARELLA

Prosciutto con la rucola
PROSCIUTTO WITH ARUGULA

Piselli al prosciutto in tegame
PEAS AND PROSCIUTTO

Prosciutto cotto in salsa di cipolla
HAM IN ONION SAUCE

SEE ALSO

*Involtini di pollo ripieni di nocciole, prosciutto e
formaggio*
CHICKEN BUNDLES WITH HAZELNUTS, HAM
AND CHEESE

La mia mozzarella in carrozza
FRIED MOZZARELLA AND SALAMI
SANDWICHES

Melanzane ripiene alla pugliese
EGGPLANT STUFFED WITH LUGANEGA, PINE
NUTS AND RAISINS

Pollo ripieno
STUFFED CHICKEN FLAVORED WITH WHITE
TRUFFLE

I may be accused of being chauvinistic, but I am sure Italy produces a greater variety of delectable foods from the pig than any other country. The products that are used in these recipes are, of course, limited to the ones that can easily be bought in this country, but if you visit any salumeria (delicatessen) in Italy you will be confronted by a manifest tribute to the pig. Wreaths and chains of small and medium sausages, cotechino and zampone (the stuffed foot of a large pig), salami of all shapes and sizes, large brown prosciutto, fat pink mortadella . . . they all hang from the ceiling like stalactites. And seductively displayed under the glass counter in front of you, giving off an appetizing smell, are the same products, cut open so as to tempt you even more. It is a sight that testifies to the creativity of the Italians in culinary matters and their love of all pork products.

Through the many centuries of privation and poverty suffered by the mass of Italian people, the pig has often been the only provider of meat, the only source of food worthy of some country celebration. Something is made out of every part of the pig. As they say in Emilia, "Il maiale è come la musica di Verdi, non c'è niente da buttar via" (a pig is like the music of Verdi, there is nothing to be thrown away). Another proverb, from the last century, says, "Se si ammazza il maiale, viene Carnevale" (when the pig is slaughtered, it's carnival time). So, indeed, it still is.

Of all the dishes that are made on the day of the maialatura—the slaughtering of the pig—the ciccioli are the best. Ciccioli are cracklings, the crisp pieces left when the fat has been melted down in huge copper pans to make lard. They are a specialty of Emilia-Romagna, although they are made all over central Italy. I remember once during the war, when we were evacuated to the countryside near Reggio Emilia, the screams of our poor friend the pig waking us up at dawn. They were forgotten by the evening when an orgy of ciccioli and bread took place in the kitchen of the nearby farm. Ciccioli are made industrially now and sold in vacuum packs. I bought some when I was in Modena recently, but any hopes I had of rediscovering the past were sadly disappointed. They were nothing like sizzling ciccioli taken straight from the copper pan.

A DISH OF CURED MEATS. A plate of affettato (cured meats) is lovely to look at in its shades of pink and red and one of the most appetizing dishes when you are hungry. It always appears at a buffet lunch in Italy and is often a classic antipasto in a northern Italian home—always at lunch, never at dinner. Nowadays it is also a quick secondo for the working mother.

You need five or six different kinds of cured meat and a large oval or round dish. The traditional meats are prosciutto crudo, ham, mortadella, coppa and two kinds of salami, a sweet one from the North, such as Milano or Varzi, and a peppery, garlicky one from the South. Buy about a quarter of a pound of each meat; this will be plenty for eight to ten people. Affettato needs to be abundant. Roll the prosciutto, make little waves with the coppa and lay the heavier cuts flat.

In Milanese homes, curls of butter are dotted around the dish and the affettato is served by itself with plenty of good white bread.

COTECHINO

A cotechino is a large sausage, about eight to ten inches long and three inches in circumference, weighing about one pound. It is an ancient type of sausage, probably of Lombard origin, but made in Emilia-Romagna as well as in Lombardy. When I recently visited a small salumificio (sausage and salami factory) in Missaglia, north of Milan, I was very interested to see that they still make a cotechino that I have not come across since my childhood, the vaniglia. It is a cotechino flavored with vanilla instead of the more classic cinnamon, a flavoring that must have been due to a whim of fashion, since by the time vanilla reached Italy from Central America cotechino had long been a staple food.

Cotechino is made with lean and fat pork meat and a fair amount of coteca or rind, hence its name. The ground-up mixture is seasoned with salt and pepper, flavored with spices and then pushed into natural pig casing. In a traditional cotechino only the rind is minced, the meat being pounded in a special mortar. After two or three months of aging the cotechino is ready to be eaten. A good cotechino is sweet and tender with a creamy texture that literally melts in your mouth.

Fresh cotechino is a better product than the precooked one. However, the advantage of the precooked cotechino is that it only takes twenty minutes to cook, against the three hours needed to cook a fresh one.

HOW TO PREPARE COTECHINO. The most usual way to serve cotechino is boiled, with lentils or mashed potatoes—a perfect winter dish. It is the dish I always serve on New Year's Day, with plenty of stewed lentils. Lentils are supposed to bring wealth all through the year, each lentil representing a golden coin according to the old superstition. We all love the dish: hot, nourishing and very Italian.

Cotechino in camicia
COTECHINO WRAPPED IN PROSCIUTTO AND STEAK • SERVES 4 TO 6

This dish from Modena (its Italian name means cotechino in a shirt) is rich and robust. Once sliced it is also very attractive, with a center of pinkish sausage surrounded by the brown of the steak.

In Emilia the wine used is Lambrusco, but Lambrusco is only good in its native land. As Victor Hazan writes in his book *Italian Wine,* "One must distinguish between the Lambrusco consumed in its native Emilia-Romagna and the export variety. The first is indeed a wine, the second a beverage." I have used a good Valpolicella, which has the faint bitterness but not the sparkle typical of Lambrusco.

Ask your butcher to cut a large piece of round steak, about one inch thick, then slice the steak in half horizontally, stopping short of a long edge so that it will open out like a book. He should then beat the steak into a nice rectangle.

1 Cook the cotechino in boiling water but remove from the heat 10 minutes before it should be done. (Precooked cotechino takes about 20 minutes, fresh about 3 hours.) Allow to cool a little and then peel and discard the casing of the cotechino.

2 Trim the steak, cutting off any gristle or fat along the edges. Lay the cotechino on the steak and wrap the steak

1 cotechino (about 1 pound)
1½ pounds round steak, thinly sliced
¼ pound prosciutto, thinly sliced
2 tablespoons unsalted butter
2 tablespoons olive oil
2 shallots *or* 1 small onion, very finely chopped
1 cup good red wine
about ½ cup meat stock (page 3)
salt
pepper

(continued)

COTECHINO WRAPPED IN PROSCIUTTO AND STEAK *(continued)*

around it in order to check its size. If the steak is too large, trim it so that the edge overlaps by no more than 1½ inches. Also trim the ends. Remove the cotechino.

3 Lay the prosciutto over the steak and then lay the cotechino on the prosciutto. Wrap the steak around to make a roll. Sew along the edge of the roll and at each end with thick cotton thread. When you finish, and before you do anything else, remember to put the needle away safely (this is typical of the little items of invaluable advice that Marcella Hazan gives in her recipes).

4 Choose an oval casserole that just fits the roll. Put the butter, oil and shallots in the casserole and heat gently until the shallots are very soft. Stir frequently.

5 Add the meat roll and brown on all sides. Do not raise the heat, or the shallot will burn.

6 Meanwhile heat the wine and when it begins to bubble pour it into the casserole. Cover with the lid. If the lid does not have a hole for the steam to escape, put it slightly askew. Cook for 1¼ hours, turning the roll over 2 or 3 times. Lift the meat out of the casserole and set aside.

7 Turn the heat up and let the liquid bubble away. Add the stock a little bit at a time, tasting after each addition, until you get the right balance of flavor. Add salt, but remember that the roll will be salty enough because of the cotechino and the prosciutto. Grind in a generous amount of pepper and boil until the sauce is rich and syrupy.

8 Carve the roll into ½-inch slices, picking out the thread as you go. Lay the slices in a heated dish and spoon the sauce over, or hand the sauce around in a heated bowl.

Potatoes are excellent with cotechino. Drunk Potatoes (page 216) go very well with it as would a dish of buttery mashed potatoes. Another good choice would be braised lentils and/or Braised Broccoli (page 201).

LUGANEGA

This sausage has ancient origins. Cicero and Varro mentioned it, and Apicius, in his *De Re coquinaria,* explained how to make it. "Crush pepper, cumin, savory, rue, parsley, condiment, and laurel berries; mix with finely chopped fresh pork and pound well with broth. To this mixture, being rich, add whole pepper and nuts. When filling casings, push the meat through carefully. Hang the sausage up to smoke." Luganega returned to fame during the Renaissance, as documented by Teofilo Folengo in his *Baldus.* "Different regions and towns send their best products to Paris for the Royal banquet, which follows the tournament held there by the King of France. Milan sends its golden cakes and its sausage, which compels the drunkard French to empty bottle after bottle."

Milan, and all Lombardy, is still very famous for its luganega, and vies with Veneto for having the largest production and consumption. The luganega of Lombardy is reputedly the best, where the palm should be awarded to Monza, the suburb of Milan more famous for its car race than for its sausage. In Missaglia, north of Monza, I went to see a salumificio (sausage factory) that still makes luganega to order, adding grated parmesan and moistening the mixture with dry white wine instead of water, in accordance with a traditional Lombard recipe.

Luganega is made from both fat and lean pork meat, preferably from the shoulder, seasoned with salt, pepper, cloves and cinnamon and pushed into a very long thin casing. In southern Italy a little chili is sometimes added to the mixture, making the luganega slightly spicy.

It is also known as salsiccia a metro (sausage by the yard), because it used to be sold by length rather than by weight. It is sold fresh, and in Italy great lengths of it are to be seen, all coiled up in a circle.

Luganega, skinned and cut into small pieces, is an essential ingredient in many dishes, such as ragù and stuffings. It is also delicious by itself, split lengthwise and grilled, or stewed in a little water and then splashed in wine flavored with sage. In a good Milanese recipe a pound of luganega is added to a pound of potatoes stewed in meat stock. It is added when the potatoes are half cooked. Some cooks prefer to blanch the luganega.

The Milanese have a little verse about their luganega which sums it all up.

Pan, vin e luganeghin
l'é on mangia divin

Which might be translated:

Bread, luganega and wine
Make a meal that is divine.

Riso e luganeghin
RISOTTO WITH LUGANEGA • SERVES 3 OR 4

A classic Lombard dish which combines, in a perfect balance of flavors, two of the best local products, rice and luganega.

1 Choose a large deep saucepan. I use a round cast-iron casserole, but any heavy-based pan will do. Heat half the butter and the shallots until the shallots are soft and just beginning to turn golden.

2 Heat the stock to a simmer.

3 Add the rice to the shallots and cook until the edges of the grains become translucent, stirring frequently. In Italian this is called toasting the rice, which gives the right idea of what is happening to it. Add half the wine and boil briskly until it has been absorbed and then pour in a ladleful of simmering stock. Stir well and cook over medium heat

5	tablespoons unsalted butter
2	shallots *or* ½ medium onion, very finely chopped
3½	cups meat *or* chicken stock (page 3)
1¼	cups Arborio rice
1	cup good red wine, such as a Barbera
½	pound luganega (or other mild pork sausage)

salt
freshly ground black pepper
freshly grated parmesan

(*continued*)

RISOTTO WITH LUGANEGA *(continued)*

until the stock has been absorbed. Continue adding stock and cooking the rice until the risotto is done.

4 While the rice is cooking, blanch the luganega in boiling water. This will get rid of excess fat. Drain and return the luganega to the saucepan. Cover with the remaining wine and simmer very gently with the lid firmly on for 7 to 8 minutes. Then transfer the sausage to a chopping board and stir the wine into the rice.

5 Cut the luganega into 1-inch pieces and mix into the rice a few minutes before it is finished cooking.

6 When the risotto is ready, turn the heat off and add the rest of the butter, cut into 2 or 3 small pieces. Cover the pan and leave for 1 minute. Stir well to make the rice creamy, adding salt and pepper to taste, and transfer to a heated dish. Serve immediately, passing the parmesan separately in a bowl.

I find that this dish is nourishing enough to be either preceded or followed only by a vegetable dish or a salad. The vegetable dish I would choose is Grilled Peppers with Anchovies, Olives and Capers (page 106) and for salad, Fennel and Orange Salad (page 119).

Luganega e peperoni in salsa

LUGANEGA AND PEPPERS IN TOMATO SAUCE • SERVES 4

If you cannot find luganega you can use any mild, coarse-grained pork sausage, not too highly spiced or herbed.

- **3 large yellow, red or orange peppers**
- **1 pound luganega**
- **2 tablespoons olive oil**
- **2 garlic cloves, peeled**
- **1/4 cup chopped parsley leaves**
- **2 cups coarsely chopped canned tomatoes**
- **6 tablespoons red wine**
- **1 teaspoon sugar**
- **salt**
- **pepper**

1 First roast the peppers in a preheated 475°F. oven until you can see the skin coming away from the pulp, about 30 minutes. Put on a soup plate to cool.

2 While the peppers are cooling, cut the luganega, if it is in one long piece, into 4-inch lengths. Grill very gently so that it will cook without hardening or burning. I use a nonstick pan under the broiler instead of the broiler pan; the sausages are farther from the heat, and the pan is quickly washed out. Cooking the sausages separately gets rid of most of the unwanted fat.

3 Meanwhile heat the oil, the garlic cloves and parsley in a sauté pan that will be large enough to hold the sausages

and the peppers. When the garlic begins to color, add the tomatoes. Bring to the boil and then add the wine, sugar, salt and pepper. Stir well and cook over lively heat. Let the sauce boil nicely for 10 minutes or so. Remove and discard the garlic.

4 By now the peppers should be cool enough to peel, Working over the same soup plate, so as to collect more of the rich juice, cut each pepper into quarters, then remove and discard all the seeds, the core and the membranes. Cut each quarter in half.

5 Cut the sausage into roughly 1-inch chunks and mix into the tomato sauce. Add the peppers and all the juice collected in the plate. Stir everything together, put a lid on the pan and cook for about 15 minutes to let the flavors blend. Check seasoning.

6 Serve with mashed potatoes, boiled rice or a golden polenta. Nothing else is needed.

✖ Start with a vegetable dish, a salad or a soup. Stuffed Onion Cups (page 84), Broiled Eggplant Stuffed with Tuna and Anchovies (page 98), Arugula and Potato Soup (page 125) or Bread Soup (page 43) would be my choice.

SALAMI

All salami is made from minced lean meat and pork fat, stuffed into a natural pig casing. The meat is usually pork, but there are a few kinds, among which salame Milano is the best known, that also contain a small proportion of beef. In Italy, some salami is made with wild boar, donkey, horse or even mule, and all are good. The meat can be flavored with garlic and chili, as in most southern Italian salami, or—in the best salami—with white wine. The meat and fat can be coarsely or finely ground, and the proportion of fat to meat varies from one kind of salami to another. Most salami is cured for two or three months, although some of the better ones are aged for twelve months.

Salami should not be sliced too thin. The rule is, the thinner the salami, the thicker the slice. When I want a piece of cacciatore, for instance, which is a small Milanese salami about five inches long and a little more than an inch across, I will cut a chunk that is about one inch thick.

Salami is usually eaten by itself or as part of an affettato—a platter of mixed cured meats (see page 70). I like salami, rather than prosciutto, with fresh figs. Sometimes a few slices of salami are added to a meat stuffing to give a stronger flavor. And there is a good recipe for a pasta sauce in which about a quarter of a pound of cubed salami is stir-fried with the cooked pasta, together with cannellini beans stewed in a tomato sauce.

Tortino di puré di patate
MASHED POTATOES BAKED WITH SALAMI AND MOZZARELLA • SERVES 4

The salami makes this a dish in its own right; it is perfect for a family supper. You can also serve it with steaks or roast chicken. If you want a vegetarian dish, eliminate the salami and add a couple of tablespoons of gruyère cheese.

1½ **pounds potatoes**
⅔ **cup milk**
4 **tablespoons unsalted butter**
1 **egg**
3 **tablespoons freshly grated parmesan**
salt
freshly ground pepper, preferably white
½ **pound mild salami, thickly sliced, cut into small cubes**
½ **pound mozzarella, cut into small pieces**
2 **tablespoons fine dried breadcrumbs**

1 Scrub the potatoes and boil them in their skins in plenty of lightly salted water. Drain and peel them as soon as they are cool enough to handle.

2 While the potatoes are cooking, heat the milk.

3 Puree the potatoes through a food mill fitted with a disk with small holes, or through a potato ricer. Do not use a food processor or blender, as these would make the potatoes gluey.

4 Preheat the oven to 375°F.

5 Add 3 tablespoons of the butter to the pureed potatoes and beat hard until absorbed, then beat in the hot milk. The longer you beat a puree, the lighter it becomes.

6 Mix together the egg, parmesan, salt and pepper in a small bowl. Add to the potato puree and beat again. Now mix in the salami and the mozzarella.

7 Butter a soufflé dish and sprinkle with half the breadcrumbs. Shake off the excess crumbs.

8 Spoon the potato mixture into the dish, sprinkle the top with the rest of the breadcrumbs and dot with the remaining butter.

9 Bake in the preheated oven for 20 minutes, until a golden crust has formed on top. If a crust has not formed, pass the dish under the broiler. Allow to stand for a few minutes before serving.

PROSCIUTTO

There is an old adage from Parma that runs, "Grasso e magro non del tutto, ecco il pregio del prosciutto." It means that the prosciutto must have the right balance of fat and lean meat. The prosciutto di Parma and that of San Daniele in Friuli are the best prosciutto crudo (raw ham). Prosciutto crudo is also made in Modena, Reggio Emilia and on many country farms in central Italy. These latter are less delicate, leaner, redder and often saltier, and for these reasons they make the most appetizing panini (sandwiches).

The first process prosciutto undergoes is salting, which is done by the maestri salatori. The prosciutto is then hung, and the long curing process, which lasts from twelve to eighteen months, begins. It is supervised by other specialists who, every so often, insert a long stick right through to the bone and then take it out and smell it. Their sense of smell must be as keen as that of a Master of Wine, since the smell tells them all they need to know about the condition and readiness of the prosciutto.

I recently visited a prosciutto factory in Langhirano, south of Parma. Langhirano is a town dedicated to the making of prosciutto because it is ideally situated in the valley of the Taro River. Breezes from the southwest blow through the valley to cullare i prosciutti (rock the prosciutto). In Langhirano and neighboring places, 7 million prosciutti are produced each year. Gino Tanzi, the owner of the factory, took me round from one cold room to the next. In his huge, dark storeroom 20,000 prosciutto hams hang from wooden posts. It was an impressive sight which, oddly enough, brought to my mind a long pergola supporting a vine loaded with huge bunches of red grapes. Signor Tanzi explained that some of the prosciutto we could see were

not "di Parma." They came from pigs reared in other regions, even abroad in Holland and Denmark; they are smaller pigs, fed on different food, which produce prosciutto that will never be granted the ducal crown of Parma, the stamp of the authentic local product. This second quality prosciutto is often sliced and vacuum packed.

Genuine prosciutto di Parma is large and makes lovely large slices which have just the right amount of fat. When it is as good as this, prosciutto does not need the usual accompaniment of melon, although this is often served as a matter of course. Green figs, perfectly ripe and con la goccia—with the milky drop, as they say—are also often eaten with prosciutto. For a change I like to wrap a quarter of a juicy ripe pear in a slice of prosciutto. While these accompaniments serve to enhance the flavor of the prosciutto as a result of the contrast of flavors, prosciutto is also used to complement other foods. The famous saltimbocca would be a totally different dish without the slice of prosciutto within the rolled veal scaloppine. Prosciutto fat is used as a base for the most delicate soffritti, and chopped prosciutto is added to many fillings for ravioli, crespelle and the like.

Prosciutto con la rucola
PROSCIUTTO WITH ARUGULA • SERVES 4

Next time you decide to serve prosciutto for your first course at a dinner party, buy some arugula to go with it instead of a melon. The piquancy of the arugula and the sweetness of the prosciutto di Parma is as good a combination of flavors as it is of colors.

¼ **pound arugula**
3 **tablespoons extra-virgin olive oil**
1 **tablespoon fresh lemon juice**
salt
pepper
½ **pound prosciutto, thinly sliced**

1 Clean and wash the arugula. Dry very thoroughly and put in a bowl. Add the oil, the lemon juice and salt and pepper to taste. Toss very well.

2 Place the slices of prosciutto either on individual plates or on a serving dish, and put the arugula on the side, around or in the middle, whatever you think looks prettiest.

(continued)

✂ This fresh and light antipasto can be followed by a robust secondo such as Osso Buco, Milanese Style (page 170) or Beef Braised in Barbera Wine (page 215).

Piselli al prosciutto in tegame
PEAS AND PROSCIUTTO • SERVES 4

The marriage of peas and prosciutto is even older than that of pasta and tomatoes and it's still one of the most successful. It originated in Rome or, at least, it is the Romans who have made it well known. There are many recipes based on this union and here is mine.

The prosciutto for this recipe should have plenty of fat on it, and it should not be too thinly sliced. The peas should come from small, plump, unblemished pods of a bright green color; large peas are not suitable for this recipe.

6 **scallions**
3 **tablespoons unsalted butter**
salt
1 **teaspoon sugar**
½ **cup vegetable stock (page 4)**
2 **pounds fresh peas, shelled
(about 2 cups)**
freshly ground black pepper
2½ **ounces prosciutto, not too
thinly sliced**

NOTE: You can, of course, replace the fresh peas with frozen petits pois (a 10-ounce package will give the right amount); thaw them before you use them. Cook them for only 3 minutes, adding only a couple of tablespoons of stock at the end.

1 Slice the scallions into tiny rings and sauté in half the butter for 1 minute. Sprinkle with a little salt and the sugar and add a couple of tablespoons of the stock. Cover the pan and continue cooking until soft.

2 Add the peas, another couple of tablespoons of the stock and some pepper. Cook, covered and over very low heat, for 10 minutes or so, until the peas are tender. Add a little more stock if necessary.

3 Cut the prosciutto into short matchsticks and add to the pan with the remaining butter and a generous grinding of pepper. Cook for a couple of minutes, stirring frequently. Check seasonings and serve.

✂ This dish is a delicious accompaniment to Veal Chops, Milanese Style (page 50) or Veal Scaloppine with Basil and Lemon (page 210).

Prosciutto cotto in salsa di cipolla

HAM IN ONION SAUCE • SERVES 4

I find that the Christmas ham can outlast its welcome. It is delicious at first, hot, then cold with turkey once or twice, but after that something must be done. One good answer is to heat it up in this sauce. Leftover tongue, fresh or pickled, responds well to the same treatment.

3 onions, thinly sliced
4 tablespoons unsalted butter
1 teaspoon salt
1 teaspoon sugar
1 pound ham
½ cup dry vermouth
1 tablespoon flour
1 cup meat *or* vegetable stock (pages 3–4)
pinch of ground cloves
freshly ground black pepper

1 Heat the onions with the butter in a sauté pan. Sprinkle with the salt and the sugar. Add 4 tablespoons of water. Put the lid firmly on the pan and let the onion cook over the gentlest heat for at least 45 minutes. Stir every now and then. Remove the lid, turn the heat up and cook the onion until it becomes colored and almost like a puree.

2 Meanwhile carve the ham and cut the slices up fairly small.

3 Splash the onion with the vermouth. Boil until half the vermouth has evaporated.

4 Blend in the flour and cook for 1 minute, stirring constantly. Add the stock and a pinch of ground cloves and bring to the boil. Continue stirring and cooking for 5 minutes over very low heat. Taste and add salt, if necessary, and plenty of pepper.

5 Add the slices of ham and heat gently for 5 minutes or so. The dish is now ready.

I think the best way to serve this is on a bed of boiled rice. Should you want a vegetable, sautéed carrots would go well with it. My choice for a primo would be Chickpeas and Arugula (page 41) or Wine-dressed Green Bean and Tomato Salad (page 120).

PANCETTA

Pancetta comes from the pancia (belly) of the pig. It is in fact the same cut of meat as bacon, but its taste is different because it is cured in a different way—pancetta is salted and lightly spiced, not smoked. Bacon can be used instead of pancetta if you blanch it in boiling water for three minutes. For il sapore Italiano genuino (the authentic Italian flavor) you should keep some pancetta in your fridge.

Pancetta is mainly used as part of a soffritto. Even though it has been partly replaced by the increased use of olive oil, the flavor of pancetta is essential in some dishes. The best known of these is spaghetti alla carbonara, others are Bolognese ragù, Milanese minestrone and Venetian pasta e fagioli (bean and pasta soup). Pancetta is also cut into chunks and skewered with liver, meat or vegetables. A new idea is to skewer cubes of pancetta with chunks of monkfish marinated in olive oil, lemon juice and garlic and cook the skewers on a barbecue. My favorite spiedini (kabobs) are of pancetta, luganega and a little piece of veal interspersed with small sage leaves. Another excellent spiedino is made with a small piece of pancetta, a small onion layer, a chunk of pork and a piece of a pepper.

There are two kinds of pancetta, pancetta stesa and pancetta arrotolata. Pancetta stesa is the belly left flat in its natural shape, like bacon, and it is mostly used in cooking. Pancetta arrotolata (rolled pancetta) contains a high proportion of lean meat and is flavored with cloves and peppercorns. It is eaten as is, at the table, or in a sandwich, and if the pancetta is good, it is delicious. Some types of pancetta are smoked, especially those from Alto Adige, Valle d'Aosta and Friuli, regions on the frontiers of Italy and thus more affected by the foreign preference for smoked food.

I buy pancetta in some quantity. I keep a piece of about a quarter of a pound in the fridge, and the rest I put in the freezer in packets of a similar weight.

Vegetables and Salads

VEGETABLES

Scodelle di cipolla ripiene
STUFFED ONION CUPS

Lattuga imbottita alla napoletana
STUFFED BIBB LETTUCE

Radicchio alla griglia col parmigiano
BROILED RADICCHIO WITH PARMESAN

Carciofi alla romana
ARTICHOKES STUFFED WITH MINT AND
PARSLEY

Risotto coi carciofi
RISOTTO WITH ARTICHOKES

Sogliole al carciofo
SOLE WITH ARTICHOKE PUREE

Melanzane al limone
LEMON-FLAVORED EGGPLANT

Pizzette di melanzane
BROILED EGGPLANT WITH PIZZA TOPPING

Melanzane ripiene alla pugliese
EGGPLANT STUFFED WITH LUGANEGA, PINE
NUTS AND RAISINS

VEGETABLES (*continued*)

Sugo di melanzana
EGGPLANT SAUCE

Rotoli di melanzane ripieni
BROILED EGGPLANT STUFFED WITH TUNA
AND ANCHOVIES

Parmigiana di melanzane
EGGPLANT PARMIGIANA

Sformato di finocchi
FENNEL TIMBALE

Finocchi del Corrado
FENNEL WITH PISTACHIO AND ANCHOVY
SAUCE

Finocchi stufati
BRAISED FENNEL

Peperoni arrostiti
GRILLED PEPPERS

Peperoni alla siciliana
GRILLED PEPPERS WITH ANCHOVIES, OLIVES
AND CAPERS

Peperoni e patate in padella
SAUTEED PEPPERS AND POTATOES

Fagottini di peperoni e coda di rospo
GRILLED PEPPER AND MONKFISH BUNDLES

Terrina coi peperoni
PEPPER-STUDDED MEAT TERRINE

La mia salsa
PLAIN TOMATO SAUCE

Sugo fresco di pomodoro
QUICK TOMATO SAUCE

Sugo di pomidoro crudo
UNCOOKED TOMATO SAUCE

Teglia di patate e pomodori
POTATO AND TOMATO PIE

Finte trippe
FRITTATA STRIPS IN TOMATO SAUCE

Tortino di crespelle pasticciate
CRESPELLE WITH MOZZARELLA AND TOMATO
SAUCE

SALADS

Trevisana coi borlotti
RADICCHIO WITH CRANBERRY BEANS

Insalata di finocchio ed arancie
FENNEL AND ORANGE SALAD

Insalata di fagiolini al vino
WINE-DRESSED GREEN BEAN AND TOMATO
SALAD

La panzanella a modo mio
PANZANELLA

SEE ALSO

Asparagi alla milanese
ASPARAGUS WITH FRIED EGGS AND
PARMESAN

Bastoncini di patate e zucchine
SAUTEED POTATO AND ZUCCHINI STICKS

Broccoli stufati
BRAISED BROCCOLI

Brodo vegetale
VEGETABLE STOCK

Cavolfiore strascinato con la mollica
CAULIFLOWER AND BREADCRUMBS WITH
ANCHOVIES, CAPERS AND OLIVES

Coda di rospo e cozze in salsa gialla
MONKFISH AND MUSSELS IN A SAFFRON
SAUCE

Giardiniera
PICKLED VEGETABLES

Insalata del Bronzino
PURSLANE, SCALLION AND CUCUMBER SALAD

Insalata di cicorino
DANDELION SALAD

Luganega e peperoni in salsa
LUGANEGA AND PEPPERS IN TOMATO SAUCE

Minestra di rucola e patate
ARUGULA AND POTATO SOUP

Minestrone alla genovese
MINESTRONE WITH PESTO

Pappardelle con le fave
PAPPARDELLE WITH FAVA BEANS

Pasta e broccoli
PASTA WITH BROCCOLI

Pasta e peperoni al forno
BAKED PASTA AND GRILLED PEPPERS

Patate ubriache
DRUNK POTATOES

Piselli al prosciutto in tegame
PEAS AND PROSCIUTTO

Polenta alla pizzaiola
POLENTA WITH PIZZA TOPPING

Polenta pasticciata alla piemontese
BAKED POLENTA WITH PORCINI

Pomodori ripieni di riso e olive nere
TOMATOES FILLED WITH RICE AND BLACK
OLIVES

Prosciutto cotto in salsa di cipolla
HAM IN ONION SAUCE

Risotto con gli asparagi
RISOTTO WITH ASPARAGUS

Rotolo di salsa di pomodoro con acciughe e ricotta
ROLLED SOUFFLE WITH TOMATO SAUCE,
ANCHOVIES AND RICOTTA

Salsa di rucola e pomodoro
ARUGULA AND TOMATO SAUCE

Spaghetti al tonno
SPAGHETTI WITH TUNA AND TOMATO SAUCE

Tagliolini e merluzzo al pomodoro
TAGLIOLINI AND HADDOCK IN TOMATO
SAUCE

Tonno alla calabrese
TUNA BAKED WITH TOMATOES, CAPERS,
BLACK OLIVES AND CHILIES

Tortino di puré di patate
MASHED POTATOES BAKED WITH SALAMI AND
MOZZARELLA

Tortino di zucchine
BAKED ZUCCHINI IN TOMATO SAUCE

Triglie al cartoccio
RED MULLET EN PAPILLOTE

Zucchine ripiene alla mantovana
STUFFED ZUCCHINI, MANTUA STYLE

great mass of colors and vegetable freshness." For me an excursion to the market is one of the highlights of my visits to Italy, and that vivid phrase from D. H. Lawrence's description of the market in Palermo exactly captures one's initial impression. When I am in Milan, my weekly assignment is to go on Monday mornings to the market in Via Kramer, around the corner from my mother's house. It was the memory of this sight that brought waves of nostalgia when

I first came to England in the early 1950s. The vegetable scene was a desert, and I felt the same as Giangiacomo Castelvetro had, over three centuries earlier. Castelvetro lived for a long time—and died—in England, having taken refuge there when he incurred the wrath of the Inquisition through his leanings toward Protestantism. He wrote with longing about the artichokes, the tender sweet peas, the lovely foliage of the beans that are grown on the balconies of Venice and through which one can glimpse the beautiful ladies as they peer between the leaves.

Vegetables

Vegetables are treated with love and care by Italians. Vegetables are stuffed and baked, they are stewed or sautéed or boiled and then strascinati (see the recipe for cauliflower on page 48) or dressed with oil for a salad. The oldest and most delicious pies are, more often than not, filled

with vegetables, and in the last decades cooks have created vegetable ravioli and many vegetable sauces for pasta, such as my broccoli sauce on page 19 or the eggplant one on page 97.

The vegetables I have chosen for this chapter are those that I connect mostly with Italy, the ones around which the Italians have been able to create outstanding recipes.

Scodelle di cipolla ripiene
STUFFED ONION CUPS • SERVES 4

Of the many good ways to stuff onions, this is my favorite. This stuffing can also be used with large tomatoes, which would be baked for 40 minutes or so. Another excellent stuffing for onions is to be found in the recipe for Bibb lettuce on page 86.

1 Peel the onions and plunge them into boiling salted water. Cook for about 15 minutes, until the outer layers are just soft, but still slightly crunchy. Drain and leave to cool.

2 Meanwhile drain the tuna and chop with the anchovy fillets, capers, garlic, chili and oregano. Put the mixture in a bowl.

3 Soak the bread in the milk for 5 minutes. Then squeeze out the milk and break up the bread with a fork.

4 Preheat the oven to 400°F.

5 When the onions are cool, cut them in half vertically through the core, and put aside 16 to 20 outer layers. Chop the remaining onion layers and sauté them in 2 tablespoons of the oil. Cook gently for 10 minutes, stirring frequently, and then mix in the bread soaked in milk. Continue cooking for 5 minutes to allow the flavor to penetrate the bread. Add this mixture to the bowl, pour over 1 tablespoon oil and mix throughly. Taste and adjust seasoning. You will probably find that there is no need for salt, and that the chili has imparted enough hotness to make pepper unnecessary also.

6 Place a smaller outside onion layer inside a larger one to make 8 to 10 onion cups. Choose a shallow ovenproof dish (I use a small rectangular metal one) in which the onion cups will just fit and brush with 1 tablespoon oil.

7 Place the onion cups in the dish, sprinkle lightly with salt and pepper and fill them with the tuna mixture. Sprinkle with the dried breadcrumbs, pour over the remaining oil and bake on the top rack of the oven for about 20 minutes, or until a light golden crust has formed on top. If necessary place under the hot grill for a few minutes to brown. Serve warm or at room temperature, neither piping hot from the oven nor freezing cold from the fridge. The flavors must be allowed to blend at the right temperature.

✕ This dish, like all others made with stuffed vegetables, can be served by itself as a primo or a secondo. I don't think it would be right as an accompaniment to meat or fish, but some hard-boiled eggs would go well if you want to make the course more substantial.

✕ You can produce a most attractive first or second course by preparing two or three different stuffed vegetables and serving them together. These onions, for instance, served with Eggplant Stuffed with Luganega, Pine Nuts and Raisins (page 96) and Tomatoes Filled with Rice and Black Olives (page 231) would make a well-balanced combination.

2 or 3 red or other sweet onions, about 1 pound
1 can (7 ounces) tuna packed in olive oil
4 anchovy fillets
1 tablespoon capers, rinsed
1 garlic clove, peeled
1 small dried chili, seeded
2 teaspoons dried oregano
2 slices bakery white bread without the crust
⅔ cup milk
5 tablespoons olive oil
salt
pepper
2 tablespoons dried breadcrumbs

Lattuga imbottita alla napoletana

STUFFED BIBB LETTUCE • SERVES 4

Bibb lettuce has the slightly bitter taste necessary to counterbalance this sweet-and-sour stuffing, and they are just the right size. This stuffing is also very suitable for grilled peppers (page 104) or for Stuffed Onion Cups (page 84).

STUFFING

6 anchovy fillets
milk
2 tablespoons golden raisins
2 tablespoons capers
2 tablespoons pine nuts
2 garlic cloves, peeled
6 tablespoons dried breadcrumbs
1 tablespoon Black Olive Puree (page 230) *or* 12 black olives, pitted and chopped
4 tablespoons extra-virgin olive oil
freshly ground black pepper

———

8 heads Bibb lettuce *or* hearts of larger types of lettuce
4 tablespoons dry white wine
2 tablespoons olive oil

1 First put the anchovy fillets in a saucer and cover with milk. The milk will sweeten the anchovies, making them more suitable for this dish. Leave for 15 minutes or so.

2 Put the raisins and the capers in a small bowl and cover with warm water. This is necessary to plump the raisins and to rid the capers of excess vinegar. Leave them for 10 minutes and then drain and dry thoroughly.

3 Put the pine nuts in a small cast-iron frying pan or other heavy pan and toast them for 2 or 3 minutes. This brings out their characteristic flavor.

4 Coarsely chop the pine nuts, raisins, capers, anchovies and 1 garlic clove and put in a bowl. Add the breadcrumbs and the olive puree or chopped olives and mix in with the extra-virgin olive oil. Season with pepper. You won't need to add any salt because of the saltiness of some of the ingredients.

5 Blanch the lettuce in lightly salted boiling water for 3 minutes. Drain, reserving some of the water. Refresh under cold water, drain thoroughly, then gently squeeze out the liquid and dry with paper towels.

6 Push the stuffing in between the leaves of each head of lettuce. Close the bunches up gently and lay them in a saucepan in which they fit cosily. Add about 4 tablespoons of the reserved cooking water from the lettuce, the wine, 2 tablespoons olive oil and the remaining garlic. Cook over low heat for 20 minutes, turning the lettuce over once. Do this very gently, using 2 spoons.

7 Transfer the stuffed lettuce to a serving dish. Remove and discard the garlic. Taste the juice and check seasoning. If it is too liquid, reduce by boiling fast until it is rich in flavor. Spoon over the lettuce. Serve warm, not hot, or at room temperature.

✖ Serve this dish by itself, as a primo or as a secondo, before a plate of Spaghetti with Clams (page 68) or Spaghetti

with Squid Stew (page 64). You could also serve the stuffed
lettuce with Stuffed Onion Cups (page 84); they complement
each other and make a more important primo for an informal
dinner party.

Radicchio alla griglia col parmigiano
BROILED RADICCHIO WITH PARMESAN • SERVES 6

This simple little recipe is a most successful combination of an old
dish with a modern topping. It is ideal for a barbecue.

For 4 people you will need 1½ pounds of radicchio, 5
tablespoons of extra-virgin olive oil and ¼ pound of the best
parmesan, such as Parmigiano-Reggiano. Cut the radicchio
heads into quarters and place them in the broiler pan. Pour
over some olive oil and season with salt and a lot of pepper.
Cook on charcoal or under a preheated broiler for 10 minutes
and then transfer to a dish and cover with flakes of parmesan.
Drizzle a little more olive oil over the top. The cheese should
just melt in contact with the hot radicchio. A perfect
antipasto.

✂ The grilled radicchio without the parmesan on top is
an excellent accompaniment to broiled meat.

ARTICHOKES

This thistle, Cynara scolymus, is the food that
most vividly symbolizes the civilized gastronomy
of the Renaissance. There was, in that period,
endless concern about novel and attractive things
to eat, and the artichoke, with its peculiar shape
and its many gradations of color, was the ideal
vegetable to serve—or to use as centerpiece.

A native of Italy, the artichoke did not cross
the Alps until Caterina de' Medici went to
France. Indeed this is one of the few foods
known to have been introduced at her behest,
whereas most merely followed the general northerly spread of Italian culture. Caterina was a great
glutton, and she had a particular weakness for
artichoke hearts. At a banquet in 1575 she ate so
many that she was taken ill. Her passion for this
aristocratic thistle spread to the French court, so
much so that Louis XIII's doctor declared that
no dinner could be considered complete that did
not include at least one artichoke dish.

It was in Paris that Charles I and Henrietta
Maria tasted their first artichokes. The Queen,

who must have inherited a passion for artichokes from her mother, another Medici, grew artichokes in the garden of her country house in Wimbledon, England. I am sure she had more success than I did when I tried my hand at growing them in Barnes, not far away. I found that, through lack of sun, my artichokes became woody before they could develop fully. By way of compensation, I enjoyed the stalks of the side shoots in creamy risottos.

In Italy there are two different kinds of artichoke, with and without thorns. The prickly artichokes come from Liguria and are the ones we eat raw. No unpleasant fuzzy choke to deal with, only tender young leaves to dip in a pool of oil. Or they are cut into very thin wedges and served mixed with radicchio, a harmonious blend of flavors in a mix of contrasting colors. The other kind are the Roman artichokes, called by the charming name of mammola because of their purplish color reminiscent of a viola mammola (a violet). In Venice the little artichokes are sometimes called canarini (little canaries), because of their pale yellow-green color.

HOW TO CHOOSE ARTICHOKES. It is easy; they should be green, showing no brown patches or tips. Ideally they should have leaves still attached to the stalk and the leaves should be silvery green and alive-looking.

HOW TO PREPARE ARTICHOKES. Artichokes can make your hands black, so before you start preparing the artichoke rub your hands very thoroughly with lemon and let the juice sink in.

Hold the artichoke in one hand and with the other break off the tough outer leaves. It is impossible to say how many layers of these tough leaves you will have to discard, since it depends on the quality, age and freshness of the artichoke. Next snap off the green part of each remaining leaf by bending it back with a sharp movement. This leaves the tender part attached to the heart, removing the stringy tough top. Continue snapping off the tough tops until you get to a central cone of pale leaves that are purplish green only at the top. Then cut off about ¾ inch of the tips of these very tender leaves. Rub all the cut parts immediately with lemon to prevent discoloration, and leave in a bowl of lemon-water. The artichokes are now ready for cooking.

Remember that the stalks, once you have removed the thick outer layer, are delicious in a soup or a risotto, or even cooked with the artichokes and eaten with them.

- -

Carciofi alla romana
ARTICHOKES STUFFED WITH MINT AND PARSLEY •
SERVES 2 TO 4 ACCORDING TO SIZE

The touch that differentiates this classic Roman recipe from other recipes for stuffed artichokes is the mint. The local mint, mentuccia romana, has very small leaves and a sweet taste. If you can, grow it in your garden; it is much sweeter than apple mint or spearmint.

1 Prepare the artichokes following the instructions above.

2 Cut off the stems evenly at the base. Remove the thick outer layer of the stems, keeping only the soft inside part.

3 Choose a sauté pan or a saucepan of the right size to hold the artichokes upright, very close together, so that they support each other. Add the stems, the lemon, garlic, parsley stems, sprigs of mint, olive oil, salt and pepper and enough water to reach two-thirds of the way up the artichokes. Bring slowly to the boil and cover the pan with a piece of foil and a tight-fitting lid. Simmer over very low heat until the artichokes are partially cooked. It is difficult to give an exact time: large artichokes will take 10 to 15 minutes, while small ones take no longer than 5 minutes.

4 While the artichokes are cooking, prepare the stuffing. Finely chop the garlic cloves, the parsley and the mint and put in a bowl. Add the breadcrumbs and the nutmeg. Season with enough salt and pepper to make the stuffing very tasty, otherwise the final result will be rather bland.

5 When the artichokes have cooled enough to be handled remove them from the saucepan. Open them up gently, like a rose, and pull out the prickly central leaves. Remove the fuzzy part of the chokes with a pointed teaspoon, being careful not to remove the delicious heart. You will find it easier to do this now, when the artichokes are partially cooked.

6 Fill the centers of the artichokes with the stuffing and put the artichokes and stems back in the saucepan. Cover with the foil and the lid and continue cooking until the artichokes are tender. To test them, pull out a leaf and eat the end. The leaf should detach very easily and the edible end should be tender.

7 Transfer the artichokes to individual plates. Strain the cooking juices into a clean saucepan and make the sauce. If it is too thin, reduce over high heat until the juices are concentrated, then turn the heat down. Add the lemon juice and the butter a little at a time while you swirl the pan around. Do not let the sauce boil again. As soon as the butter has melted, spoon a little sauce over the artichokes and put the remaining sauce in a sauceboat to pass around.

✕ This is an appetizing first course which can be followed by most dishes, particularly by a roast. It is also a delicious main course for a family supper.

4 small artichokes

COOKING BROTH

1 lemon, sliced
1 garlic clove, peeled
2 or 3 parsley stems
2 sprigs of mint
4 tablespoons olive oil
salt
pepper

STUFFING

1 or 2 garlic cloves, peeled
⅔ cup fresh parsley leaves
½ cup mint leaves
2 tablespoons dried breadcrumbs
pinch of freshly grated nutmeg
salt
freshly ground black pepper

SAUCE

2 teaspoons lemon juice
1 tablespoon unsalted butter

Risotto coi carciofi

RISOTTO WITH ARTICHOKES • SERVES 4 OR 5

This recipe from my mother's *ricettario* (recipe book) works well even with the older, tougher specimens of artichoke often available. This is because you cook all the tough woody parts separately and then puree them. Remember to rub your hands very thoroughly with half a lemon before you start preparing the artichokes, as otherwise they will make your skin black.

3 medium artichokes
1 lemon, sliced
salt
2 tablespoons olive oil
1 garlic clove, peeled and chopped
2 tablespoons chopped fresh parsley
salt
freshly ground black pepper
3½ cups light meat stock (page 3)
2 shallots *or* 1 small onion, chopped
4 tablespoons unsalted butter
1½ cups Arborio rice
¼ cup heavy cream
½ cup freshly grated parmesan

NOTE: If you are short of time you can eliminate the puree. Boil the tough leaves and stalks and add the drained liquid to the meat stock.

1 Prepare the artichokes according to the instructions on page 88. You must be sure to remove all the hard part of the leaves, because they stay woody no matter how long you cook them and would spoil the final dish. Remove all the outer layer of the stalk until you reach the soft part in the middle. Put all the inedible tough outer leaves and the parings from the outer stalk in a bowl of water containing 2 slices of lemon.

2 Cut the cleaned artichokes in half from top to bottom, scoop out and discard the fuzzy choke and then cut each half, which now consists of the heart and few soft leaves, into very thin vertical slices. Cut the peeled stalks into rings. Put the slices and rings in another bowl of water containing 2 slices of lemon.

3 Drain the outer leaves of the artichoke and put them in a saucepan. Cover with water, add ½ teaspoon salt and bring to the boil. Simmer for about 50 minutes and then lift all the solid parts out of the liquid. Reserve the liquid and puree the artichoke through a food mill into a bowl. I am afraid this is rather a hard job, but you cannot use the food processor for this operation because the woody and stringy parts must be eliminated. Set the puree aside.

4 While the outer leaves of the artichoke are cooking, heat the oil with the garlic and parsley in a sauté pan. Add the artichoke slices and rings and sauté over moderate heat for 10 minutes, stirring very frequently. Add ½ cup boiling water and salt and pepper to taste. Turn the heat down, cover the pan tightly and cook for 20 minutes or so, until the artichoke is tender.

5 Now begin to cook the risotto. Heat the stock and add the water in which the outer parts of the artichoke have cooked. Keep the liquid at a low simmer.

6 Sauté the shallots in butter until soft. Add the rice and sauté for 2 minutes until the rice becomes transparent. Add 1 ladleful of simmering stock and cook until it has been

absorbed. Add another ladleful and continue in this way until the rice is cooked. If you run out of stock, use hot water. Remember to stir the rice often, but not the whole time since you want the risotto to form a slight crust at the bottom of the pan—the best part.

7 Halfway through the cooking of the risotto add the artichoke puree. When the rice is nearly done add the sliced artichokes with all their juices. Stir very well.

8 When the rice is done, turn off the heat and add the cream and half the cheese. Taste and check seasoning. Spoon the risotto into a heated deep dish to make a lovely greenish mound and serve at once, with the rest of the parmesan in a bowl on the side.

✘ Risotto must be made at the last minute. For this reason follow it with a dish of meat or fish that you can prepare in advance. Cold Roast Veal with Herbs (page 206) or Sweet-and-Sour Shoulder of Lamb (page 223) would both be very suitable. If you want fish, which goes so well with artichokes, I can recommend the Red Mullet en Papillote (page 60), an easy and effective recipe.

Sogliole al carciofo
SOLE WITH ARTICHOKE PUREE • SERVES 4

This is a recipe I owe to Rita Stancescu, a Venetian friend who is an excellent cook and who prepared many remarkable meals for us when we had an apartment in Venice. The apartment was near the Ca' d'Oro and whenever possible I started the day by visiting my two favorite places. First I would go to the church of San Crisostomo, near Rialto. The perfect harmony of its architecture and the beauty of the painting of the three saints by Sebastiano del Piombo never fail to revive my spirits. Then I would retrace my steps and take the gondola ferry from Santa Sofia across the Canal Grande to shop at the Rialto market. Waiting for the ferry— or standing somewhat precariously in it—I would talk to the Venetians, who are the greatest chatterboxes in the whole of Italy.

At the market my first call was Sprizza, the cheese shop, for ricotta, mozzarella and the best crescenza ever. Then I walked in wonder up and down those amazing fish stalls seething with glistening fish, sometimes asking questions of the fishmongers and

(continued)

always comparing prices. My expedition ended among the vegetable stalls, in the open space along the Canal. We used to spend most Easters in Venice, just the right time for the primizie (the season's new vegetables), prominent among which were the local small artichokes.

The combination of artichoke and fish is a very old one, and very good it is too. What differentiates Rita's recipe from the usual ones is that the artichokes are pureed, and it is this that makes the recipe suitable for larger, tougher artichokes. In the original recipe the fish used is John Dory. Since that's unavailable here, I tried the recipe with sole, and it works very well.

Ask your fishmonger to fillet the fish for you, rather than buying prepared fillets. The fish that is already filleted is often yesterday's (at best), and you cannot see the part that gives its age away.

3 medium artichokes
lemon juice
3 tablespoons olive oil
½ garlic clove, peeled and very finely chopped
½ cup chopped fresh parsley
2 tablespoons fresh chervil *or* 1 teaspoon dried chervil
pinch of freshly grated nutmeg
salt
pepper
2 tablespoons unsalted butter
3 pounds sole, filleted (about 1½ pounds fillets)
⅔ cup heavy cream
4 tablespoons freshly grated parmesan cheese

NOTE: You can prepare the artichoke puree well in advance and chill for up to 3 days, or freeze it.

1 Prepare the artichokes as directed on page 88. Cut the artichokes in half, scoop out and discard the fuzzy choke and then cut into thin vertical slices. Put these slices in a bowl of lemon-water. Remove and discard the tough outer layer of the stalks, cut the soft inside into rings and add to the slices in the bowl.

2 Heat the oil with the garlic and herbs in a sauté pan for about 1 minute. Add the artichoke slices and the stalk rings. Pour in about ½ cup hot water and add the nutmeg and salt and pepper to taste. Cover the pan tightly and cook for about 45 minutes at the gentlest simmer (I use a flame disperser). Stir every now and then and add a couple of tablespoons of hot water whenever the artichokes seem too dry.

3 Preheat the oven to 400°F.

4 Puree the artichokes and all the cooking juices through a food mill—quite hard work, but essential. A food processor does not do the job nearly as well, because it does not get rid of any remaining woody parts of the artichokes. Return the puree to a clean bowl.

5 Choose a shallow ovenproof dish just large enough for the fillets to lie in a single layer. Grease the dish with half the butter. Sprinkle the fish with salt and pepper on both sides, place it in the dish in a single layer and dot with the rest of the butter. Cover tightly with foil and bake in the oven for about 10 minutes.

6 While the fish is cooking, heat the artichoke puree and mix in the cream and the cheese. Taste and check seasoning.

7 Spoon the puree over the fish, cover with the piece of foil and return to the oven for another 5 to 10 minutes. Allow the dish to cool for a few minutes out of the oven before bringing it to the table.

✂ This is an elegant dish which calls for an equally chic first course. My choice would be Fish Soup (page 57). If you object to two fish courses, start with Tagliatelle with Mascarpone (page 146) or with your best quiche.

✂ No other vegetable is necessary, but you can serve a few steamed or boiled potatoes, which go very well with the dish.

EGGPLANTS

The eggplant is a first cousin of the tomato, with which it so often and so successfully combines. But the eggplant grew in Italy long before the arrival of its American cousin. It reached Sicily from the East during the Middle Ages, and apparently grew wild there. The Sicilians did not eat eggplants, however, fearing them to be poisonous. It was only during the famine that followed the Norman invasion at the turn of the millenium that they were driven to try them. The story goes that they first tested eggplants on their goats, who ate them and survived. But the doubts remained, and eggplants were even accused of causing madness. In the sixteenth century, in fact, the Italian word for eggplant, melanzana, was thought to derive from the Latin malum insanum, meaning unhealthy apple.

The eggplant was also known by other names. Messisbugo, in the sixteenth century, was the first to write about it; in his *Libro novo* he called it *mollegnane or pome disdegno* (literally, scornful apple). A century later Bartolomeo Stefani wrote *L'Arte di ben cucinare,* in which he said of eggplants, "When they are perfect they should be purple in color and as smooth as ivory." Stefani called them aventani, whereas the great nineteenth-century food writer Pellegrino Artusi gave them the name of petonciani. A common thread related to the supposed aftereffects of eating eggplants may link these two names, since aventani is perhaps derived from vento, meaning wind, while petonciani could be derived from peto, which means fart.

When Artusi wrote his famous book *La Scienza in cucina e l'arte di mangiar bene* (it has been reprinted well over 100 times), eggplants were only just beginning to be popular; in fact, as he wrote, "Eggplants and fennel were hardly seen in the market in Florence forty years ago." They are now popular in all regions, although most of the preparations are from southern Italy. Eggplants grow best in the south, where the rainfall is very low and the temperature very high in the summer. These conditions produce fruit with a pulp that is full of flavor, just as they do with tomatoes. When you buy eggplants, choose ones that are firm and unblemished, with a smooth, glossy skin.

The recipes I have chosen show the versatility of this vegetable, and many more can be devised by the creative cook. Grilled eggplant slices are the healthier version of the old-fashioned yet unsurpassably delicious melanzane fritte (eggplants deep-fried in oil). I often cover my eggplant cubes, previously sautéed in olive oil and butter, with a plain béchamel flavored with parmesan and then bake the dish for about ten minutes. This is a simple yet delicious recipe in which the taste of the eggplant is emphasized. Eggplants are also ideal for stuffing and baking in the traditional way. The stuffing is based on the pulp of the eggplant sautéed in oil, with different ingredients added.

HOW TO PREPARE EGGPLANTS. Eggplants can be large and bulbous, long and thin or small and round, and their color can vary from deep purple to a creamy ivory. They all have the same taste, and they all taste better if salted before cooking. Salting the eggplants gets rid of most of their bitter liquid; they are thus sweeter, they fry quicker, absorbing less oil, and they remain crisper. The salt is mixed in with the cubed or sliced eggplants, which are then put in a colander and weighted down with a heavy bowl or pan, or placed on a slanting wooden board. I usually peel eggplants unless they are to be stuffed, although I should point out that most of the vegetable fibers are in the skin.

Melanzane al limone

LEMON-FLAVORED EGGPLANT • SERVES 4 AS AN ACCOMPANIMENT

This is the lightest and freshest eggplant dish I know. Prepare the vegetable stock in advance if you haven't any ready in the freezer.

1 pound eggplant
salt
about ⅔ cup vegetable stock (page 4)
1 tablespoon lemon juice
rind of ½ lemon
2 garlic cloves, peeled
3 teaspoons chopped fresh marjoram *or* 2 teaspoons dried oregano
2 tablespoons extra-virgin olive oil
freshly ground black pepper

1 Wash the eggplant and cut into small cubes, without peeling. The texture of the skin makes the cubes more pleasant to eat and it keeps them in a neat shape. Place the eggplant in a colander, sprinkle with salt and leave for no longer than 1 hour or it will become too soft. Squeeze out the juice and dry with paper towels.

2 Choose a medium sauté pan or frying pan and heat ½ cup of the stock, the lemon juice, lemon rind, garlic and marjoram. Bring to the boil and simmer gently for 5 minutes. Add the eggplant and cook over moderate heat, turning it over every now and then. You might have to add more stock during the cooking, which will take about 10 minutes. When the eggplant is ready there should be practically no liquid left.

3 Remove and discard the garlic and the lemon rind.

4 Transfer the eggplant and any cooking liquid to a bowl. Toss with the oil. Taste and add pepper and salt if necessary. You may like to add a little more lemon juice. The dish can be served warm or at room temperature.

This dish goes very well with any roasted or grilled meat or with grilled fish. It can also be served as a first course, or after a hearty primo such as Spaghetti with Squid Stew (page 64) or Risotto with Luganega (page 73).

✕ A dinner which is rather fun is a dinner au citron. Start with Risotto with Lemon (page 27), followed with this eggplant, and finish with Lemon Sorbet (page 188) or with my favorite lemon meringue pie—Jane Grigson's in her *Fruit Book*.

Pizzette di melanzane
BROILED EGGPLANT WITH PIZZA TOPPING • SERVES 4

Here grilled slices of eggplant stand in for the bready base of a pizza. This is a cheerful and tasty first course or side dish. I prefer to top the eggplant slices with tomato sauce, which I always have in the fridge. But if you haven't any, and no time to make it, place a small spoonful of chopped canned tomatoes, a little salt and a touch of garlic over each slice, and drizzle it with a teaspoonful of extra-virgin olive oil.

1 Wash and dry the eggplants. Peel them and cut lengthwise into slices about ½ inch thick, no less. Sprinkle with salt and leave on a slanting board to drain for about 1 hour.

2 Heat the broiler.

3 Dry the eggplant slices with paper towels. Cut each slice across in half. Brush each slice with olive oil on both sides and place on an oiled piece of foil in the broiler pan. Broil for about 3 minutes on each side until golden brown; you might have to turn the heat down to prevent the eggplant cooking too fast.

4 Meanwhile cut the mozzarella into slices slightly smaller than the eggplant slices and about ⅓ inch thick.

5 Preheat the oven to 400°F.

6 Transfer the foil with the eggplant slices onto a baking sheet. Lay a slice of mozzarella over each eggplant slice and top with a dollop of tomato sauce and with some dried oregano rubbed between your hands. Sprinkle with lots of pepper and bake until the mozzarella has melted, about 5 minutes. Serve hot or at room temperature.

2 eggplants, about ¾ pound each
salt
olive oil
¾ pound mozzarella
1 cup Plain Tomato Sauce (page 112)
1 tablespoon dried oregano
freshly ground black pepper

Melanzane ripiene alla pugliese

**EGGPLANT STUFFED WITH LUGANEGA, PINE NUTS AND RAISINS •
SERVES 4**

The stuffing in this recipe brings together an unusual combination
of ingredients: sausage and golden raisins.

2 eggplants, about 1 pound
each

salt

2 tablespoons golden raisins

4 tablespoons extra-virgin
olive oil

1 large garlic clove, peeled and
finely chopped

½ small onion *or* 1 shallot, very
finely chopped

½ celery stalk, preferably with
its leaves, very finely chopped

2 pounds spicy luganega *or*
other coarse-grained pure
pork spicy sausage, skinned
and crumbled

4 tablespoons soft white
breadcrumbs

2 tablespoons pine nuts

2 tablespoons capers, rinsed
and dried

1 egg

1 tablespoon dried oregano

2 tablespoons freshly grated
pecorino romano *or*
parmesan

freshly ground black pepper

1 large ripe tomato, peeled and
seeded

1 Wash and dry the eggplants, cut them in half
lengthwise and scoop out all the flesh with the help of a sharp
small knife and then with a small pointed teaspoon, leaving
about ½-inch border all around. Be careful not to pierce the
skin.

2 Coarsely chop the pulp of the eggplant and place in a
colander. Sprinkle with salt, mix well and leave to drain for
about 2 hours.

3 Sprinkle the inside of the eggplant shells with a little
salt, place the shells upside down on a board and leave to
drain.

4 Put the raisins in a bowl, cover with warm water and
leave for about 20 minutes. Drain and dry them.

5 Put 2 tablespoons of the oil, the garlic, onion and
celery in a frying pan and sauté over low heat until soft,
stirring frequently. Add the sausage and cook gently for 20
minutes.

6 Meanwhile, squeeze the liquid from the chopped
pulp of the eggplants and dry thoroughly with paper towels.
Add to the pan and fry gently for a few minutes, stirring
frequently.

7 Preheat the oven to 375°F.

8 Add the breadcrumbs to the mixture in the frying pan
and, after 2 to 3 minutes mix in the pine nuts. Cook for
another 30 seconds and then transfer to a bowl.

9 Add the capers, egg, oregano, cheese, pepper and
raisins to the mixture in the bowl and mix very thoroughly.
Taste and adjust salt.

10 Pat dry the inside of the eggplant shells and place
them, one next to the other, in an ovenproof dish, greased
with 1 tablespoon of the remaining oil. Fill the eggplant shells
with the mixture.

11 Cut the tomato into strips and place 2 or 3 strips on
the top of each eggplant half. Pour over the rest of the oil in
a thin stream. Cover the dish with foil and bake for 20
minutes. Remove the foil and bake for another 20 minutes.
Serve warm, about an hour after the eggplants come out of
the oven.

✖ The stuffed eggplants can be served as a first course or a light second course. They make a lovely Mediterranean dish with other stuffed vegetables. I like to serve them as a secondo with Stuffed Onion Cups (page 84) and Stuffed Bibb Lettuce (page 86). For a primo, serve the Pasta with a Garlicky Béchamel (page 202) or any of the risottos in this book, except Risotto with Luganega.

- -

Sugo di melanzana
EGGPLANT SAUCE • SERVES 4

When I first tasted this sauce, at La Meridiana in London, I was baffled. There seemed to be hints of several different flavors in it, suggesting many ingredients. Not so; the sauce is in fact made from eggplant and olive oil, and nothing else. It is the ideal dressing for meat ravioli, which is how it was served at La Meridiana, or for a lovely dish of homemade tagliatelle.

For 4 people you will need a large eggplant (about ¾ pound) and 4 tablespoons of extra-virgin olive oil. Prick the eggplant with a fork in a few places and grill it over charcoal, or over a direct flame using a wire-mesh disk, or under the broiler. Turn it around until the skin is charred all over. When it is cool enough to handle, peel it and squeeze out as much of the bitter juice as you can. Put the eggplant in a food processor and when the eggplant is pureed, add the olive oil through the funnel with the processor still going. Do this very slowly, as you do for mayonnaise. Season with salt and a really good amount of pepper. When the pasta is cooked, mix a couple of tablespoons of the pasta water into the sauce before you pour it over the tagliatelle.

- -

Rotoli di melanzane ripieni
BROILED EGGPLANT STUFFED WITH TUNA AND ANCHOVIES • SERVES 4

This dish makes a delicious first course, with a most interesting combination of tastes and textures. The secret here is to use a light homemade lemon mayonnaise; a strong vinegary sauce would kill the characteristic eggplant flavor.

2 eggplants, about ¾ pound each

salt

4 tablespoons extra-virgin olive oil

2 garlic cloves, peeled and mashed

pepper

1 can (7 ounces) tuna packed in olive oil

2 anchovy fillets

1 tablespoon capers, rinsed and dried

3 tablespoons mayonnaise, preferably homemade with lemon juice

hot-pepper sauce

NOTE: You can prepare the recipe in advance through Step 4, and then spread and roll the eggplant slices just before eating them.

1 Wash and dry the eggplants. Cut them lengthwise into slices no thinner than ⅓ inch or they might crack and burn while grilling. Put the slices on a slanted board and sprinkle with salt. Leave them to drain for at least 1 hour. Rinse the slices and pat dry.

2 Put the olive oil in a soup plate and add the garlic and a generous amount of pepper. Coat the eggplant slices with the oil and place on a broiler pan.

3 Heat the broiler and when hot place the pan under it. Cook the eggplant on both sides until tender, but not burned. Keep a watch and turn down the heat if necessary. Allow to cool.

4 Meanwhile prepare the stuffing. Process the tuna with the anchovy fillets and the capers until smooth. Transfer to a bowl and add the mayonnaise gradually and a few drops of hot-pepper sauce. You may not need to add all the mayonnaise; stop when you reach the consistency of a thick mousse. Taste and adjust seasonings.

5 Spread some of the tuna mixture on each eggplant slice and roll it up jelly-roll fashion.

❧ The rolls are very good surrounded by sliced ripe tomatoes that have been lightly dressed with extra-virgin olive oil and salt.

❧ To follow you can serve most meat or fish dishes. I recommend fish because I am used to, and like, the Italian custom of serving a meal composed of complementary, rather than contrasting, dishes. Monkfish and Mussels in a Saffron Sauce (page 56) or Stewed Octopus (page 65) would be my choice.

Parmigiana di melanzane

EGGPLANT PARMIGIANA • SERVES 4 TO 5

This is one of the most popular of all eggplant dishes. If you do not like fried food, you can broil the eggplant slices. If, however, you salt the eggplant slices for at least 2 hours (see the remarks on page 94) and keep the oil at the right temperature during the frying, the eggplant will absorb hardly any oil during the frying.

A tip I have learned from Marcella Hazan is to soak the mozzarella in oil. This improves the texture of the factory-made mozzarella that is mostly available nowadays.

4 or 5 eggplants, about ¾ pound each
salt
½ pound mozzarella, finely chopped or grated (1 cup)
5 tablespoons olive oil
1 cup coarsely chopped canned plum tomatoes
1 garlic clove, peeled and mashed
a few fresh basil leaves, torn, *or* 1 teaspoon dried oregano
freshly ground black pepper
vegetable oil for frying
½ cup freshly grated parmesan
2 hard-boiled eggs, sliced

1 Wash and peel the eggplants and slice them lengthwise about 3/16 inch thick. Sprinkle generously with salt, put in a colander and leave to drain for 2 hours or longer. Rinse under cold water and dry thoroughly with paper towels.

2 Put the grated mozzarella in a bowl, drizzle on 1 tablespoon of the olive oil and leave to soak for 30 minutes or longer.

3 Put 1 tablespoon of the olive oil in a small saucepan together with the tomatoes, garlic and basil. Add salt and pepper and cook at a lively simmer for 5 minutes. Puree the sauce through a sieve or a food mill.

4 Pour enough vegetable oil in a frying pan to reach 1 inch up the side of the pan. Heat the oil and when very hot (test it by immersing the corner of an eggplant slice: it should sizzle) put in as many eggplant slices as will fit in a single layer. Fry to a golden brown on both sides (this will take about 5 minutes) and then retrieve the slices with a slotted spoon and drain on paper towels. Repeat until all the eggplant is fried.

5 Preheat the oven to 400°F.

6 Smear the bottom of a shallow baking dish with 1 tablespoon of the olive oil. Cover with a layer of eggplant, spread over a little tomato sauce and some mozzarella. Sprinkle with a lot of freshly ground pepper and with some parmesan. Spread over a few slices of the hard-boiled egg and then cover with another layer of eggplant. Repeat these layers until all the ingredients are used up, finishing with a layer of eggplant. Pour over the remaining oil and bake in the preheated oven for about 30 minutes.

Like many other vegetable dishes, Eggplant Parmigiana can be either a primo or a secondo; it can even

(*continued*)

be an accompaniment to a steak or roast chicken, although personally I would find this excessive. If you want to serve it as a first course, either Braised Shoulder of Pork with Herbs and Garlic (page 203) or Sweet-and-Sour Shoulder of Lamb (page 223) would be suitable as a secondo. I like to serve the eggplant as a secondo for the family or at an informal dinner, preceded by Bread Soup (page 43) or Risotto with Shellfish (page 28).

FENNEL

"It is said that serpents are very fond of fennel, and that after feeding on this plant they do not get any older." Thus wrote Bartolomeo Sacchi, known as Platina, in the fifteenth century, and after listing fennel's many therapeutic properties he wrote, "It is therefore advisable to eat fennel, whether raw or cooked." I love fennel, both the herb and the bulb, and as I eat it I cherish the hope that, like Platina's snakes, I may discover the secret of eternal middle age! I grow the herb in the garden with great ease, and I buy the bulbs whenever I see some that look fresh enough. Unfortunately the fennel you buy outside Italy is not as flavorful as the fennel in Italy.

In the past fennel was eaten at the end of the meal, sometimes with a little salt, being considered a very healthy food with which to finish a heavy meal. This habit has more or less disappeared, except for some places in Tuscany, where wedges of fennel are still placed on the table with apples and tangerines. But fennel is still eaten a great deal in Italy, as a vegetable or in salad; in fact, because of its versatility, it is the most popular winter vegetable.

Fennel is one of the best ingredients for a Piedmontese bagna caôda—crudités dipped in a hot garlicky sauce, or for a Roman pinzimonio (page 118). It is also excellent cooked. Try stewing it in milk and butter, or in a thin tomato sauce. A favorite of mine in winter is fennel baked with béchamel, parmesan and nutmeg, while another is tagliatelle dressed with a creamy sauce of stewed fennel.

Fennel is best in the autumn and winter months. When you buy fennel for eating raw, choose the round squat bulbs in preference to the flat, elongated ones. They are crisper and sweeter. For cooking, either variety is suitable. See that the bulbs have no brown or wilted patches and that the bottom is white.

When you prepare fennel, start by removing any brown or wilted parts. Then cut the fennel according to the recipe and wash thoroughly in cold water. For cooking you will need about three large heads for four people; if you are going to eat them raw, two will be enough.

VEGETABLE TIMBALES. "A sformato, a dish which figures largely in Italian home cooking but never in restaurants, is a cross between a soufflé and what we should call a pudding." Thus wrote Elizabeth David in *Italian Food,* first published in 1954. And how right she was so many years ago, when nobody outside Italy, or even outside northern Italian families of a certain milieu, knew what a sformato (timbale) was. In my home, sformati of different vegetables, often mixed in sections in the same mold, were the usual entremets at dinner parties. They replaced fish on giorni di magro (fast days) when a sformato would precede sea bass or porgies.

My impression is that nowadays sformati are rarely served at home while, with slight modifications, they have become the most fashionable fare to be had in a restaurant, where they appear in individual portions and are called sformatini or timballini. One reason why a sformato is less often served at home is that the usual meal now consists of only three courses, and the Italians like a minestra for the primo and meat or fish for the secondo. The entremets has, by and large, ceased to exist, so where can a sformato appear?

I find that, in fact, a sformato makes a good supper dish en famille, or a perfect start to a dinner party. It looks most impressive when served, and it is less nerve-racking for the hostess than a soufflé, since it will not collapse. If you butter a mold very carefully and *very* generously, and sprinkle it all over with breadcrumbs, you will have no difficulty in unmolding it.

A sformato can be made with green beans, with fresh or dried peas, with carrots, artichokes, spinach, eggplants, in fact with most vegetables that are cooked first and then chopped or puréed. In the past, eggs and béchamel were used for binding, but now that béchamel is out of fashion, cream is often used instead. However, I find the old recipe better. A sformato can be served with various sauces, the most common being a tomato sauce, perfect with a sformato of green beans or of eggplants, and a fonduta (page 143), my favorite with spinach or with fennel. These can also be served with a rich finanziera, a velouté sauce from Piedmont containing chicken giblets, prosciutto and mushrooms.

You can make individual sformatini by using ramekins. Unmold them on individual plates and surround them with a little sauce. The recipe here is for a large sformato.

Sformato di finocchi

FENNEL TIMBALE • SERVES 6

1 Cut away the green tops, the stalks and any bruised or brown parts of the outside leaves of the fennel. Reserve a handful of the green top. (Do not throw all the rest away; it will make a good soup for the family with the addition of a potato or two.)

2 Cut the fennel bulbs lengthwise into slices about ¼ inch thick. Wash the slices, and the reserved fennel top, in cold water and dry with paper towels.

3 Melt 2 tablespoons of the butter in a frying pan. When the butter begins to foam, add the fennel and cook for 5 minutes. Add salt and half the milk. Cover the pan and cook very gently until the fennel is tender, about 20 minutes. Keep a watch on the fennel and add a little water if it becomes too dry.

4 Chop the fennel by hand or in the food processor to a very coarse puree. Transfer to a bowl.

5 Preheat the oven to 375°F.

6 Make a fairly thick béchamel sauce (see page 4) with the remaining butter, the flour and the rest of the milk.

1½ **pounds fennel bulbs**
4 **tablespoons unsalted butter**
salt
1¼ **cups milk**
3 **tablespoons flour**
pinch of freshly grated nutmeg
freshly ground pepper, preferably white
3 **eggs**
5 **tablespoons freshly grated parmesan**
3 **tablespoons dried breadcrumbs**

NOTE: You can cook the fennel in advance, even the day before, and make the sformato just before serving.

(*continued*)

Flavor the béchamel with grated nutmeg and some pepper and then add to the fennel in the bowl.

7 Beat the eggs together lightly with a fork and add to the fennel mixture together with the parmesan. Mix very thoroughly, then taste and adjust the seasoning.

8 Butter a 2 quart ring mold very generously. If you are nervous about unmolding the sformato, line the base of the ring with parchment paper and butter the paper. Sprinkle the mold with the breadcrumbs and then shake off the excess crumbs.

9 Spoon the mixture into the prepared mold. Place the mold in a baking dish and fill the dish with very hot water to reach two-thirds of the way up the side of the mold. Place in the preheated oven and cook for about 45 minutes, until a thin skewer or a toothpick inserted into the middle of the sformato comes out dry.

10 Allow to stand for 5 minutes. Loosen the sides of the sformato with a metal spatula and place a round dish over it. Turn the dish and the mold over, shake the mold lightly and lift it off. Remove the paper, if you were using it.

11 Fill the hole in the sformato with some sauce, and spoon a few tablespoons around it. Serve the rest of the sauce in a warm sauceboat.

✖ You can follow this sformato with fish; Steamed Fish with Fresh Herb Sauce (page 205) would be nice. If you prefer meat, serve Osso Buco, Milanese Style (page 170). If you want to serve the sformato as a second course in a vegetarian dinner, start with Stuffed Reginette (page 21) or Risotto with Lemon (page 27).

Finocchi del Corrado
FENNEL WITH PISTACHIO AND ANCHOVY SAUCE • SERVES 4

I am at a loss to describe the taste of this superb dish which I adapted from an eighteenth-century recipe by Vincenzo Corrado, my favorite food writer. Corrado had the perfect touch when dealing with vegetables, to which he dedicated more of his writings than did any other writer of the past. The dish leaves you delighted yet puzzled as to how such an unlikely combination of flavors could blend with such complete harmony. Those, at least, were my feelings when I first made the dish.

1 Remove the bruised and brown parts of the fennel, as well as the stalks and the feathery tops. Cut the fennel into quarters, wash them and then cut them into very thin segments.

2 Put the wine, bay leaves, cinnamon, peppercorns and 1 teaspoon of salt in a saucepan. Add the fennel and enough water to cover. Bring to the boil and cook, covered, at a steady simmer until the fennel is tender but still al dente. Drain and then put the fennel into a deep dish.

3 For the sauce, blanch the pistachios in boiling water for 20 seconds and then peel them. Put them in a mortar and add all the anchovies, sugar, a generous amount of nutmeg, the olive oil, vinegar and grated lemon rind. Pound to a paste with a pestle, using a rotary motion, then taste and add enough lemon juice to achieve the desired amount of bite. You can use a food processor for this operation.

4 Spoon this sauce over the fennel, cover with plastic wrap and leave it in the refrigerator for at least 24 hours. Bring the dish back to room temperature before serving. You can decorate with a few sprigs of the feathery tops.

✂ This fennel is good as an accompaniment to grilled or boiled fish, or with cold roast beef, veal or chicken. But I think it is ideal by itself as a first course, when the full complexity of its flavor can best be appreciated.

1½ pounds fennel bulbs
 1 cup dry white wine
 2 bay leaves
2-inch piece of cinnamon stick
 8 peppercorns, bruised
salt

SAUCE

 2 tablespoons pistachio nuts
 2 anchovy fillets
 1 teaspoon sugar
freshly grated nutmeg
 3 tablespoons extra-virgin olive oil
 2 teaspoons white wine vinegar
grated rind and juice of ½ lemon

- -

Finocchi stufati
BRAISED FENNEL • SERVES 4

The old-fashioned way of cooking vegetables in Italy is to braise them. This recipe will demonstrate how such slow cooking intensifies the flavor. The fennel becomes unbelievably tasty, although crunchy-vegetable fanatics might not approve of the texture.

1 Trim the fennel, removing any brown parts as well as the stalks and the feathery tops. (These last two can be used for a soup.) Cut the fennel lengthwise into quarters, then slice the quarters into wedges about ½ inch thick. Put in a colander and wash under cold running water. Drain and dry thoroughly with paper towels.

1¾ pounds fennel bulbs
 4 tablespoons unsalted butter
about 1 cup vegetable *or* meat stock (pages 3–4)
salt
pepper

(*continued*)

2 Choose a sauté pan large enough to hold the raw fennel comfortably. Melt the butter and when it acquires a golden tinge, add the fennel and fry gently for about 10 minutes, turning it over and over to insaporire (make tasty) on all sides.

3 Add enough stock to cover the bottom of the pan. Cover with a tight-fitting lid and cook over very low heat for at least 30 minutes, until the fennel are very tender indeed. You might have to add a little more stock during the cooking if the fennel gets too dry. By the time it is finished there should be just a little liquid left: the fennel should certainly not be swimming in it. The fennel should be pale gold in color. Add salt and pepper to taste and serve.

PEPPERS

The first peppers to reach Europe in the wake of the returning conquistadors were much too fierce for the European palate. On January 15, 1493, Christopher Columbus wrote in his diary, "In Haiti my men found a lot of aji which the natives use as pepper, but which merits a much higher value, as aji can be considered a dish in its own right for anyone who can bear its very strong taste." The popularity of this plant spread far and wide, and peppers became a favorite in the Middle East and India within a hundred years of the discovery of the New World. They took longer to establish themselves in Europe, although it is not clear exactly when they became popular in Italy. Peppers were certainly cultivated and eaten in southern Italy quite early on, but they were evidently considered a lowly vegetable not worthy of the attention and creativity of chefs and writers.

I have not been able to find any mention of peppers in Italian cook books until 1847, when a recipe for stuffed peppers was written by Ippolito Cavalcanti Duca di Buonvicino in his excellent book, *Cucina teorico-pratica,* published in Naples in that year. It is a simple recipe for roast peppers stuffed with a classic Neapolitan stuffing of breadcrumbs, capers, olives, oregano, anchovy fillets, parsley and garlic, a recipe still very popular to this day. It is the stuffing used in the recipe for Bibb lettuce on page 86. Nowadays peppers are recognized as one of the most interesting and rewarding of vegetables, and they cheer every vegetable stand with their bright, pulsating colors.

BUYING PEPPERS. Peppers should be smooth and shiny, without wrinkles. The heavier the pepper, considering its size, the better it is, because it is meatier. Color is an indication of ripeness. Thus, when green peppers ripen, they become red or yellow. I prefer those that are ripe and sweet, although in some dishes it is right to include green peppers as well, not only for the appearance of the dish but because it may need the more pronounced flavor of the green pepper.

HOW TO GRILL PEPPERS. I like to skin peppers as I find the skin hard to digest and often tough. To skin peppers that are to be eaten raw, I use a swivel-action peeler; if the pepper is meaty it's not too difficult. To skin peppers that are going to be stuffed or cooked, you can either grill them, char them over a direct flame or roast them in a very hot oven (475°F) for about 20 minutes. When the skin is blistered and charred, put them aside to cool. As soon as they are cool enough to handle, peel them and pat them clean with paper towels. Don't put them under the tap or the delicious juices will be washed away with the charred bits. To remove the seeds, cut away the stalk, cut the peppers in half and brush out all the seeds with paper towels.

Grilled peppers have a richer flavor than roast peppers, and although they tend to become more limp, I prefer to grill them even when they are to be stuffed. Instead of stuffing the peppers whole I cut them in half first and then stuff each half.

In September and October, when peppers are cheap, I grill quite a few and put them in jars with a few garlic cloves, then fill the jars with olive oil. They come in very useful as a first course on their own, with maybe a couple of hard-boiled eggs, or as an accompaniment to roast pork. They keep for at least three months, at least I believe they do, although in my home they never last that long!

Peperoni arrostiti
GRILLED PEPPERS • SERVES 4

When I serve these peppers on their own I like to dress them with a sauce based on olive oil and garlic with anchovy fillets (I sometimes add capers as well). The sauce should be cooked for a couple of minutes so that the garlic and anchovy flavors combine well and become less pervasive. It is very important that the sauce cook over very low heat or the garlic will burn and the anchovy turn bitter. The ideal saucepan to use is a small earthenware pot that can be put directly on the heat. Earthenware has the property of distributing the heat all over the container and retaining it for a long time.

1 You can grill the peppers over charcoal, or over direct flame using a wire mesh holder. If you cook with electricity, use the broiler. Put the peppers on the flame or charcoal and grill them all over. As soon as the side in contact with the heat is charred, turn the peppers around until all the surface, including the top and bottom, is charred. When all the skin is charred, take the pepper off the flame, otherwise the meat will begin to burn and you will be left with paper-thin peppers.

2 Let the peppers cool and then remove the skin; it will come off very easily as long as the peppers have been well grilled. (Although many food writers suggest that putting the peppers to cool in plastic or paper bags makes them easier to peel, I find this totally unnecessary.) Cut the peppers in half,

4 red or yellow bell peppers (about 1½ pounds)
6 anchovy fillets
3 garlic cloves, peeled
2 tablespoons fresh parsley
1 small dried chili, seeded
4 tablespoons extra-virgin olive oil

(*continued*)

remove the stalk and seeds and then cut them lengthwise in strips. Put them on a dish.

3 If you are using salted anchovies, bone and wash them. Dry them with paper towels. Pound and mash the anchovy fillets together with the garlic, parsley and chili in a mortar, or chop very finely

4 Put the oil and the anchovy mixture in a very heavy pot and heat very slowly while stirring and pounding the whole time until the mixture is mashed. Spoon over the peppers and leave to marinate for at least 4 hours. The longer you leave them, up to a week, the better they get. Serve plenty of bread with them.

Peperoni alla siciliana
GRILLED PEPPERS WITH ANCHOVIES, OLIVES AND CAPERS • SERVES 4

If I had to name my favorite vegetable dish, this would certainly be one of the principal contenders. It is more like a relish than a vegetable dish, with all the flavors blending beautifully together during the lengthy cooking. In fact, I find the dish is even better if made a day in advance.

4 large bell peppers (about 1½ pounds)
1 medium onion, finely sliced
2 garlic cloves, peeled and chopped
3 tablespoons extra-virgin olive oil
salt
vegetable *or* light chicken stock (pages 3–4)
2 tablespoons balsamic vinegar *or* red wine vinegar mixed with 1 teaspoon sugar
2 tablespoons chopped fresh oregano *or* 1 tablespoon dried oregano
16 black olives, pitted and cut into strips
4 anchovy fillets
1½ tablespoons capers, rinsed
pepper

1 Grill and peel the peppers as described on page 104.

2 Cut each pepper into quarters, remove the core, seeds and membrane and then cut into 1-inch strips.

3 Put the onion, garlic and oil in a sauté pan. Sprinkle with salt and add 2 tablespoons stock. Cook gently, covered, until the onion is so soft as to be like a puree. Uncover the pan and continue cooking until the onion turns gold. This will take about 40 minutes.

4 Add the peppers, 2 tablespoons stock and the vinegar. Cook, uncovered, for 30 minutes, stirring occasionally. Add a couple of tablespoons of hot water or hot stock if the peppers seem to become too dry.

5 Add the oregano, olives, anchovies, capers and pepper and continue cooking for another 20 minutes or so, until all the flavors have blended into a rich sauce. You should keep the heat very low indeed for this final cooking or the anchovies will acquire a bitter taste. Serve warm or at room temperature.

✴ This is a versatile dish, perfect as a secondo by itself with plenty of crusty bread, or as a primo followed by a robust dish of meat or fish such as Beef Braised in Wine Vinegar (page 222) or Stewed Octopus (page 65). It is also an ideal accompaniment to cold roast beef or a roasted bird, either for a lunch party or as a buffet side dish.

- -

Peperoni e patate in padella
SAUTEED PEPPERS AND POTATOES • SERVES 4

In this recipe from southern Italy, the peppers impart their characteristic flavor and firm texture to a bowl of sautéed potatoes. It is particularly good with roast pork, such as the Braised Shoulder of Pork with Herbs and Garlic (page 203).

1 Peel the potatoes and cut into thin slices. Wash and dry them thoroughly. Keep them wrapped in a kitchen towel to prevent them from browning as you prepare the peppers.

2 Wash the peppers and cut them into quarters. Remove seeds, white ribs and cores and cut into 1-inch pieces. Dry and set aside.

3 Chop the garlic, chili and parsley together very finely.

4 Put half the oil in a heavy frying pan, add half the garlic, chili and parsley mixture and sauté over medium heat for 30 seconds, stirring constantly. Add the potatoes and continue cooking for about 5 minutes. At this stage you should turn the potatoes over very frequently. Use a fork, as this breaks them up less than a spoon. Turn the heat down a little and sauté until the potatoes are tender, at least 30 minutes. Stir frequently and add a couple of tablespoons of hot water whenever they stick to the bottom of the pan.

5 While the potatoes are cooking, put the remaining oil, garlic, chili and parsley in another large frying pan. Sauté for 30 seconds and then mix in the peppers. Cook over medium heat until the peppers are cooked but still somewhat crunchy, which will take about 20 minutes. Stir and shake the pan frequently during the cooking.

6 Add salt to the potatoes and to the peppers, and mix well. Transfer both the vegetables to a warm bowl and mix together thoroughly. Serve at once.

1 pound waxy potatoes
1 pound yellow and red bell peppers
2 garlic cloves, peeled
1 dried chili, or more according to taste, seeded
2/3 cup parsley, preferably flat-leaf
5 tablespoons olive oil
salt

NOTE: You can cook the peppers in advance, but I prefer to cook the potatoes as nearly as possible at the last minute, since reheated potatoes taste of reheated potatoes. Don't forget, though, that potatoes will keep warm for nearly half an hour in their pan, tightly covered with a lid.

- -

Fagottini di peperoni e coda di rospo
GRILLED PEPPER AND MONKFISH BUNDLES • SERVES 4

Once when I was testing this recipe and had not made a first course, I put some steamed potatoes around the fish to help satisfy our hunger. They were perfect with the fish and, in fact, I've always served them since then.

4 large bell peppers, red and/or yellow (about 1½ pounds)

salt

pepper

1½ pounds monkfish

3 tablespoons extra-virgin olive oil

5 tablespoons dry white wine

1 garlic clove, peeled

1 chili

1 Grill and peel the peppers as directed on page 104. Set aside the smallest pepper and cut the other 3 in wide strips: you need 8 of them. Remove core, seeds and membrane. Sprinkle each strip with salt and pepper.

2 Preheat the oven to 425°F.

3 Remove both the dark skin, if still on, and the transparent skin from the fish and cut into 8 chunks. Sprinkle with salt and pepper. Wrap a strip of pepper around each piece of monkfish and lay the bundles in a well-oiled oven dish; the bundles should fit snugly. (I use a small lasagne dish.) Drizzle 1 tablespoon of the oil over all and cover with foil. Place the dish in the oven and cook for 10 minutes.

4 Meanwhile prepare the sauce. Clean the remaining pepper and chop coarsely. Put it in a small saucepan with the wine, garlic and chili.

5 When the fish is done, pour all the cooking juices into the small pan with the sauce. Turn the oven heat down to 325°F and put the fish back in the oven, but without the foil.

6 Cook the sauce gently for 10 minutes, stirring occasionally. Remove and discard the garlic and chili and puree the sauce in the food processor. Add the remaining oil slowly through the funnel with the machine running.

7 Place 2 bundles on each of 4 plates and spoon a little of the sauce around the bundles.

✂ As a first course I recommend Fish Soup (page 57) or, for hearty eaters, Spaghetti and Mussels en Papillote (page 66). This would be a typically Italian meal, where both courses are based on fish. If you are serving the bundles as a first course and want to follow with something different, choose Pork Tenderloin with Berries, Almonds and Balsamic Vinegar (page 227) or any other meat dish with a distinct flavor. After the pepper sauce, you won't be able to taste a delicate dish.

Terrina coi peperoni
PEPPER-STUDDED MEAT TERRINE • SERVES 8

This terrine is just right for a summer buffet. I find it is also a very useful standby for weekend lunches when you come in late and have to feed a hungry family in ten minutes flat. The terrine keeps very well in the fridge for three or four days, wrapped in foil.

1 First roast the peppers in a hot oven (475°F) until the skin is soft and the peppers can be easily peeled, about 25 minutes. If you prefer you can grill the peppers over a flame instead of roasting them, but I find roasting gives the peppers the right texture for this terrine. When you have peeled them, cut into quarters and remove the core, seeds and membrane and then cut into ½-inch pieces.

2 Turn the oven down to 375°F.

3 Put the meat in a bowl, add the parmesan, eggs and garlic. Mix well and then add the peppers, salt and a generous grinding of pepper. Remember that this dish is eaten cold, and cold food needs more seasoning. Mix again very thoroughly. I find this is best done with your hands, so that you can feel when the two kinds of meat have blended and the pepper pieces are evenly distributed.

4 Brush a 1-quart metal loaf pan with the oil. Transfer the meat mixture into the pan and press down well with the palm of your hand, then bang the pan on the work surface to get rid of any remaining air bubbles. If the terrine has pockets of air trapped in it, it is likely to break when you slice it.

5 Cook in the oven for at least 1 hour. (The terrine will shrink away from the sides of the pan.) Pour off the juices and allow to cool.

6 For a family lunch, slice the terrine at the table. If you want to be more formal, prepare the dish in the kitchen, garnishing the sliced terrine with black olives or cornichons.

✄ Any salad goes well with this terrine, but I particularly like a potato salad, dressed with a thin lemony mayonnaise, or Wine-dressed Green Bean and Tomato Salad (page 120). A lovely dish of spaghetti or a creamy risotto can be the first course. Try Spaghetti with Tuna and Tomato Sauce (page 60), Spaghetti with Clams (page 68) or one of the vegetable risottos (pages 30 and 90).

3 red, yellow and green bell peppers (about 1 pound)
1 pound lean ground beef
½ pound ground pork
⅓ cup freshly grated parmesan
2 eggs, lightly beaten
1 small garlic clove, peeled and very finely sliced
salt
freshly ground black pepper
1 tablespoon olive oil

TOMATOES

Although it is hard to imagine Italian food without the tomato, Italian cooking had already reached great heights of sophistication and was spreading its influence throughout Europe 150 years before this fruit existed in Italy. The tomato, a native of Peru and Mexico, was brought to Europe by the returning conquistadors and first reached Italy at the end of the sixteenth century. It was only in the late seventeenth century, however, that tomatoes began to gain popularity, and then only in southern Italy, where the best varieties were produced. As late as 1770 the Irish traveler Patrick Brydone, writing from Sicily, reported, "They have likewise a variety of flowering shrubs; particularly one in great plenty which I do not recollect ever to have seen before. It bears a beautiful round fruit of a bright shining yellow. They call it Il Pomo d'Oro or golden apple."

It was around that time that tomatoes began to appear in Italian kitchens. The earliest recipe for a tomato sauce for dressing pasta was written in Naples by the eighteenth-century food writer Francesco Leonardi, while his contemporary Vincenzo Corrado, also a Neapolitan, combined tomato with mutton, with prosciutto and with other ingredients. Slowly through the nineteenth century, and then at a much faster pace through the twentieth, tomatoes became a common ingredient, often grafted onto traditional recipes such as the Milanese osso buco or the Veronese sopa coada, a thick soup made with pigeon and vegetables.

"The word tomato now embraces the best and the worst of the vegetable kingdom"—thus writes Jane Grigson in her admirable *Vegetable Book*. Without a doubt it has become very difficult to buy good tomatoes. During the winter months it is even better to use canned tomatoes rather than out-of-season fresh ones which offer poor value for the money. When you buy canned tomatoes, shop around for a good brand and then stick to it. Canned tomatoes are improved by adding a teaspoon of sugar and a teaspoon of tomato paste when you cook them.

Tomatoes do not keep well for more than a few days. The refrigerator is really too cold for them, since the ideal temperature for storing tomatoes is 50°F.; it is best, therefore, to buy no more than you can use within three or four days at most.

The best way to eat a good tomato is to cut it in slices or chunky wedges and dress it with extra-virgin olive oil, salt and pepper. Oregano or basil leaves and a touch of garlic add to the pleasure.

Tomatoes can be stuffed in many ways. Tomatoes Filled with Rice and Black Olives (page 231) are good, but try them also filled with tuna and mayonnaise, or filled with raw rice and then baked. The great nineteenth-century cookery writer Artusi suggests baking them, cut in half and dressed with a knob of butter, plenty of pepper and a little salt, to be served as an accompaniment to roast or grilled meats. One of my favorite dishes consists of plum tomatoes, peeled and cut in half and filled with extra-virgin olive oil, a cube of Italian mozzarella and a leaf of basil. Before you fill them, sprinkle a little salt on the inside and leave them in the fridge, cut side down on a plate or board for half an hour.

Finally I should mention the use of tomatoes as a condiment. Even one ripe tomato, if it is good, adds flavor to meat or fish, as well as an attractive tinge of color. And a soup is often improved by adding a chopped tomato to the basic soffritto.

HOW TO PEEL TOMATOES. Being Italian, I peel tomatoes only when I am going to cook them. A good tomato with a thin, tender skin should not be peeled. Unfortunately the new breed of tomatoes have tough skins tasting of grass, and these definitely need peeling. To peel tomatoes, pour boiling water over them and leave for 15 to 30 seconds, according to their ripeness. Then lift them out and drop them into a bowl of cold water. In Italy we remove all the seeds, but the tomatoes there contain much more pulp. Cut the tomato in half and squeeze: enough seeds and juice will come out.

MY FAVORITE TOMATO SAUCES. To make a good tomato sauce you can either cook the tomatoes for a very short time, or let them bubble for at least 40 minutes. There is a reason for this wide variation in cooking time. Tomatoes only begin to release their acid liquid after they have cooked for about ten minutes, and it takes half an hour of lively simmering to evaporate this liquid altogether. So if you have very tasty tomatoes, make the Quick Tomato Sauce (page 113). For less good tomatoes, choose the recipe that calls for lengthy cooking, Plain Tomato Sauce (page 112). And if you want the full freshness of the tomatoes with your pasta or rice, do not cook them at all, as in the recipe for Uncooked Tomato Sauce (page 113).

SUNDRIED TOMATOES. These are small tomatoes, usually from Calabria. There they are split open, sprinkled with salt and laid on bamboo racks to dry in the hot sun. When the water in the tomatoes has evaporated, they shrivel up and their flavor becomes very concentrated. These tomatoes, previously soaked in water, give any tomato dish, sauce or soup, a very strong and delicious flavor.

You can buy them in jars, covered with olive oil, or dried. If you buy them dried, and I would advise you to do so, cover them with a mixture of equal parts of boiling water and vinegar and leave them for about one hour. Then turn them over and leave them for an hour and a half. They are now ready to be prepared. Drain them and lay them on a kitchen towel to dry, then pat them with paper towels.

Put the tomatoes in a glass jar in layers with oregano, chopped garlic, little pieces of anchovy fillets and one or two dried chilies, according to taste. Cover with extra-virgin olive oil. For one pound of dried tomatoes you will need about one to one and a half cups of olive oil. The oil should cover the top layer. Check that there is no air trapped between the layers by sliding a metal spatula down the side of the jar. These tomatoes make a quick and most delicious little antipasto served by themselves or with grilled peppers. They are also the most appetizing treat when you feel hungry!

La mia salsa

PLAIN TOMATO SAUCE • MAKES ABOUT 2½ CUPS

This is a basic tomato sauce, which I often make in large quantities when tomatoes are good and cheap. Make it with plum tomatoes when they are available, as they are plumper and tastier. I freeze the sauce in plastic containers of various sizes which then come in very handy for recipes that only call for a couple of tablespoons. I use it in meat and fish dishes, I add it to soups and I dress pasta with it, adding a couple of tablespoons of extra-virgin olive oil or a good lump of butter when I reheat the sauce.

When added to a meat dish, the sauce must cook with the meat for a long time to allow the flavors to combine. This sauce is also perfect for a ragù, when it has to cook for even longer, as Eduardo de Filippo reminded us in a poem he wrote in his native Neapolitan dialect. It is called "O Rraù di Mamma" (Mama's ragù), and concerns the views of a newly married man on this subject, as expressed somewhat forcefully to his young wife. Loosely translated, what he says is, "Only mama made ragù the way I like it, and since the day we married we have kept on talking about it. I am not difficult, and it's not something to quarrel about. But do you really think that what you make is ragù? I eat it just for something to eat, but may I tell you something? This is just meat with tomato sauce." What withering scorn!

Wash and cut 2 pounds of tomatoes into large pieces. Put them in a heavy-based saucepan and add 1 celery stalk, 1 medium onion and half a carrot, all cut into pieces, plus 1 or 2 garlic cloves, 2 sprigs of parsley, 2 sage leaves, a sprig of thyme and some salt. I do not add the pepper at this stage. If the tomatoes are insipid I also mix in 1 teaspoon of tomato paste and 1 teaspoon of sugar. Bring the mixture to the boil and cook, uncovered, over low heat for 40 to 50 minutes, stirring frequently. Keep an eye on the sauce and do not let it stick to the bottom of the pan; if necessary add a little vegetable stock or hot water. By the end of the cooking the sauce should be quite thick and all the liquid should have evaporated. Put the sauce through a food mill or a sieve; this, rather than a food processor, gives the best consistency. If you want to use a food processor you will have to peel and seed the tomatoes before you put them in the pan. When the sauce is pureed, add some freshly ground pepper and check the salt.

Sugo fresco di pomodoro
QUICK TOMATO SAUCE • MAKES 2 CUPS

This sauce is cooked for a very short time so that the tomato flavor is retained. It is good with pasta or gnocchi or to accompany boiled meat, or grilled or steamed chicken or fish.

3 cups canned San Marzano tomatoes
1 garlic clove, peeled
2 shallots
1 teaspoon sugar
2 tablespoons vegetable stock (page 4)
salt
freshly ground black pepper
6 fresh basil leaves, torn
4 tablespoons extra-virgin olive oil *or* 3 tablespoons unsalted butter

1 Empty the tomatoes into a strainer, leave for 5 minutes and then coarsely chop the tomatoes.

2 Finely chop the garlic and shallots. Put them in a pan with the sugar and the stock. Cover and cook very gently until the onion is soft, by which time the stock will have more or less evaporated.

3 Add the tomatoes to the pan. Season with salt and pepper. Bring to the boil and cook uncovered for 5 minutes at a lively heat.

4 Add the basil and either olive oil or butter, according to your taste.

Sugo di pomodoro crudo
UNCOOKED TOMATO SAUCE • MAKES 1½ CUPS

A classic recipe, in Italy this sauce is used only with spaghetti or spaghettini. I also like to dress boiled rice with this sauce, especially for a summer meal.

1½ pounds ripe tomatoes, preferably plum tomatoes
4 tablespoons extra-virgin olive oil
1 garlic clove, peeled and very finely sliced
12 fresh basil leaves, coarsely torn, *or* ½ cup fresh parsley, preferably flat-leaf
salt
pepper
freshly grated parmesan (optional)

1 Peel the tomatoes as described on page 110. Cut in half and squeeze out some of the seeds and juice. Cut into thin strips and put in the bowl in which you are going to serve your spaghetti or rice. Add the oil, garlic and basil leaves. If you are using parsley, chop it, but not too fine, and add to the bowl. Season with salt and pepper. Leave to marinate for at least 1 hour.

2 When the spaghetti or the rice is cooked, drain well and then toss thoroughly in the sauce. I do not like parmesan with this dish, but if you do, it should be served separately.

Teglia di patate e pomodori
POTATO AND TOMATO PIE • SERVES 4

This is a different and very Mediterranean way of using leftover boiled or steamed potatoes. Make this dish when you can get really good tomatoes.

Take 6 or 7 medium cooked potatoes and 1 pound of the best ripe tomatoes. Slice the potatoes into ¼-inch rounds and put them in a well-oiled shallow ovenproof dish. Chop ½ cup parsley, 1 garlic clove, 1 dried chili, 1 tablespoon rinsed and dried capers and—if you like them—about 6 black olives. I use 1 tablespoon Black Olive Puree (page 230) instead of the olives. Put the chopped ingredients in a bowl and add 2 tablespoons of your best olive oil. Spread half this mixture over the potatoes. Peel the tomatoes as described on page 110. Cut them in half, squeeze out the seeds and then roughly slice or chop them. Spread them on top of the potatoes and then spoon over the rest of the parsley mixture. Dribble a little oil all over the top and bake in a preheated hot oven (400°F.) for 30 to 40 minutes. Serve warm, not straight from the oven.

Finte trippe
FRITTATA STRIPS IN TOMATO SAUCE • SERVES 3 OR 4

The odd name of this recipe from Rome, "fake tripe," is explained when you see the dish: the strips of flat omelet look like strips of tripe stewed in a tomato sauce. I love eggs however they are cooked and this is one of the best ways of cooking them I know.

1 Heat the butter and the oil in an 8-inch sauté or frying pan. When the butter foam begins to subside, add the celery and onion and cook very slowly for 5 minutes, stirring frequently. Add the tomatoes and salt. Cook, uncovered, over low heat for 30 minutes, stirring occasionally, then add pepper and the basil. Mix well and check seasoning. If the sauce becomes too thick, add a couple of tablespoons or more hot water during the cooking. The sauce should have no liquid by the end of the cooking.

2 Preheat the oven to 400°F.

3 While the sauce is cooking, lightly beat the eggs with the parmesan, a little salt and a lot of freshly ground black pepper.

4 Lightly butter a 10 × 12-inch baking dish. Sprinkle with a little flour all over the buttered surface and then shake off excess flour. Pour the egg mixture into the pan and tilt it to spread the mixture evenly. Place the pan in the oven and bake until the frittata is set but still soft, about 8 to 10 minutes. You will, in fact, notice the smell of cooked egg when it is ready.

5 Gently ease the frittata from the pan with the help of a spatula. Turn the pan upside down onto a wooden board and let the frittata fall on it. Allow to cool a little and then loosely roll the frittata up, jelly-roll fashion. Cut into ½-inch strips and mix gently into the sauce. Cook for 2 or 3 minutes to allow the frittata to soak up the flavor of the sauce.

✖ This is a good family secondo which goes well with sautéed or steamed zucchini, or with Sautéed Potato and Zucchini Sticks (page 211). The dish can also be served as a first course, to be followed by any meat dish or a vegetable pie.

1 tablespoon unsalted butter
2 tablespoons olive oil
½ celery stalk, very finely chopped
½ small onion, very finely chopped
1¼ cups coarsely chopped canned plum tomatoes, with their juice
salt
pepper
6 fresh basil leaves, torn into small pieces

FRITTATA

6 eggs
2 tablespoons freshly grated parmesan
salt
freshly ground pepper
butter
flour

Tortino di crespelle pasticciate
CRESPELLE WITH MOZZARELLA AND TOMATO SAUCE • SERVES 4 TO 6

Although this dish contains two of the most humble ingredients of Italian cooking—tomatoes and mozzarella—its presentation makes it very elegant. It looks like a cake made of baked lasagne, but the crespelle give the dish a softer consistency and a more subtle taste. It is a stunning dish whether you serve it as a first course for a dinner party or for a light lunch followed by a green salad.

You can prepare the crespelle a day or two in advance and refrigerate them. They can also be frozen, separated with sheets of wax paper and wrapped in plastic wrap. Thaw before using. The tomato sauce, too, can be prepared well in advance. It keeps in the refrigerator for up to three days, or it can be frozen. The dish, however, must be assembled just before going into the oven or the pancakes will become too soft.

The crespelle can also be layered with a mixture of spinach,

(*continued*)

¾ cup flour

salt

  2 eggs

  1 cup and 2 tablespoons milk

  2 tablespoons unsalted butter

TOMATO SAUCE

  6 tablespoons olive oil

  2 tablespoons unsalted butter

½ small onion *or* 1 shallot, coarsely chopped

  1 garlic clove, peeled and chopped

½ celery stalk, coarsely chopped

  1 small sprig of parsley

  3 cups canned tomatoes with the juice from the can

  1 teaspoon tomato paste

½ teaspoon sugar

salt

freshly ground black pepper

BECHAMEL SAUCE

  2 tablespoons unsalted butter

  3 tablespoons flour

1¼ cups milk

———

  1 cup grated mozzarella

milk

  4 tablespoons freshly grated parmesan

  2 tablespooons chopped fresh basil

freshly ground black pepper

  1 tablespoon unsalted butter

ricotta and béchamel or with ham, mushrooms and béchamel. In fact, any filling you fancy is suitable as long as it has the consistency of heavy cream. You can even turn it into a dessert by making a sweet filling of crème pâtissière, with very finely sliced poached pears and slivered almonds.

The quantities given here are for four hungry young people, or for six more normal appetites, when served as a first course. If you want to serve more people, it is better to make two cakes rather than to pile up too many crespelle.

1 To prepare the pancakes, sift the flour with a little salt into a bowl. Drop in the eggs and beat, while gradually adding the milk, until the surface of the batter is covered with bubbles. You can also put the ingredients in a blender or food processor and blend until smooth. Let the batter stand for at least 30 minutes; it does not matter if you leave it for longer.

2 When you are ready to make the pancakes, melt half the butter and stir it into the batter. Transfer the batter into a pitcher or measuring cup.

3 Heat a cast-iron frying pan with an 8-inch bottom and add a small knob of the remaining butter. (If you have a nonstick pan you don't need to add any butter). Swirl the butter around the pan to grease the bottom.

4 When the pan is hot, turn the heat down to moderate. Stir the batter and pour just enough batter to cover the bottom in a very thin layer, while tipping the pan quickly in all directions. Pour the excess batter back into the pitcher. Cook until pale gold and then turn the pancake with a spatula and cook the other side very briefly. Slide onto a plate or board. Remove the pan from the heat before you pour in more batter or it will set before it can spread. You should be able to make about 8 to 10 pancakes, but you may have to add a tiny bit of butter every so often when the pan appears dry.

5 Prepare the tomato sauce. Put the olive oil, butter, onion, garlic, celery and parsley in a heavy saucepan and sauté gently until soft, about 10 minutes, stirring frequently.

6 Add the tomatoes, the tomato paste, sugar, salt and pepper. Bring to the boil while breaking up the tomatoes with a spoon. Cook, uncovered, at a steady low simmer for 1 hour. The sauce should be quite dense at the end. If the sauce gets too thick, add a couple of tablespoons of hot water during the cooking. Puree the sauce through a food mill or in a food processor. Taste and check for salt.

7 Make the béchamel following the instructions on page 4. Mix thoroughly into the tomato sauce. Keep warm.

8 Put the mozzarella in a small bowl with a little salt and cover with milk. Leave for 30 minutes or so.

9 Preheat the oven to 350°F.

10 Butter a round 8-inch ovenproof dish or the base of an 8-inch flan or cake ring generously and place it on a baking tray.

11 Drain the mozzarella and squeeze out most of the milk. (Keep the milk for the cat!)

12 Place a pancake in the dish and spread with a generous tablespoon of sauce. Put a few small lumps of mozzarella here and there and sprinkle with a little parmesan, basil and black pepper. Cover with a second pancake and repeat these layers until you have used up all the ingredients. The topping must be sauce, basil, parmesan and pepper.

13 Melt the butter in a small saucepan and then pour it slowly over the mound, while making small deep incisions with a small knife for the butter to seep through.

14 Cover the dish with foil or with a cake tin and place in the oven for about 15 minutes. Remove the foil or cake tin and bake for another 10 minutes. Allow the dish to stand out of the oven for about 5 minutes before serving. If you are using the base of a flan or cake ring, slide the tortino onto a round dish and serve.

✗ If you serve this tortino at a dinner party, you should follow it with something quick to make, to compensate for the time you dedicated to the tortino. Cold Roast Veal with Herbs (page 206) or Steamed Fish with Fresh Herb Sauce (page 205) are both good ideas.

Salads

In Italy all vegetables are likely to be served as salads. These may either be raw vegetables, such as lettuce or endive, tomatoes, cucumbers, fennel, artichokes and so on, according to the season, or they may be cooked vegetables, such as green beans, potatoes, zucchini, spinach or cauliflower.

Whatever the salad may be, the traditional dressing is olive oil, wine vinegar (or in some cases lemon juice), salt and sometimes pepper. These ingredients are added directly to the vegetables already in the bowl. Green salad is often dressed at the table, since the dressing must be added at the last minute or the salad will "cook," that is, lose its crispness. The dressing is an integral part of an Italian salad, not an addition.

It is difficult to state how much oil or vinegar is needed in a salad, since it depends on the salad itself, as well as on the fruitiness of the oil and the acidity and strength of the vinegar. Green beans, for example, need less oil than potatoes or lettuce, whereas cucumbers and beets require more vinegar or lemon juice. The only way to solve the problem is to taste and correct the seasonings before serving. As a rough guide, however, you will need one tablespoon of vinegar and four tablespoons of olive oil for a salad for four people, plus salt and pepper to taste.

PINZIMONIO

The best way to serve raw vegetables is the pinzimonio. The raw vegetables used are peppers, young artichokes, celery, fennel, zucchini—in short, most of the crunchy vegetables that are in season. A lovely dish of these vegetables, sliced or cut, is put in the middle of the table, and everyone is given a little bowl containing a few tablespoons of the best olive oil, coarse salt and black pepper. Nothing else. They then take a few vegetables, dip them in the oil and enjoy their pinzimonio.

The dish originated in Rome, as did its name, which comes from pinzare (to pinch), referring to the pinching of the vegetables between the thumb and forefinger, and monio from matrimonio (marriage), the union with the oil.

GREEN SALAD. The number of different kinds of salad greens displayed in shops and supermarkets in Italy is proof of their popularity. At any time of the year there are at least ten varieties, all fresh and inviting. Traditionally green salads are served on their own, although I have recently come across some successful combinations: red radicchio and thin wedges of raw artichokes; mâche with grilled peppers; and finely sliced cicorino (dandelion) with cubes of tomatoes and cucumbers.

Green salad must be thoroughly washed and then well dried. Everybody has his or her own way of adding the dressing; mine is to put the vinegar into the salad spoon, add the salt to it and sprinkle over the salad, at the same time rapidly stirring the vinegar and salt in the spoon with the salad fork. I add the oil last, since if it were added first it would coat the salad leaves and prevent the vinegar from penetrating. A grinding of pepper, and ecco fatto—it is done—and ready to be mixed.

However you choose to dress your salad, it must be tossed many times after adding the seasonings. Some people swear that 36 times is the secret for a successful salad! It is said that you need four people to dress a salad: a generous one to pour the oil, a wise one to sprinkle the salt, a miser to add the vinegar and a patient soul to toss it.

RADICCHIO

This pretty head is now in the shops nearly all year round. It does cheer our salad bowls with its mauvish red color, but pretty though it is, mass-produced radicchio lacks the delicious bitter flavor of the original varieties. What it has instead is its property of keeping crisp and fresh for days and, consequently, its ready availability.

In modern cooking, both in Italy and outside, a number of recipes have been created for radicchio: gnocchi, lasagne, sauces and even sweets (I will spare you my comments about the last). And in 1985 a book called *Il Radicchio in cucina* was published; its author, Armando Zanotto, is a chef who gathered or created no fewer than 617 recipes, all based on this ultra fashionable vegetable!

Trevisana coi borlotti
RADICCHIO WITH CRANBERRY BEANS • SERVES 4

While there is a strong contrast in the texture of these two ingredients, their flavors blend beautifully. Cooked or canned beans are reheated first so that they absorb the oil more readily.

Heat 2 cups of cooked or canned cranberry beans very gently with a couple of tablespoons of water until hot. Transfer the beans to a bowl and dress them with 2 tablespoons extra-virgin olive oil. Leave them to cool while you wash and dry ½ pound radicchio very thoroughly. Place the radicchio leaves around a round dish. Chop a garlic clove and put it in a small bowl. Add a couple of tablespoons extra-virgin olive oil and season with salt and pepper to taste. You can add 1 tablespoon lemon juice or wine vinegar if you wish; I prefer to use only oil, salt and pepper. Pile the beans within the circle of the radicchio and drizzle the garlic dressing all over the salad.

NOTE: Canned pinto beans may be substituted for cranberry beans. Always drain and rinse canned beans before using.

Insalata di finocchio ed arancie
FENNEL AND ORANGE SALAD • SERVES 4

In Sicily there are two kinds of salad containing oranges. One is with onion and the other is the one given here. I was told this recipe by my Sicilian travel agent, a real buongustaio (bon viveur) to whom I am grateful both for cheap tickets to Italy and for original Sicilian recipes. In Sicily the green used is the heart of a young romaine lettuce or of a bunch of escarole. I use Belgian endive as well because it is on the market when fennel is at its best.

2 medium fennel bulbs, preferably the sweeter round kind

2 large oranges

1 large Belgian endive *or* the inner leaves of escarole

juice of 1 small lemon

3 tablespoons olive oil

salt

12 black olives

1 Remove the stalk, green foliage and any bruised or brown parts from the fennel bulbs. (Keep them for a soup, except, of course, the brown bits.) Cut the bulbs in half

(*continued*)

lengthwise, and then cut them across into thin slices. Wash the slices, drain and dry them thoroughly, then put them in a bowl.

2 Peel the oranges to the quick and slice them across on a plate so as not to waste any of the juice. Cut the smaller slices in half and the larger slices into quarters. Add to the fennel in the bowl together with the juice collected on the plate.

3 Cut the endive into rings or the escarole leaves into short pieces. Wash and dry thoroughly and then add to the bowl.

4 Beat the lemon juice and the olive oil together, add salt to taste and pour over the prepared vegetables. Toss very well. Taste and adjust salt. (Pepper is never added to this kind of salad in Sicily: its hotness would clash with the sweetness of the fennel and the orange.)

5 Transfer the salad to a deep dish and scatter the olives over it, or serve straight from the bowl.

Insalata di fagiolini al vino
WINE-DRESSED GREEN BEAN AND TOMATO SALAD • SERVES 4

1 pound green beans
salt
2 tablespoons good dry white wine

SAUCE
½ teaspoon Dijon mustard
1 tablespoon dry white wine
1 tablespoon lemon juice
3 tablespoons extra-virgin olive oil
salt
hot-pepper sauce

———

3 tomatoes, peeled
6 fresh chives

This is an excellent recipe from the book *Dieta e fornelli* by Romana Bosco, a leading Italian cook, and Giorgio Calabrese, a dietician. The beans and tomatoes are dressed with wine, some of which is poured over the beans while they are still hot. This gives flavor to the beans as well as softening the taste of the wine.

1 Top and tail the beans and then wash them thoroughly, rubbing them against each other. Cook in plenty of boiling salted water. Drain as soon as they are ready; they should be still crunchy. You can literally smell when they are cooked, as the particular aroma of cooked beans begins to arise just at that moment. Splash them immediately with wine.

2 To make the sauce, put the mustard in a small bowl and dilute with wine and lemon juice. Add the oil gradually beating hard and thoroughly with a fork to emulsify the sauce, then add salt and hot-pepper sauce to taste.

3 Slice the tomatoes and place them in the center of a dish, surrounding them with the beans. About half an hour before serving, spoon the sauce over the vegetables and then snip the chives all over the tomatoes. Serve at room temperature.

Romana Bosco suggests serving this salad as a first course—a very good idea. As a secondo my choice would be Grilled Pepper and Monkfish Bundles (page 108) or Osso Buco, Milanese Style (page 170).

La panzanella a modo mio

PANZANELLA • SERVES 6

Panzanella is the traditional poor man's salad, based on bread. When we had a farmhouse in Chianti, it was our luncheon fare. A large earthenware pot full of panzanella was put on the scrubbed table under the fig tree, the air heavily scented with fig leaves and wild mint. The fig tree was next to the well which for years served as our fridge, until electricity was brought to the house. Dangling in the cool water, at the end of a rope, was a fiasco of Chianti, while a pull on another rope brought up a bucket containing a watermelon. Panzanella, anguria e vino—an ideal trio for the perfect lunch.

Back in London, I couldn't find the pan sciocco (unsalted country bread) needed for a good panzanella. Panzanella was forgotten until I came across Marcella Hazan's recipe, made with croutons. From that recipe I developed mine, in which bread moistened with olive oil is toasted, not fried. This panzanella is very pretty to look at, especially if you serve it on a white dish, or on white plates, so as to set off the vivid greens and reds of the vegetables. It will remind you of Matisse's palette.

½ red onion
salt
½ cup extra-virgin olive oil
2 garlic cloves, peeled and bruised
1 chili pepper
6 slices pain de campagne (country-style bread), without the crust
½ large yellow bell pepper
2 tomatoes, ripe but firm
½ cucumber, peeled
1 cup basil leaves, torn into small pieces
1 tablespoon capers, rinsed and dried
2 anchovy fillets
2 tablespoons wine vinegar
freshly ground black pepper

1 At least an hour before you want to serve the panzanella, slice the onion into very thin rings, put the rings in a bowl and cover with cold water. Add a pinch of salt and leave to soak. (This is not necessary if you don't mind the strong flavor of raw onion.) Put the olive oil in another bowl, add the garlic and the chili and leave to infuse for the same length of time.

2 Preheat the oven to 400°F.

(*continued*)

PANZANELLA (*continued*)

NOTE: You can prepare everything in advance up to Step 6.

3 Put the bread slices on a baking sheet and brush them with a little of the spiced olive oil. Place in the preheated oven for about 8 minutes. When the bread is toasted, remove and leave it to cool.

4 Wash the pepper, remove the core, seeds and ribs and cut into ½-inch cubes. Wash the tomatoes and cut into the same size morsels, eliminating the seeds. Do the same to the peeled cucumber. Put the chopped vegetables in a bowl and add the basil.

5 Drain and dry the onion rings and add to the bowl.

6 Remove the garlic and chili from the oil.

7 Chop the capers and the anchovy fillets and add to the oil together with the vinegar and pepper and salt to taste. Mix well and pour this sauce on the vegetables. Stir thoroughly and then taste and adjust the seasoning.

8 Put a slice of bread on each plate and spoon some of the vegetable mixture over each slice. Serve at once.

✖ Panzanella makes a delightfully fresh first course for a summer lunch, and you can follow it with any fish or meat dish as long as it is of the robust kind, such as Cold Roast Veal with Herbs (page 206) or Tuna Baked with Tomatoes, Capers, Black Olives and Chilies (page 59). It is also an attractive side dish for a buffet party or salad for a barbecue, when you would toast your bread, moistened with the flavored olive oil, on the hot embers.

Edible Wild Things

WILD MUSHROOMS

Funghi in umido
BRAISED MUSHROOMS

Coniglio alle erbe e funghi secchi
RABBIT WITH HERBS AND DRIED PORCINI

Funghi al forno
BAKED MUSHROOMS WITH ANCHOVIES AND
CAPERS

TRUFFLES

Pollo ripieno
STUFFED CHICKEN FLAVORED WITH WHITE
TRUFFLE

SEE ALSO

Ceci e rucola
CHICKPEAS AND ARUGULA

Fonduta piemontese
PIEDMONTESE FONDUE

Polenta pasticciata alla piemontese
BAKED POLENTA WITH PORCINI

Prosciutto con la rucola
PROSCIUTTO WITH ARUGULA

EDIBLE WEEDS

Pasta con la rucola
PASTA WITH ARUGULA

Minestra di rucola e patate
ARUGULA AND POTATO SOUP

Salsa di rucola e pomodoro
ARUGULA AND TOMATO SAUCE

Insalata di cicorino
DANDELION SALAD

Risotto alle ortiche
RISOTTO WITH NETTLES

Insalata del Bronzino
PURSLANE, SCALLION AND CUCUMBER SALAD

I talians are passionate about food for free. Their walks need an aim, be it to collect wild greens, wild mushrooms, berries or flowers.

Edible Weeds

In my childhood the prati (open fields) outside Milan were only half an hour's bicycle ride from our house in the center of the city. Many a happy Sunday was spent with friends picking nettles, dandelions, wild beets, daisies and poppies. Then home with bulging baskets, whose contents were quickly made into delicious salads and lovely little bouquets for the table. I still pick dandelions, nettles and sorrel whenever I am in the country.

ARUGULA

Rucola (arugula) grows wild in southern Italy and has always been used a lot in the local cooking, but it only became known in Milan and Turin with the invasion of the southerners in the 1960s, when they came north to find work. In ancient Rome it used to appear on the tables of the gourmands and the gourmets, just as it does now. It was mainly used in sauces together with other herbs, or in a vegetable pie called moretum. This must have been a popular dish; it was even described in a poem written by Septimus Serenus, a contemporary of Virgil. Only in recent decades, however, has it found favor with the food faddists of the world. Strange to say, not a single recipe listing arugula appeared in Italian cookery books until about ten years ago. Southern Italians are very chauvinistic people where food is concerned. As with provolone, which they brought north and which afterwards began to be manufactured near Milan because of the demand from the new "locals," arugula began to be cultivated to satisfy their cravings. The cultivated variety of arugula is less pungent or tingly on the tongue than the wild, and its taste has a more distinct resemblance to cabbage. This cabbagey taste is rather overwhelming when the arugula becomes old, so be sure to use the young, tender leaves.

Pasta con la rucola
PASTA WITH ARUGULA • SERVES 4

The Calabresi love to eat these two favorite foods together. The pasta used is ziti or macaroni broken into 1½-inch lengths.

Start cooking about ¾ pound of pasta. While it is boiling, wash and dry about ½ pound of arugula and stir-fry it in 5 tablespoons of the best extra-virgin olive oil, with 2 bruised garlic cloves and 1 or 2 chilies. Add a couple of tablespoons of the pasta water to the arugula and then transfer the drained pasta to the pan and fry it for a minute or two. Put some grated pecorino romano on the table to sprinkle on the pasta. Don't forget to remove the garlic and the chili before you serve the pasta.

If you find the arugula too pungent for your taste, blanch it before you fry it.

Minestra di rucola e patate
ARUGULA AND POTATO SOUP • SERVES 4

The grated cheese for this soup should be pecorino romano, which has the right pungency to match the arugula. If you cannot buy pecorino, use good freshly grated parmesan.

1 Wash and dry the arugula and remove any thick stalks. Cut it roughly into strips.

2 Coarsely chop the parsley, chili and garlic and put them in a heavy pot with 2 tablespoons of the oil. I use an earthenware pot, so that the garlic won't burn. Sauté over gentle heat until you begin to smell the garlic aroma.

3 Peel and cut the potatoes into about ½-inch cubes and add to the pot. Stir them in the soffritto until they are shiny and slightly translucent and then add the arugula. Stir and cook for 2 or 3 minutes.

4 Meanwhile heat the stock or water. (You should always heat any liquid before pouring it over partly cooked potatoes, since a cold liquid will harden them.) Pour into the soup pot and stir, adding salt if necessary. Turn the heat down as low as possible and let the soup simmer for 40 minutes or so. Taste and check seasoning.

5 Put 1 or 2 slices of the slightly stale bread into each soup bowl and ladle the soup over them. Pour the rest of the oil directly into each bowl and pass the grated cheese separately.

¼ pound arugula
½ cup fresh parsley leaves
1 small dried chili, or more according to taste
2 garlic cloves, or more according to taste
3 tablespoons extra-virgin olive oil
½ pound potatoes
6 cups vegetable stock (page 4) *or* water
salt
pepper
4 to 8 slices day-old pain de campagne (country-style bread)
freshly grated pecorino romano, if available, *or* parmesan

NOTE: If you prefer, you can make the soup with pasta, instead of bread, by adding ½ cup of ditalini 10 minutes before the soup is ready.

Salsa di rucola e pomodoro

ARUGULA AND TOMATO SAUCE • MAKES 1 CUP

Toward the end of last autumn I found I still had a lot of arugula in my small London garden. So, rather than let the frost destroy this delicious and versatile green, I collected it all and prepared this arugula and tomato sauce (which freezes well). In this sauce the arugula loses some of its pungency through being combined with the raw tomato. Although the sauce is not a very pretty color, its taste is most appealing, sweet and herby at the same time.

I first had this sauce some years ago at the Locanda dell'Angelo near Sarzana, in Liguria. In 1983 the owner and chef of that restaurant, Angelo Paracucchi, was invited by Gault et Millau to open a restaurant in Paris, the Carpaccio—surely the greatest accolade any foreigner could receive from the French. In his book, *Cucina Creativa all' Italiana*, Angelo Paracucchi suggests this sauce as an accompaniment to boiled fish or meat. I also like it on hard-boiled eggs, but perhaps that's just because I like eggs, whether by themselves or dressed with a delicious sauce such as this!

½ **pound tomatoes, very firm and not fully ripe**
½ **cup roughly chopped arugula leaves**
sliver of peeled garlic
1 **small dried chili, seeded**
1 **tablespoon balsamic vinegar**
salt
pepper
5 **tablespoons extra-virgin olive oil**

NOTE: This sauce can be kept in the refrigerator for up to 3 days or it can be frozen.

1 Peel the tomatoes as described on page 110. Cut them into quarters and squeeze out the seeds and watery juice. Put in a food processor and add the arugula, the garlic, chili, balsamic vinegar and a little salt and pepper. Process for 15 seconds.

2 Scrape down the sides of the workbowl and process until smooth and thick, while gradually adding the oil, as for mayonnaise.

DANDELIONS

In Italy one of the pleasures of early spring is a trip to the countryside to collect dandelions. It is quite usual to have a salad of dandelions, or to eat them cooked. In many western countries this is not so, but in the past, it seems, they were more popular. In Eliza Acton's *Modern Cookery for Private Families,* first published in 1845, there is a section headed "TO DRESS DANDE-LIONS LIKE SPINACH, OR AS A SALAD (Very Wholesome)." The first part of it reads:

This common weed of the fields and highways is an excellent vegetable, the young leaves forming an admirable adjunct to a salad, and much resembling endive when boiled and prepared in the same way, or in any of the modes directed for spinach. The slight bitterness of its flavour is to many persons very agreeable;

and it is often served at well-appointed tables. It has also, we believe, the advantage of possessing valuable medicinal qualities.

Eliza Acton served her blanched dandelions dressed with melted butter. I prefer them strascinati (literally, dragged) in a frying pan with two or three tablespoons of extra-virgin olive oil, a garlic clove and maybe a little chili. Both the garlic and chili must be removed before serving. You will need about one pound for two or three people. Another way is to serve them at room temperature dressed in extra-virgin olive oil, lemon juice, salt and pepper.

If you are going to cook your dandelions, it is best to pick very young leaves. This is because, as with any greens, the flavor is released in cooking. In the case of dandelions this means that their bitter flavor will be more noticeable cooked than raw.

Eliza Acton gives many invaluable hints and tips, and I end with one of these. "A very large portion of the leaves will be required for a dish, as they shrink exceedingly in the cooking." I would add that they also shrink when you dress them raw and serve them as a salad.

Insalata di cicorino
DANDELION SALAD • SERVES 4

Dandelions are also excellent raw, and this is how I suggest you prepare them.

For 4 people you will need about 4 cups of dandelion leaves. Wash the leaves thoroughly, and gather as many leaves as will fit in your fist. Shred them very finely. The narrower the strips, the nicer the salad. Put them in a bowl, cover with cold water and add some salt. Leave for 1 hour or so. This removes some of the bitterness of the dandelion. About 30 minutes before serving, drain and dry the dandelion thoroughly and put in a salad bowl. Mix 2 tablespoons red wine vinegar, 3 tablespoons extra-virgin olive oil, salt and pepper to taste and, if you want, 1 teaspoon of Dijon mustard which goes well with dandelion. Spoon into the salad. Toss well (36 times is the magic number!) and leave for 20 minutes. This will "fatigue" the salad, as the French say, which I find improves its flavor. Add some sliced red onion on the top.

NETTLES

It seems a sad waste that these eminently edible weeds should be eaten so little when in many places they grow in some profusion. During my childhood in Milan, nettles were eaten in many guises, the most usual being in a soup with rice, riso e ortiche. A similar dish is the pasta con le ortiche made in Apulia.

Nettles are good when young and bright green. Pick only the young shoots, when the sting is minimal, and pick a lot since, like spinach, they boil down to very little. Nettles are covered with stinging hairs which lose their sting when boiled. Wear gloves when picking and washing them. When you pick them you will be surprised by the smell they give off. It always reminds me of that milky-sweet Mediterranean scent of fig leaves, and this is indeed the flavor nettles have when young.

Risotto alle ortiche
RISOTTO WITH NETTLES • SERVES 4

The sweet, delicate taste of nettles is just discernible in this moist, creamy risotto. Pick a large bag of tender nettle shoots in April or early May. It will boil down much as spinach does. Don't forget to wear your gloves when you pick them and when you clean and wash them. Cooking removes their sting. The same recipe can be made with very young spinach, but don't use the larger and older spinach as its taste is too coarse.

1 pound nettle shoots
salt
2 shallots *or* 1 small onion, very finely chopped
4 tablespoons unsalted butter
4 cups vegetable stock (page 4) *or* light meat stock (page 3)
1½ cups Arborio rice
4 tablespoons heavy cream
½ cup freshly grated parmesan

1 Pick the leaves and shoots of the nettles and discard the stalks. Wash in 2 or 3 changes of water. Put the nettles in a saucepan with 1 teaspoon of salt and boil over high heat until cooked. You don't need to add any water; as with spinach, the water that comes from the leaves is enough. When cooked, drain, reserving the liquid. Set aside, keeping the nettles in a sieve placed over the bowl containing the nettle water.

2 Sauté the shallots or onion in half the butter very gently, until the onion is soft.

3 Heat the stock to the simmer.

4 Squeeze all the liquid out of the nettles into the bowl. Coarsely chop the nettles and add to the shallots. Sauté for a minute, stirring constantly, then add the rice and fry it until the edges of the grains become translucent.

5 Pour the nettle liquid into the simmering stock. Add about ⅔ cup stock to the rice. Mix well. The rice will soon absorb the stock. Then add another ladleful of stock and continue in this manner until the rice is done. Stir frequently, but not all the time. The better the rice, the longer it takes to cook: Arborio superfino takes at least 20 minutes from when it is put in the pan.

6 Remove the pan from the heat, add the cream, the rest of the butter and half the cheese. Leave it to rest for a couple of minutes and then stir vigorously; this makes the risotto mantecato (creamy) as any risotto should be. Transfer to a heated dish and serve at once, passing the remaining cheese separately.

With one exception, the dishes suggested to follow the Risotto with Asparagus (page 30) would also be suitable after this risotto—Porgy en Papillote (page 55) or Chicken with Orange (page 176). The exception is Cold Roast Veal with Herbs (page 206), although if you wanted to give a theme to your party, in this case green, it would do well.

PURSLANE

This annual, Portulaca oleracea, has small fleshy leaves that grow in bunches. It has a pleasant flavor, mild yet with a touch of sourness reminiscent of young spinach. The pretty green leaves are succulent and very satisfying to the bite. Eat them in a tomato salad, as is done in southern Italy, or mixed with broiled and peeled peppers, as Jane Grigson suggests in her *Vegetable Book.*

Yan Kit So tells me purslane is sold in Chinese shops under the name of yin choy. Although not easy to buy, purslane grows very easily in the garden, and in the northeast of America it grows like a weed, reseeding itself year after year.

Insalata del Bronzino

PURSLANE, SCALLION AND CUCUMBER SALAD • SERVES 4

This salad is so delicious that it inspired the sixteenth-century painter Bronzino to write this little poem:

> Un'insalata di cipolla trita
> Colla porcellanetta e citrioli
> Vince ogni altro piacer di questa vita

Which might be translated:

> A salad of chopped onion
> With purslane and cucumber
> Beats any other pleasure in life

about ½ pound purslane
4 scallions, white parts only
½ cucumber
4 tablespoons extra-virgin olive oil
salt
freshly ground black pepper
lemon juice to taste

1 Remove the leaves of the purslane and wash thoroughly. Drain and dry well. Put the leaves in a salad bowl.

2 Slice the scallions into thin rings and add to the bowl.

3 Slice the cucumber very thin and add to the salad.

4 Dress with the oil, salt and pepper and add lemon juice to your taste. Toss well and serve immediately.

Wild Mushrooms

Mushroom hunting is a solitary activity whose secrets you share only with the wind and the trees. I even balk at writing about how many good species of wild mushrooms I find during a day's outing around London! I have some Milanese friends who not long ago sent us a postcard from Scotland, where they had gone to see that country's many sights. A week later another card arrived from the same place. They had discovered the treasure of the Scottish woods: wild mushrooms everywhere, and in great abundance. They were utterly amazed that no one else was in sight,

no one either picking the mushrooms or preventing them from picking all they wanted.

When we had a house in Chianti, the caccia (hunt) for mushrooms started just after the objectionable caccia of the birds, with its continuous salvoes of gunfire and flurry of birds and hares. I used to go up the Apennines with Remo, a local farm-worker who, like me, preferred the silent hunt for mushrooms. He knew all the species which grew there, but we collected mainly porcini (cèpes) and chanterelles, which are by far the best. Back in London I tried limiting my search to these two species, but soon enough I was collecting any edible mushrooms. There simply weren't enough cèpes and chanterelles.

HOW TO PREPARE MUSHROOMS.
Mushrooms should not be peeled, and they should be washed as little as possible. (It is a fallacy to think that field mushrooms are only good if they peel easily.) I wipe mushrooms with damp paper towels and cut away the base of the stalks and any blemished parts. The spongy underside of the caps of cèpes is good, and should not be removed unless soggy and mushy. All mushrooms should be sautéed quite briskly in oil and/or butter until they have absorbed all the fat. The heat should then be turned down and the mushrooms will then release their liquid. Most wild mushrooms release more liquid than cultivated ones. This liquid will evaporate with a brisk cooking, but you must be careful not to overcook the mushrooms. Some mushrooms, the incomparable chanterelles for instance, are spoiled by prolonged cooking, while others such as cèpes need a minimum of fifteen to twenty minutes' cooking to release their aroma.

DRIED PORCINI

These are available in many supermarkets and in all Italian shops. Before you buy them, look into the packet if you can; the pieces of dried cèpes should be large and well formed, not small and crumbly. Dried porcini are expensive, but even as little as three-quarters of an ounce gives a dish more flavor than five times that many cultivated mushrooms.

HOW TO RECONSTITUTE DRIED MUSHROOMS. Soak the mushrooms in hot water for at least 20 minutes. I prefer to pour boiling water over them and leave them for 15 minutes or so. The liquid, filtered through damp paper towels, is usually added to the dish for extra flavor. If you add a few dried porcini to some cultivated mushrooms for stronger flavor, sauté the porcini first for 5 minutes before you add them to the mushrooms.

- -

Funghi in umido
BRAISED MUSHROOMS • SERVES 3 OR 4

This dish is made in Italy with an assortment of wild mushrooms, of which porcini (cèpes) are the major component and the tastiest. I have made it using a selection of mushrooms found in the shops—both cultivated and wild—plus a handful of dried porcini. It is a perfect accompaniment to braised meat or game dishes, although I also like these mushrooms by themselves, hot, with a soft polenta, or cold, as an antipasto, with crusty bread.

1 Put the porcini in a bowl and pour over about ⅔ cup boiling water. Leave them until soft, about 15 minutes.

2 Clean the mushrooms. Unless they are very dirty, wipe them with damp paper towels rather than washing them, then cut them into thick slices.

3 Lift the dried porcini gently out of the water. Wash them under running water if you find some grit still attached.

½ **cup dried porcini (about 1 ounce)**
1 **pound mixed mushrooms**
2 **shallots** *or* **1 small onion**
4 **tablespoons olive oil**
1 **tablespoon unsalted butter**
1 **garlic clove**
2 **tablespoons tomato paste**
2 **tablespoons chopped fresh parsley**
salt
pepper

(continued)

Cut them into pieces of about the same size as the fresh mushrooms.

4 Filter the porcini liquid through a sieve lined with damp paper towels.

5 Chop the shallots or onion and put them in a large sauté pan and sauté in the oil and butter until soft. Put a toothpick into the garlic clove (this is to help recognize the garlic when you have to remove it later) and add to the shallot together with the tomato paste. Cook, stirring constantly, for 1 minute and then add the mushrooms and the porcini. Cook at a lively heat for 5 minutes or so, turning them over to coat in the cooking juices.

6 Add the parsley and salt and pour over the porcini liquid. As soon as the liquid begins to boil, turn the heat down and cook, uncovered, for 20 minutes, stirring frequently, until soft and just resistant to the bite. Season with pepper and check salt. Serve hot, warm or even at room temperature.

Coniglio alle erbe e funghi secchi
RABBIT WITH HERBS AND DRIED PORCINI • SERVES 3 OR 4

In Liguria rabbit has always been the most popular meat. Every villager has a row of rabbit hutches at the back of the house, and the occupants of these all finish, sooner or later, in the pot. With them in the pot are the herbs that grew nearby during their brief lives. I remember as a child, when we spent our summer months on the Riviera, feeling so sorry for the local children when their pet rabbit —they all had one—would disappear. They knew perfectly well that it would reappear the next day at lunch in a different guise. With the total lack of sentimentality of country people, they would eat it and pass comment on how much, or little, they liked the way it was cooked, without a word about what the dish used to be.

The other main ingredient of this dish is porcini, another favorite of the Ligurian people. It is the porcini that set this recipe apart from the more common dish of rabbit with herbs. I use dried porcini, since the fresh ones are difficult to obtain. The rabbit can be tame or wild. Tame rabbit is less tasty but more tender, and it takes much less time to cook. Ask the butcher for the liver and heart of the rabbit.

1 Use the saddle, legs and back of the rabbit. The ribs, head and shoulder can be used to make stock for another dish.

2 Combine the wine, juniper berries, bay leaf, parsley, peppercorns, celery, carrot, onion and garlic for the marinade. Put the rabbit in a single layer in a bowl, preferably earthenware, cover with the marinade and leave for at least 6 hours, overnight if possible. Leave the bowl out of the fridge, unless the weather is very hot. The wine in the marinade will prevent the meat from going bad.

3 Lift the rabbit out of the marinade and dry thoroughly with paper towels. Strain the marinade and reserve.

4 Soak the porcini in hot water for at least 30 minutes. (If you pour boiling water over them you only need to leave them to soak for 15 minutes.) Lift them out, rinse if there is still some grit on them, and dry them.

5 Chop the garlic, shallots, all the herbs and the porcini together, or process for a few seconds. Heat the oil in a large Dutch oven and sauté the mixture very gently for 10 minutes. Add the rabbit and cook over low heat for 10 minutes, turning the pieces over every so often.

6 Add about 1 cup of the strained marinade and reduce over high heat. Blend the flour with the stock and add to the pan. Sprinkle with salt and pepper. Cover and cook slowly until the rabbit is done, between 45 minutes and 1½ hours, depending on the rabbit. Remove the pieces from the pan and keep warm in a low oven.

7 Clean and chop the liver and heart and add to the pan. Cook over a lively heat for 2 minutes or so. Spoon the sauce over the rabbit.

✖ I like to serve polenta with this dish, but then not everyone likes polenta as much as I do! Boiled rice is a good alternative. As a first course, Grilled Peppers with Anchovies, Olives and Capers (page 106) or Bread Soup (page 43) would do very well.

1 rabbit, about 3 pounds, including heart and liver, cut up

MARINADE

1½ cups white wine
5 juniper berries, bruised
1 bay leaf
2 or 3 parsley stems
4 peppercorns, bruised
1 celery stalk, cut in pieces
½ carrot, cut in pieces
½ onion, thickly sliced
2 garlic cloves, peeled and bruised

———

½ cup dried porcini (about 1 ounce)
1 garlic clove, peeled
2 shallots
1 cup mixed fresh herbs: parsley, marjoram, thyme, basil, sage, rosemary, celery tops
3 tablespoons olive oil
1 tablespoon flour
½ cup meat stock (page 3)
salt
pepper

Funghi al forno

BAKED MUSHROOMS WITH ANCHOVIES AND CAPERS • SERVES 4

You can now find a few different species of cultivated mushrooms in the best supermarkets; for this dish you will need at least three, plus the dried porcini. I use some common cultivated field mushrooms, and—my favorite—some pleurottes. These, Pleorotus ostreatus, have a delicate taste that resembles the taste of white truffles. You can also add some shiitakes, although personally I find them too pricey for what they are. You could also use only cultivated mushrooms, although the final taste would not be very rich. The dried porcini, on the other hand, although expensive are worth every penny. You need only a little bit to make all the difference. They have a distinct aroma without having the rather heady and overwhelming flavor of some wild species.

The breadcrumbs can be either white or brown. Both are suitable as long as they are made from good bread.

½ **cup dried porcini (about 1 ounce)**

1½ **pounds mixed wild mushrooms**

1 **cup fresh parsley leaves, preferably flat-leaf**

2 **garlic cloves, peeled**

4 **anchovy fillets**

1 **dried chili, seeded**

2 **tablespoons capers, rinsed and dried**

½ **cup extra-virgin olive oil**

salt

pepper

1 **cup fresh breadcrumbs**

1 Soak the dried porcini in a cupful of boiling water for 15 minutes or so. Lift them out gently and sift through to make sure there is no grit stuck to them. Cut up the larger pieces. Strain the liquid into a little pan through a sieve lined with damp paper towels. Add the porcini and cook very gently for 10 minutes to soften them.

2 Preheat the oven to 375°F.

3 Wipe the mushrooms with paper towels and then slice them. Put them in a bowl. Add the porcini.

4 Chop the parsley, garlic, anchovies, chili, and capers and put them in a small bowl. Add 5 tablespoons of the oil and season with salt and pepper to taste. Mix well and then spoon this sauce over the mushrooms. Mix very thoroughly; your hands are the best tool for doing this.

5 Grease a shallow ovenproof dish with a little of the remaining oil. Pile the mushrooms into the dish. Sprinkle the breadcrumbs over the top and drizzle with the remaining oil.

6 Bake for about 30 minutes. The top will have formed a crust and the mushrooms will be just tender, but still retain their shape. Serve the dish cool or tepid: it will be much nicer then, when all the flavors have blended.

✄ Serve this dish as a first course, or with roast beef or chicken, hot or cold.

Truffles

Truffles—tartufi in Italian—are fungi, many species of which are found in northern and central Italy. The only three species that are of importance gastronomically are the Tuber magnatum (the white truffle or tartufo d'Alba), the Tuber melanosporum (black truffle or tartufo di Norcia, which the French call truffe du Périgord) and the Tuber aestivum or scorzone. This latter, also known as tartufo d'estate or maggengo, is not on a par with the white or the black truffle, and it differs from them in that it matures in the summer. It has a delicate and quite pleasing flavor, but it is rather bland. It is mostly used in pâtés, sausages, terrines, truffle paste, and so on. In the context of this book, I am mainly concerned with the white truffle, which is found only in Italy.

Truffles have been known in Italy since the beginning of history. The Romans were passionate about them and studied them in great detail. Pliny, Martial and Juvenal wrote treatises about truffles, while Apicius collected recipes for them. Nero ate truffles in abundance, calling them cibus deorum (food of the gods). After the fall of the Roman empire, truffles were ignored even by the monks, who preserved so much of the Roman civilization. It is said that they did so deliberately because they considered truffles to have aphrodisiac properties—hardly an encouragement to chaste living.

During the Renaissance, however, the truffle once again became king of the high table. The Emperor Charles V enjoyed truffles at the dinner prepared in his honor by Bartolomeo Scappi, chef to Cardinal Campeggi, who was entertaining the Emperor. The truffles were stewed in bitter-orange juice and also served simply raw in salad. In the eighteenth century, hunting parties were organized to search for tartufi. Dogs, rather than pigs, were used in Piedmont, and tartufi were found in amazing quantities. It was at that time that all the European royal houses were asking the House of Savoy for experienced men and trained dogs to search for truffles. In 1751 Carlo Emanuele III sent George II two trifolai (truffle hunters) and eight dogs to search for truffles in Windsor Park. Truffles similar to the tartufi d'Alba were found in moderate quantities. (In 1986 a sizeable truffle was found in a garden in Dover!)

Black truffles, too, were much more common in the past than they are now. William Whetmore Story, an American who lived in Rome in the 1860s, gives a graphic description of the market in Piazza Navona. There were, he wrote, "excellent truffles. They grow in great quantities in the country around Rome, and especially at Spoleto, and used to be very cheap before the French bought them up so largely for the Parisian markets."

I am old enough to have enjoyed truffles in good quantities as a child. Before Mass on Sundays we used to go and buy truffles from the stalls under the arches in the Piazza del Duomo. I was allowed to carry the parcel, and during Mass I held it under my nose, the penetrating aroma of truffles mixing deliciously with the heavy scent of the incense. A salad that used to be served in my home at lunch parties was made up as follows: one third of a dish was covered with sliced ovuli, the choicest wild mushrooms, another third with parmesan flakes and the remaining section with sliced tartufi d'Alba. The three parts were dressed with olive oil, lemon juice, salt and pepper.

Truffles cannot be cultivated like other fungi. Pliny the Elder wrote "nascuntur et seri non possunt" (they grow but cannot be cultivated). And this is still so, despite endless researches into the matter. White truffles grow in symbiosis with poplars, willows, littleleaf lindens, hazel bushes, oaks and hornbeams, in places around a thousand feet high where rains in August and September keep the soil moist. They are usually found only a few inches below the ground. They are roughly globular in shape and can be as large as one foot in diameter. These are the real diamonds, since their price per gram increases in direct proportion to their size. There is a closed season for collecting truffles which starts on a certain date in October and ends in December. Truffles are at their best in early November, when they are fully ripe and their flavor is well developed. They keep only for a very short time, but they can be preserved or pounded into a paste and mixed with other ingredients.

I advise any of you who are interested in food to buy a truffle at least once in your lifetime, and handle it and absorb its aroma. To prepare a truffle you must brush it with a soft brush, gently but thoroughly, then rinse it quickly and dry it well. Since truffles are so expensive, they should be served in the best possible way—raw for white truffles, cooked for black ones. White truffles are added to a dish of tagliatelle that has been dressed only with butter and parmesan. They are also added to a creamy risotto, to a rich fonduta piemontese or to a fresh carpaccio. Black truffles mixed with anchovy fillets and garlic make a divine sauce for spaghetti, spaghetti alla norcina. They also change an everyday trout into an haute-cuisine dish when they are used to stuff the fish.

The price of truffles has always been exorbitant, but in 1987 there was a shortage and the price jumped to 6000 lire a gram, three times what it had been the year before. At this price a small fresh truffle weighing an ounce would cost about $120! There are, however, a number of brands of puree on the market, some of which are excellent, containing only truffles and olive oil; others, less expensive, also contain porcini.

There is one place above all others where you will find everything you could wish for concerning truffles and other fungi. (Whether you can afford what you will find there is another question!) It is a shop in Milan, at Via Anfossi 13, called La Nuova Casa del Fungo e del Tartufo, and it belongs to Maurizio Vaglia and Carlo Urbani, who is known as King of the Truffles. There you can buy every kind of tartufo, while listening to Maurizio, a Piedmontese, who will extol the merits of the tartufo bianco piemontese. His wife, who comes from Norcia in Umbria, will interrupt to tell you that they are nothing compared to the real tartufo nero from around *her* hometown. A typical example, this, of the Italians' regional chauvinism when it comes to food and cooking. Even if you don't want to buy anything, go there and have a chat with this charming couple; you will witness the almost religious fervor with which Italians discuss matters of gastronomy.

Pollo ripieno

STUFFED CHICKEN FLAVORED WITH WHITE TRUFFLE • SERVES 8

For a long time I was prevented from making this recipe from my mother's ricettario (recipe book) because the white truffles, essential to this dish, were too expensive. Now truffles can be bought in the affordable form of a paste. The bird my mother used was a capon.

This is a demanding dish which involves quite a few hours of work. You must remove the carcass and the thigh bones of the chicken, leaving only the drumsticks and the wings. Although a lengthy job, it is not difficult. The boned chicken, once back in its original shape, looks lovely—soft and plump—and it is easy to carve. You will also have the carcass for making the stock. Prepare the stuffing a day in advance to allow the flavors to blend together.

1 Bone the chicken as described on the next page, then prepare the stuffing.

2 Soak the sweetbread in a bowl of cold water with a teaspoonful of salt and a slice of lemon for 1 hour. This will remove any blood. Drain, rinse and dry well with paper towels.

3 Trim the liver, then wash and dry it. Do the same with the sweetbread.

4 Put the butter and the shallot in a small frying pan and sauté gently for 2 or 3 minutes. Add the liver and "stiffen" it for a couple of minutes. Remove the liver from the pan and place on a chopping board. Put the sweetbread in the pan, sauté for 2 minutes and then transfer to the chopping board. Chop the liver and sweetbread very finely and then transfer to a bowl. Add the cooking juices.

5 Cut the prosciutto into small pieces or strips and add to the bowl. Mix in the truffle paste, herbs, marsala, egg, cinnamon, nutmeg, cloves and salt and pepper to taste.

6 Put the bread in the food processor and chop into crumbs. Add to the bowl. Mix very thoroughly with your hands until you have a homogenous mixture. It will have a rich smell, imbued with the flavors of all the ingredients.

7 Preheat the oven to 400°F.

8 Lay the chicken skin side down on a board and put the stuffing in place of the carcass you have removed. Shape the stuffing into an oval and wrap the skin around it, slightly overlapping one edge over the other.

9 Sew up the skin, from the neck to the tail, with a trussing needle and some heavy thread. Put a skewer through the knees of the legs, and another along the seam of the tail, to help keep the chicken in place. Truss, starting from the neck end, and tie the string around the soft body to keep it in shape, fixing the string to the skewers.

10 Melt the butter in a small saucepan.

11 Rub salt and pepper over the bird and moisten all over with some of the butter, using a pastry brush. Place the chicken on a rack in a roasting pan and put the pan in the oven. Cook until the breast is pale gold, about 20 minutes.

12 Heat the wine and pour over the chicken.

13 Cut a piece of cheesecloth large enough to cover the chicken breast and soak in the remaining melted butter. Cover the breast with the buttery cheesecloth and continue roasting until the chicken is cooked, about 1½ hours. Turn the heat down to 350°F after about 1 hour. You must baste the chicken every 15 to 20 minutes.

1 chicken *or* small capon, 5 to 6 pounds

STUFFING

½ pound calf's *or* lamb's sweetbread

salt

slice of lemon

¼ pound calf's liver

1 tablespoon unsalted butter

2 tablespoons chopped shallot *or* onion

¼ pound prosciutto, preferably in 1 or 2 thick slices

1 tablespoon truffle paste

6 tablespoons chopped fresh parsley, rosemary, sage and thyme

⅔ cup marsala *or* medium dry sherry

1 egg

pinch of ground cinnamon

pinch of freshly grated nutmeg

pinch of ground cloves

pepper

4 slices crustless bakery white bread

———

6 tablespoons unsalted butter

salt

pepper

½ cup dry white wine

NOTE: The dish can also be made without boning the chicken, by pushing the stuffing, in reduced quantity, into the cavity. The result, although less time-consuming, is also less impressive.

(continued)

STUFFED CHICKEN FLAVORED WITH WHITE TRUFFLE *(continued)*

14 When the bird is cooked, transfer it to a heated serving dish and keep warm in a cool oven. Skim off the clear fat that floats on the surface of the cooking liquid and deglaze the liquid with a couple of tablespoons of water. Boil rapidly and scrape the cooking residue loose. Check seasoning and strain into a heated bowl or sauceboat.

15 To serve, bring the dish to the table for everyone to see. Then remove the legs and wings and carve the stuffed body with a very sharp knife, beginning at the neck end. Slice the legs and thigh and give each guest a stuffed slice and a piece of meat. Serve with the sauce.

NOTE: If you have any stuffing and chicken left over, chop finely and mix with some chopped cooked spinach or nettles and some ricotta or béchamel, and use it as a stuffing for crespelle or cannelloni. To make about 10 cannelloni, enough for 4 people, you will need about 1¼ pounds of stuffing. Bake covered with béchamel in the usual way for 20 minutes in a hot (375°F.) oven.

This chicken can be accompanied by any vegetable you would serve with roast chicken. But if you would like to emphasize the truffle taste, pass round a dish of Braised Mushrooms (page 131). And if you want to be really Milanese accompany the chicken with timbales made with plain risotto (page 26).

The first course must be elegant too. A soup made with the stock from the carcass is ideal. My first choice would be Passatelli (page 50), which is quick and easy to prepare. For something simpler still, serve prosciutto with melon or your favorite salad, but nothing too garlicky or too piquant.

HOW TO BONE A CHICKEN. First, cut off the wingtips and wipe thoroughly inside and out with paper towels. Put the chicken, breast down, on a board and make a deep incision all the way down its back, from the neck to the tail, using a boning knife or some other sharp pointed knife. Begin detaching the flesh from the bone at the neck end, using your fingers as well as the knife to pry the flesh from the bone. When using the knife, keep the point and the sharp edge toward the bone and away from the skin of the chicken, since it is essential not to pierce the skin. Loosen the flesh around the bone in the shoulder and cut through the joint. Cut away and remove the wishbone. Pull the flesh from the rib cage and pry it free with your fingers, until you reach the crest of the breastbone. As you progress down the back you will meet the saucer-shaped hip joint. Loosen the meat all around the thigh and cut through the drumstick joint. The skin and flesh with the wings and drumsticks should now be attached to the carcass only by the crest of the breast bone. Cut the skin away, being particularly careful as the skin is very thin on the crest. Remove any flesh from the carcass and place it in the boned chicken. The chicken is now ready to be stuffed.

Cheese

Gnocchi alla parigina
CHOUX PASTRY GNOCCHI

Fonduta piemontese
PIEDMONTESE FONDUE

Salsa al gorgonzola
GORGONZOLA SAUCE

Mascarpone all'aceto balsamico
MASCARPONE WITH BALSAMIC VINEGAR

Tagliatelle al mascarpone
TAGLIATELLE WITH MASCARPONE

Tiramisù
TIRAMISU

La mia mozzarella in carrozza
FRIED MOZZARELLA AND SALAMI
SANDWICHES

Polpettine alla pizzaiola
CROQUETTES STUFFED WITH MOZZARELLA IN
TOMATO SAUCE

Asparagi alla milanese
ASPARAGUS WITH FRIED EGGS AND
PARMESAN

Zucchine ripiene alla mantovana
STUFFED ZUCCHINI, MANTUA STYLE

Torta salata di ricotta
RICOTTA, BASIL AND OLIVE TART

Rotolo di salsa di pomodoro con acciughe e ricotta
ROLLED SOUFFLE WITH TOMATO SAUCE,
ANCHOVIES AND RICOTTA

Cassata siciliana nuda
RICOTTA CAKE

Ricotta alla mentuccia
RICOTTA WITH MINT

SEE ALSO

Crema di mascarpone e olive verdi
MASCARPONE, OLIVE AND GRUYERE SPREAD

Involtini di pollo ripieni di nocciole, prosciutto e formaggio
CHICKEN BUNDLES WITH HAZELNUTS, HAM
AND CHEESE

Parmigiana di melanzane
EGGPLANT PARMIGIAN

Passatelli
PASSATELLI

Pesto
PESTO

Pizzette di melanzane
BROILED EGGPLANT WITH PIZZA TOPPING

Polenta alla pizzaiola
POLENTA WITH PIZZA TOPPING

Polenta pasticciata alla piemontese
BAKED POLENTA WITH PORCINI

Radicchio alla griglia col parmigiano
BROILED RADICCHIO WITH PARMESAN

Reginette imbottite
STUFFED REGINETTE

Risotto in bianco
RISOTTO WITH PARMESAN

Tagliolini e merluzzo al pomodoro
TAGLIOLINI AND HADDOCK IN TOMATO
SAUCE

Tonnarelli alla polpa di granchio
TONNARELLI WITH CRAB SAUCE

Torta di noce alla crema di mascarpone
WALNUT CAKE WITH MASCARPONE CREAM

Tortino di crespelle pasticciate
CRESPELLE WITH MOZZARELLA AND TOMATO
SAUCE

Tortino di puré di patate
MASHED POTATOES BAKED WITH SALAMI AND
MOZZARELLA

A catalogue published in 1977 listed 451 different Italian cheeses. Across the length and breadth of Italy there are many different pastures and methods of cheese-making, and countless local dishes are made with these various cheeses.

The origins of Italian cheese-making are ancient, and rooted in legend. In the *Odyssey,* Homer, who is thought to have lived between the seventh and sixth centuries B.C., describes the arrival of Odysseus in Polyphemus's cave in Sicily in which "there were baskets laden with cheeses." After the Cyclops had returned with his herd of goats and ewes, "he sat down to milk his ewes and bleating goats, which he did methodically, putting her young to each mother, as he finished. He then curdled half the white milk, gathered it all up and stored it in wicker baskets."

By Roman times the craft of cheese-making was firmly established in Sicily, and Sicilian cheeses came to be well known all over the empire. The Romans soon discovered that animal rennet could replace the natural curdling of the milk, and the Sicilians became expert in the dosage of rennet. Even during the barbarian invasions, cheese-making remained an important activity; eventually around the turn of the eleventh century some of what are now traditional cheeses began to take shape.

The first farm known to have been mainly devoted to cheese-making appeared near Parma in the thirteenth century, and by the sixteenth century Italian cheeses had found a place on the tables of the nobility all over Europe. Cheeses appear in most of the menus and dishes of the great chefs. The common people, too, used cheeses to enrich their simple soups, flavor their meat croquettes and dress their plain buckwheat polenta. Toward the end of the nineteenth century cheese production became an important industry. Some cheeses disappeared; others became the cheeses we know now.

Most of today's well-known cheeses are made in northern Italy, and most of them are used as table cheeses as well as in local dishes, either as formaggi da grattuggia (grating cheeses) or as formaggi da cucina (cooking cheeses), according to their properties. Bel paese, for instance, is a good melting cheese that can replace mozzarella. Some local soft cheeses are delicious for dressing polenta and gnocchi. In Sicily, ricotta salata (salted ricotta) is mixed into a tomato sauce for pasta.

In this chapter I focus on the most common cheeses used in cooking that can be found in American shops and supermarkets: fontina, gorgonzola, mascarpone, mozzarella, parmesan and ricotta.

Gnocchi alla parigina
CHOUX PASTRY GNOCCHI • SERVES 4

These very delicate gnocchi are the best vehicle for a sauce containing cheese. In spite of being Parisian in origin, as their name indicates, they are very popular in northern Italian homes, and possibly better known there than they are in Paris.

Choux pastry gnocchi are easier to make than potato gnocchi. You can dress them with some parmesan and flavored butter or with Gorgonzola Sauce (page 145). They are also delicious with a very thin béchamel to which three tablespoons each of grated parmesan and grated gruyère are added at the end.

1 Put the milk in a saucepan, add the butter and 1 teaspoon of salt; cook until the milk begins to bubble around the edges.

2 Take the pan off the heat and add the flour, all at once. Beat very hard with a wooden spoon until well blended and then return the pan to the heat and cook, over low heat, beating the whole time. This will cook the flour, thus ridding it of the unpleasant raw taste. Beat until the paste begins to

1 cup milk
6 tablespoons unsalted butter
salt
1 cup sifted flour
¼ teaspoon freshly grated nutmeg
2 tablespoons freshly grated parmesan
4 eggs
Gorgonzola Sauce (page 145) or ½ cup grated parmesan and 2½ tablespoons melted butter flavored with garlic and sage

(*continued*)

**CHOUX PASTRY
GNOCCHI** (*continued*)

NOTE. The dish can be prepared a few hours in advance through Step 7, covered with plastic wrap and left to stand at room temperature. Bake for about 25 minutes to allow the gnocchi to get hot all through.

NOTE: Another excellent way to dress the gnocchi is with this cream mixture. First season the gnocchi with a couple of tablespoons of parmesan. Then melt 1 tablespoon butter in a small saucepan and add 1 cup of light cream. Heat the cream mixture and then spoon it over the gnocchi. Bake for about 15 minutes in the preheated oven and serve with more parmesan on the side.

make a sizzling noise, about 3 minutes, then remove from the heat. (If you add the flour when the liquid is boiling very fast it may form a few hard lumps that are very difficult to dissolve. If this happens, put the mixture in a food processor and process until the lumps have disappeared.)

3 Mix in the nutmeg and parmesan and allow to cool for about 5 minutes, beating very frequently.

4 Add one egg to the paste and beat until thoroughly incorporated. Do the same with all the other eggs, incorporating one egg at a time and beating quite hard after each addition. This paste needs a lot of beating to aerate it. I use an electric beater for about 10 minutes in all. At the end the paste will be very glossy and smooth.

5 Choose a large and wide saucepan or casserole of at least 3 quarts capacity. Fill the pan with water and bring to the boil. Add 1 tablespoon of salt.

6 Preheat the oven to 350°F.

7 Turn the heat down so that the water in the saucepan is only just simmering. Pick up teaspoonfuls of the mixture and, with the back of another teaspoon, slide them into the simmering water. (You could also pipe the mixture through a pastry bag fitted with a plain ½-inch tube and cut it into 1-inch lengths.) Cook the gnocchi in two batches. They will soon come to the surface. Cook for about 1 minute and then lift them out with a slotted spoon and place on a clean cloth to dry. Transfer the gnocchi to a generously buttered ovenproof dish on which you have spread a couple of tablespoons of gorgonzola sauce or the grated cheese and melted butter. Choose a large shallow dish so that the gnocchi can be spread out in a single layer.

8 When all the gnocchi are cooked, spread the remaining sauce over and bake in the oven for about 15 minutes. Allow to rest for 3 to 4 minutes before serving.

✖ This is a delicate first course which could be followed by Sole with Artichoke Puree (page 91) or by Sautéed Veal Scaloppine with Peaches (page 179). These gnocchi are also lovely used as an accompaniment to meat. Try them, lightly dressed with butter only, with Roast Quail with Balsamic Vinegar (page 226) or Stuffed Chicken Flavored with White Truffle (page 136).

FONTINA

Fontina is a semisoft cheese made from cow's milk. It is produced in large round shapes. It has a very characteristic flavor that is redolent of the wild herbs and flowers of the high pastures of Valle d'Aosta where the farm-made fontina is produced. There is also an industrially produced variety of fontina. Both kinds of this cheese have FONTINA VALDOSTANA stamped on the crust.

The origins of fontina are very old. It is known to have been made in the fifteenth century —the name fontina appears in a list of cheeses made in Valle d'Aosta—and is thought to date back to Roman times. From the eighteenth century on, fontina was considered important enough to be listed in various local documents and inventories. At that time it was often called fontine.

There are many theories concerning the origin of the name. Some writers maintain that it comes from a mountain called Fonti near Aosta, while others see it as a derivative of fondere (to melt). This is, in fact, the most important property of fontina: it melts beautifully. For this reason the experts argue that fontina is not a table cheese, and should only be used as a condiment, traditionally for polenta and potato gnocchi, or to make fonduta (fondue).

Fonduta piemontese
PIEDMONTESE FONDUE • SERVES 4 TO 6

Fontina cheese is the principal ingredient of this delectable sauce. The other characteristic ingredient is white truffle. I use truffle paste, but the sauce is very good even without it. If you are lucky enough to have a white truffle, it should be added, thinly sliced, at the very end, just before serving the sauce.

The sauce must be made at the last minute, or the cheese will become thick and gluey. It takes about fifteen minutes once you put boiling water into the lower part of a double boiler or in a pan into which you can fit another metal container to make a bain-marie. I add a little flour to stabilize the emulsion, as this sauce is rather tricky to make.

Fonduta piemontese is traditionally served in soup bowls with crostini (croutons) or toasted bread slices handed around. I also like it with polenta or rice. A rice mold is particularly attractive.

To prepare rice in a mold, cook about 1½ cups of long-grain rice until al dente. Dress with a tablespoon of butter. Generously butter a 6-cup ring mold and sprinkle with breadcrumbs. Shake off excess crumbs and spoon the rice into the mold, pressing it down to avoid holes. Turn the mold over onto a round dish. Spoon the fonduta into the hole and around the rice. If you do not have a ring mold you can easily shape the rice with a spoon.

(*continued*)

2 cups diced fontina (about ¾ pound)

about 1 cup milk

4 tablespoons unsalted butter

1 tablespoon flour

3 egg yolks

3 tablespoons truffle paste (optional)

freshly ground black pepper

1 About 6 hours before you want to serve the fonduta, dice the fontina. Put in a bowl and add enough milk just to cover the cheese.

2 About fifteen to twenty minutes before serving, put the butter in the top half of a double boiler, add the fontina with the milk and set on simmering water.

3 Beat the flour into the egg yolks and then add to the cheese and milk mixture, while beating constantly with a wire whisk. Continue cooking and stirring until the fontina has melted and the sauce is very smooth, creamy and shiny. Mix in the truffle paste and add the pepper. Salt is not necessary because the cheese gives enough saltiness to the sauce. Do not cook any longer or the cheese will become stringy. Serve in heated soup bowls.

GORGONZOLA

Gorgonzola, the northern Italian cheese par excellence, is one of the oldest of cheeses. It is thought to date from Roman times, and its association with the town of Gorgonzola was officially recognized in 1251. Gorgonzola used to be a country town to the east of Milan, but it is now part of the outer suburbs of that city. It was once, but is no longer, a stopping place for the cattle on their journey home in the autumn after spending the summer months on the high pastures of Valsassina. The cows were tired—*stracche* in Milanese dialect—from the long journey, and it was then that the various stracchini cheeses were made, of which gorgonzola is the most popular and the best known outside Italy.

The center of its production is now in Novara, a province of Piedmont, which is where the Consorzio Gorgonzola is situated. All producers of gorgonzola must belong to the consortium, which protects the use of the name. Each cheese is stamped on the crust with the identification number of the farm or factory of origin.

Gorgonzola is made from a hot and a cold curd of cow's milk from two different milkings. These are put into round molds ten to twelve inches in diameter, and very thin metal needles are inserted into the cheese and then removed. The resulting tiny holes aerate the cheese and encourage the formation of the mold. The aging, about 50 days, used to take place in caves in Valsassina and Val Brembana, two alpine valleys northeast of Milan. Now only farm-produced gorgonzola is aged in this way. The industrially produced cheese available outside Italy is aged in storerooms in which similar atmospheric conditions are reproduced.

At its best, gorgonzola is cream colored, with blue-green veins that become more marked toward the center of the cheese. It has a fat content of about 45 percent. Its pleasing, aromatic taste varies from mellow in the gorgonzola dolce, such as dolcelatte, to piquant in the gorgonzola piccante. Experts agree that the latter is superior.

Gorgonzola is mainly a table cheese, though recently it has started to be used in cooking, principally as the main ingredient in many sauces for pasta or gnocchi.

Salsa al gorgonzola

GORGONZOLA SAUCE • MAKES 1 CUP

I like to use this sauce to dress Choux Pastry Gnocchi (page 141). This recipe makes enough for 4 servings of gnocchi or pasta.

1 Cut the gorgonzola into small pieces.

2 Heat the butter, sage and garlic in a small saucepan. When the butter has just melted, add the cheese, the cream and a good grinding of pepper. Cook, stirring the whole time, until the cheese has melted. Simmer for 1 minute. Taste and check if salt is needed: because of the saltiness of the cheese it probably will not be. Remove and discard the sage and garlic before using the sauce.

2 ounces gorgonzola

2 tablespoons unsalted butter

4 fresh sage leaves *or* ½ teaspoon dried sage

1 garlic clove, peeled

½ cup heavy cream

freshly ground black pepper

salt (optional)

MASCARPONE

When I was a child in Milan, a woman came to the house every Tuesday selling ricotta piemontese and mascarpone. I can still see her dressed in black with a black and white scarf around her head. On her arm she carried a flat basket packed with cheeses wrapped in muslin, ricotta at one end and mascarpone at the other. A steelyard hung from her shoulder, and the cheeses were placed on its large brass pan and weighed. How I looked forward to her Tuesday visits, and how I loved the smell and the whiteness and, best of all, the taste of those cheeses! I ate them as, at their best, they should still be eaten—with a little sugar.

Luigi Cherubini, the author of a dictionary of the Milanese dialect written in 1839, endorses this. In the entry for mascarpone he wrote:

A kind of milk product obtained from cream that is boiled and treated, as soon as it comes to the boil, with a moderate dosage of vinegar or acetic acid. It is of the same consistency as butter and of a very white color. . . . It is usually eaten simply sweetened with sugar; gourmands however enjoy it even mixed with rosolio [a sweet liqueur made with herbs or rose petals] or rum, or dressed in many other ways. The word mascarpone apparently owes its origin to the Spanish expression "Mas cher bueno."

Cherubini is usually very reliable on the etymology of Lombard words, but here, I think, he fails. I feel that the origin of the word suggested by the contemporary food historian Massimo Alberini must be right; the word, he says, comes from mascarpa, a type of ricotta made in the province of Como and referred to in a document dated 1168.

Until recently mascarpone was little known outside Lombardy and Piedmont. Mascarpone, the creamiest of cheeses, could only be made in the cold months, from November to February, and it had to be consumed within a few days. Now modern food technology has changed all that by means of the high-temperature process that makes mascarpone a "long-life" product. Mascarpone is now made all year round and keeps several weeks, with the result that it is popular throughout Italy and is well known in Britain, Germany and the United States.

The packaged mascarpone does not have

the same taste as the fresh, and highly perishable, mascarpone that can still be bought in the best delicatessens in Milan. But long-life mascarpone is better than no mascarpone.

Mascarpone is made from milk that comes from cows that have been fed on fresh or naturally dried forage, which retains the aromas and flavors of herbs and flowers. The sterilized milk is pumped into tanks where it stays until the cream rises to the top. The cream then passes into the inner part of a double-walled tank where it is heated by steam that is pumped through the outer container. Citric acid and tartaric acid are added, and the cream, which is stirred the whole time, soon becomes viscous. This is now mascarpone, which is pumped into cooling chambers where it stays for twelve hours. It is then ready to be poured into containers, which carry an expiration date.

The recipes given here are my favorites. You can also mix mascarpone with other cheeses. Try mashing it with Roquefort or gorgonzola, or add some grated parmesan or pecorino romano to it for a delicious dip. Mascarpone is an excellent substitute for butter with smoked salmon, tuna, caviar or truffles, or with green olives as in the recipe given here. You can serve it with a couple of teaspoons of cocoa powder, a little powdered coffee and enough honey or sugar to suit your taste. Simplest of all, though, and perhaps still best is fresh mascarpone as I ate it when a child—just with a little sugar.

Mascarpone all'aceto balsamico
MASCARPONE WITH BALSAMIC VINEGAR • SERVES I

This new dessert is based on two of the most ancient ingredients in Italian cooking, mascarpone and balsamic vinegar.

For each person you need ½ cup mascarpone, sugar to your liking—I add 1¼ to 1½ teaspoons—and about 2 teaspoons of vinegar. Try 1 teaspoon of the vinegar, taste and then add a little more until you get the right balance between the sugar and the vinegar. That's all; so easy, yet so good.

Tagliatelle al mascarpone
TAGLIATELLE WITH MASCARPONE • SERVES 3 TO 4

This is an old recipe from Pavia, a university city in southern Lombardy. Pavia is the birthplace of several excellent traditional recipes that are based on such local products as mascarpone. Strangely enough, there is not the wealth of good local restaurants that one might expect, and when I go to Pavia to see my son, who teaches at the university, I stop off at the market to buy the ingredients I will need to cook a meal in his apartment. I am known at the stall selling cheese and salami, where the owner calls me "la mamma del professore," since I go there to buy prosciutto, salami and luganega to bring back to England, as well as the fresh mascarpone with which to make this dish for lunch. It is a heavenly dish, especially if you make your own tagliatelle. This sauce takes less time to make than the tagliatelle takes to cook.

TAGLIATELLE

1⅓ cups unbleached flour
2 eggs
salt

---

1 cup mascarpone
1 tablespoon unsalted butter
pinch of grated nutmeg
freshly grated black pepper
2 egg yolks
½ cup freshly grated parmesan
extra parmesan for serving

NOTE: If you do not wish to make your own tagliatelle, you may substitute ¾ pound store-bought fresh tagliatelle or ½ pound dried tagliatelle.

1 Prepare the tagliatelle following the instructions on pages 8–9. Stop thinning out the sheets of pasta at the next-to-the-last notch.

2 Put the mascarpone, butter, nutmeg, and pepper in a serving bowl. Place the bowl in the oven and turn the heat on to very low.

3 Beat the egg yolks with half the parmesan in another bowl.

4 Drop the pasta into salted boiling water and cook in the usual way, remembering that if the tagliatelle is homemade and still soft, it will only take about 1½ minutes to cook.

5 Mix about ¼ cup of the pasta water into the mascarpone.

6 Drain the tagliatelle as soon as they are ready, reserving some of the water in a small pitcher.

7 Transfer the tagliatelle to the bowl containing the mascarpone mixture, toss thoroughly and then add the egg yolk mixture. Mix again and check the seasoning. It should not need any salt because of the amount of parmesan in the mixture. Grate a little more nutmeg on top and bring straight to the table together with the little pitcher of reserved water. This dish calls for some more parmesan, passed around separately.

The pitcher full of pasta water is a Neapolitan touch about which I was reminded recently by a friend. He told me that at the home of his Neapolitan grandmother the cooking water was always brought to the table in a little earthenware pitcher (earthenware retains heat). The hot water is for people who like their pasta more slippery. This sauce and the Mascarpone, Olive and Gruyère Spread (page 231) are typical of sauces that often need the addition of a little water. Another well-known sauce of this kind is carbonara.

Tiramisù

TIRAMISU • SERVES 6 TO 8

This is a dessert of recent birth yet it is already very popular, perhaps even more so abroad than in Italy. I often make tiramisù without the coffee or the chocolate and substitute white rum or Grand Marnier for the brandy. I find it lighter and more pleasant, but this may be because I am not mad about chocolate. Of course it is then no longer a real tiramisù, nor could it be called such, since coffee and brandy are the two ingredients that account for the name tiramisù, which means pick-me-up.

½ cup strong espresso coffee *or* 1½ teaspoons instant coffee dissolved in ½ cup water
3 tablespoons brandy
3½ ounces bitter chocolate
3 egg yolks
4 tablespoons sugar
1¼ cups mascarpone
2 egg whites
14 to 16 savoiardi *or* about 20 ladyfingers
coffee beans, for garnish

NOTE: You can make tiramisù in a glass bowl. It looks stunning, with the layers of pale and dark brown seen through the glass, and the top speckled with the grated chocolate.

1 Mix together the coffee and the brandy.
2 Grate about a quarter of the chocolate and cut the rest into small pieces.
3 Beat the egg yolks with the sugar until the mixture is very pale and forms a ribbon. Fold in the mascarpone, a tablespoon at a time.
5 Whisk the egg whites until stiff, then fold them into the mascarpone and egg yolk mixture.
6 Put a layer of ladyfingers on an oval dish. Dip a pastry brush into the coffee and brandy mixture and soak the ladyfingers with it.
7 Spread about 4 tablespoons of the mascarpone cream over the cake and scatter with the pieces of chocolate. Cover with a layer of ladyfingers, soak with coffee and brandy and continue to make similar layers until you have used up all the ingredients. Finish with a layer of mascarpone cream. Place the dessert in the refrigerator for at least 6 hours.
8 Before serving, sprinkle with the reserved grated chocolate and decorate with coffee beans.

MOZZARELLA

The popularity of pizza has made this cheese well known the world over, but only a few people have tasted the real mozzarella, made from buffalo's milk. It was first made in Campania and Latium from the milk of the Indian water buffalo (a cousin to the American bison), which was introduced to Italy in the sixteenth century. And it is in those regions that one can still come across the real thing. The area around Battipaglia and Paestum is dotted with cheese factories that advertize, "Qui la Vera Mozzarella di Buffala" (Real Buffalo Mozzarella Sold Here). I would not like to guarantee that all the factories I noticed on a recent visit to Paestum and the Cilento peninsula make their mozzarella from buffalo's milk, but the small caseificio (cheese factory) I visited certainly did

The caseificio was near the ruins of the Greek city of Velia, which flourished in the fifth century B.C. at the same time as Paestum further north. Like Paestum, Velia was an important port from which the goods that had arrived overland from the legendary Sybaris on the Ionian coast were shipped to the western Mediterranean. Unlike Paestum, however, Velia today remains largely buried. It stands at the foot of the hills overlooking the peaceful and fertile countryside of the "happy land," as the Romans later called Campania, a land that yields a wealth of pleasures besides the real mozzarella that I was looking for.

My caseificio was totally dedicated to the production of mozzarella, although in its little shop I bought good provolone and caciocavallo made nearby. The casaro (cheese-maker) was standing next to a large vessel in which a mechanical paddle was churning round and round. The rennet had already been added and the so-called pasta filata (plastic- or stretched-curd cheese) was in the process of being made. This is done by covering the crumbled curd with boiling water, which forces all the whey out with the rotary movement of the paddle. The casaro has to watch carefully and add boiling water from time to time. When a thread is formed, the cheese is mozzato—cut away from the original lump (hence the name of the cheese)—and put through an extruding machine. There three girls were breaking off pieces of pasta filata, which they quickly shaped into smooth, glistening golf balls and threw into a basin nearby. These were the delicious buffaline.

Mozzarella made with buffalo's milk has a fresher, more fragrant and yet more intense flavor than mozzarella made with cow's milk. Its texture is also different; it is more compact and it squeaks when you cut it, oozing milky whey. If you find buffalo mozzarella, do not waste it by using it for cooking, but eat it as it is. The mozzarella found in supermarkets and shops in this country is made from cow's milk. It is shaped like a squashed ball. The Italian mozzarella is more expensive than the domestic, but it has a better flavor and keeps a better texture in cooking. In Italy there are other shapes of mozzarella, mostly made from cow's milk. There are trecce (braids), ovolini (little eggs), ciliege (cherries) and bocconcini (morsels), these latter being the most popular after the squashed ball shape.

Mozzarella can be eaten raw, by itself or with vegetables, tomatoes being the best. In Italy this combination is known as insalata caprese. But because of its binding property the main use of mozzarella is in cooking. Here I can let you in on a couple of secrets. Packaged mozzarella loses much of its flavor when cooked and often becomes a mass of stringy white rubber. For this reason I follow Marcella Hazan's useful suggestion, which is to grate the mozzarella and mix it with a couple of tablespoons of olive oil for an hour or two before using it. If the dish you are making is not based on olive oil, use milk instead. The other secret is to add only a limited amount of mozzarella to the dish, and to achieve the desired cheesy flavor by adding some mild cheddar cheese, thus avoiding too much of the white rubbery substance. Do not lay thick slices of mozzarella on the top of a dish, such as pizza, that you are going to bake. Either grate the mozzarella or cut it into small pieces or thin strips and scatter them around. Another way is to tuck thin slices of mozzarella underneath the tomatoes or any other ingredient that goes in the dish.

La mia mozzarella in carrozza
FRIED MOZZARELLA AND SALAMI SANDWICHES • SERVES 2 TO 4

Mozzarella in carrozza is one of the most delicious creations of the inventive Neapolitans. They slice their mozzarella, made from buffalo's milk, sandwich it between two slices of white bread and fry it. But while the fresh mozzarella sold in this country melts in the same way as the mozzarella sold in Naples, it has far less flavor. For this reason I add a slice of good Italian salami to the sandwich.

The quantities in this recipe are enough for four people as a primo. If you serve mozzarella in carrozza as a secondo the quantities are enough for two or three, depending on their appetites.

½ pound fresh mozzarella
pepper
about ½ cup milk
⅔ cup flour
2 eggs
salt
8 slices day-old white bread, about ¼ inch thick
4 to 8 slices Italian salami, according to size, not too thinly sliced
salt
oil for frying

1 Cut the mozzarella into slices of the same thickness as the slices of bread. Season with pepper.

2 Put the milk in one soup plate and the flour in another.

3 Break the eggs into a third soup plate, add salt and pepper and beat lightly.

4 Cut the crust off the bread. Dip one side of each slice of bread very briefly in the milk. Put 1 slice of mozzarella and 1 or 2 slices of salami (according to thickness) between the dry sides of the bread. Pin with toothpicks at 2 ends of each sandwich.

5 Put enough oil in a wok or a large frying pan for the sandwiches to be deep-fried. Heat until very hot but not smoking.

6 Meanwhile dust each sandwich lightly with flour and dip in the beaten eggs, coating both sides and letting the excess egg flow back into the plate.

7 Fry the sandwiches until golden and crisp and then turn them over and fry the other side. The mozzarella should just begin to melt. Drain in a dish lined with paper towels and serve immediately.

Polpettine alla pizzaiola

CROQUETTES STUFFED WITH MOZZARELLA IN TOMATO SAUCE •
SERVES 4

These Mediterranean-tasting meat croquettes contain mozzarella
and are cooked in a tomato sauce. The mozzarella melts inside and
sometimes oozes out to mix with the tomato sauce. In Italy a sauce
is called alla pizzaiola when it contains only tomatoes and oregano.
The mozzarella here is an integral part of the meat, not of the sauce.

1   To prepare the tomato sauce, sauté the onion in 3
tablespoons olive oil, using a heavy 8-inch frying pan or sauté
pan. (Using a frying pan rather than a saucepan will make the
water in the tomatoes evaporate faster, thus concentrating
the flavor of the sauce.) Add a pinch of salt; this releases the
liquid in the onion and prevents the onion from browning.
Cook the onion until it becomes soft, stirring frequently.

2   Meanwhile finely chop the garlic and celery together
and add to the onion. Cook for a minute or so and then add
the tomato paste. Cook, stirring constantly, for 1 minute. Add
the tomatoes and the sugar and plenty of pepper. Simmer for
about 35 minutes until the sauce is thick and the oil has
separated from the tomatoes. Add a couple of tablespoons of
hot water if the sauce becomes too thick and begins to stick
to the pan.

3   While the sauce is cooking, remove the crust from the
bread and soak it in a little milk for 5 minutes or so. Squeeze
out and put in a bowl.

4   Beat the egg lightly with salt and pepper. Put the
meat in the bowl with the soaked bread and add the beaten
egg. Mix very thoroughly; this is best done with your hands.

5   Divide the meat mixture into 8 portions. Make these
into fairly flat, round shapes and pat them hard to release any
pockets of air.

6   Slice the mozzarella and cover 4 portions of the meat
mixture with the slices, leaving a clean edge all round. Place
the other 4 portions of meat on top and press all around the
edges, to seal in the cheese.

7   Heat 2 tablespoons olive oil in a nonstick pan and fry
the polpettine until a lovely dark crust has formed. Turn
them over and fry the other side, then transfer to the pan
with the sauce. Add a couple of tablespoons hot water to the
pan in which you fried the meat, boil rapidly and then pour
this juice into the tomato sauce. Sprinkle with the oregano.

TOMATO SAUCE

½ cup finely chopped onion
 3 tablespoons olive oil
salt
 1 garlic clove, peeled
 1 celery stalk with leaves
 2 teaspoons tomato paste
1½ cups canned plum tomatoes
     or 1¼ pounds fresh ripe
     tomatoes, peeled and with
     the seeds removed
 1 teaspoon sugar
freshly ground black pepper

CROQUETTES

 2 slices good-quality bakery
     white bread
milk
 1 egg
salt
pepper
 1 pound lean ground beef
½ pound mozzarella

———

 2 tablespoons olive oil
 2 tablespoons fresh oregano or
     1 tablespoon dried oregano

(continued)

CROQUETTES STUFFED WITH MOZZARELLA IN TOMATO SAUCE (*continued*)

Cover the pan and cook for 20 minutes, so that the flavors of the meat, mozzarella and tomato blend together.

✖ I like steamed and boiled potatoes with these polpettine, or tagliatelle dressed with a knob of butter. If you want to serve a green vegetable as well, some steamed or sautéed zucchini would be lovely. It would then make a very satisfying piatto unico (one-course meal).

PARMESAN

The terminology of the various cheeses that are loosely known as parmesan is more precise in Italy than elsewhere. There are in fact four distinct cheeses of this kind, and their generic name is not parmesan, but grana. They are all very hard cheeses with a grainy texture (grana means grain), but while abroad they are all likely to be called parmesan, in Italy each of the four is called by its own name. These names describe each grana by its place of origin: thus grana lodigiano from Lodi; grana piacentino from Piacenza; and grana padano from the Po valley (from the river's Latin name, Padus). The exception is the genuine parmesan, Parmigiano-Reggiano. These cheeses are all made the same way, the differences arising from the different forage on which the cows are fed, so that their milk differs from place to place. They are all made into the huge wheels you no doubt have seen, with the crust stamped very clearly with the name of the grana in question.

I often buy grana padano in Pavia, one of the centers of its production, when I go there to visit my son. It is an excellent cheese, used as a table cheese when young and in cooking when aged. In Pavia I can also find the very rare grana lodigiano, which I like as a table cheese; it is softer and more mellow than the other grana cheeses. Giacomo Casanova, who enjoyed good food, although he is perhaps better known for his other appetites, noted in his famous diaries that, "Lodi was renowned for its cheese, known all over Europe as parmesan."

Grana piacentino is a very old cheese and used to be well known throughout Europe, challenging the supremacy of its rival, Parmigiano-Reggiano. Many people through the ages have paid tribute to this cheese, one of the earliest, so the story has it, having been Hannibal. The cheese, in fact, is said to have been the cause of his defeat at Capua. On passing through Piacenza, Hannibal acquired a quantity of grana piacentino and then spent his days gorging himself on it instead of rearming against the Romans. A nice story, even if a trifle hard to believe. What is certain is that grana piacentino is an excellent cheese.

The birthplace of parmesan proper lies in an area between Reggio Emilia and Parma that was once part of the Duchy of Parma. For this reason parmesan was originally called, simply, parmigiano. Then Reggio rightly claimed its share of the provenance and the name was changed to Parmigiano-Reggiano. Parmigiano-Reggiano is made in strictly defined areas in the provinces of Reggio Emilia, Parma, Modena, Bologna and Mantua.

Parmesan, like the other grana cheeses, is still produced in small factories, called *caselli,* where a maximum of sixteen wheels are made in a day. When I was in Parma recently I was taken to visit one of these caselli by Avvocato Giorgio Bernardini, the secretary of the very efficient Consorzio Parma Alimentare. We went to a casello outside Parma where the cheese-maker, Signor Mariani, showed me around. I saw how the milk from that morning's and the previous evening's milkings is partly skimmed and then curdled with rennet, after which it is scooped out into molds, each one for about 60 to 70 pounds of cheese. Each of these molds contains about 450 quarts of milk! Then comes the cheese-maker's most difficult task: the salting. Enough salt has to be added to preserve the cheese, but not so much as to spoil the flavor. The salted wheels are then cured in huge, cool storerooms where they are stacked in long lines on shelves reaching up to the high ceiling.

While I was in one of the storerooms, a stately robot was performing its twice-weekly ritual of wiping the sweat, produced by the salting, from each of the cheeses. The machine walked between two guide rails. It stopped, two long arms emerged, retrieved a cheese and placed it on a platform where it wiped one side, turned it over and wiped the other side. The cheese was then replaced, and the monster moved on.

There are three grades of parmesan, named according to the length of time they have matured. The youngest parmesan, the nuovo, which is good as a table cheese, may be one year old. Parmigiano vecchio has aged for between one and a half and two years, while the stravecchio, which is parmesan at its best, has aged for at least two to two and a half years or more.

The origins of parmesan are unknown. We know that by the fourteenth century it was already considered an excellent cheese. Boccaccio, describing the pleasures of the Paese di Bengodi (the Land of Good Cheer) in *The Decameron*, writes, "et eravi una montagna di formaggio grattugiato sopra la quale stan genti, che niuna altra cosa facevan che fare maccheroni et ravioli." (And on a mountain all of grated cheese dwelt folk who did nought else but make macaroni and ravioli.) There can be little doubt that the cheese in question was parmesan, and it can be seen that the successful union of pasta and parmesan was already popular. Parmesan was also used a lot during the high Renaissance, when it was usually served at the end of the meal with truffles, fennel, cardoons, grapes and pears.

In Emilia, where parmesan always appears as a table cheese, parmesan with pears has remained a favorite end to a meal. Elsewhere, the habit of serving parmesan with various fresh fruits or vegetables has quite recently started to come back into fashion. Not long ago I was served peeled quarters of juicy pears rolled in grated parmesan. It was a new sensation but, truth to tell, I would have preferred to combine the two myself.

The most lordly way of presenting parmesan I have come across was at a wedding in Reggio Emilia. At the bottom of the grand staircase of the family's palazzo stood a huge half-wheel of perfect parmesan. A few special parmesan knives were placed around it, and as we dug into the cheese, waiters handed us glasses of champagne. The custom of handing round a piece of the best parmesan with drinks has spread from Emilia-Romagna to other regions. Recently I had the impression that a large scheggia (splinter) of golden parmesan next to the bottle of champagne is now de rigueur as a snack. It is also the best way to savor a good glass of Chianti.

Parmesan is not appreciated only for its taste. Some aficionados love its smell, as Squire Trelawny of *Treasure Island* did. He used to keep a snuffbox full of grated parmesan in his pocket, and from time to time brought it to his nose with great relish.

Its table use notwithstanding, parmesan is mainly regarded as a grating cheese and, because of its melting qualities, a good cooking cheese. Of all cheeses it is the one without which Italian cooking would not be really Italian. It is used a lot, though never indiscriminately, with pasta, soups and risottos. In Emilia and Romagna there are a few meat dishes that call for parmesan and even a dish made with sole, while in Lombardy parmesan is added to vegetables sautéed in butter, to asparagus and to leeks (see on page 154).

Most gratin dishes need parmesan, on which subject a word of warning. Parmesan sprinkled by itself on the top of gratin dishes will acquire a bitter taste when exposed, dry, to the heat. My secret for a better topping is to use only a couple of tablespoons of parmesan and to mix it with dried breadcrumbs. Put the rest of the parmesan in the sauce or in between the layers of the other ingredients.

HOW TO BUY AND STORE PARMESAN. Good parmesan is pale buff in color with a crumbly texture and a rich yet mellow flavor. When you come across parmesan in this perfect condition you should buy a large piece and then divide it into wedges of about half a pound each. Do this, not by cutting, but by pushing the point of a knife into the cheese: it will break apart following its natural structure. Wrap the wedges in foil, except one for immediate use, and put them in the freezer. Parmesan keeps its flavor quite well when frozen, the main effect of freezing being that, once thawed, it crumbles more easily. Wrap the reserved piece in a double thickness of cheesecloth and place it in the vegetable drawer of the fridge. The cheesecloth will allow the cheese to breathe and prevent the formation of mold on the outside for up to a month or so.

Don't throw away the crust of your parmesan: scrape it thoroughly and add it to a minestrone, a pasta and bean soup or any other vegetable soup that needs lengthy cooking.

Asparagi alla milanese
ASPARAGUS WITH FRIED EGGS AND PARMESAN • SERVES 4

This is my favorite supper dish in the spring, when the first local asparagus appear on the market. It might be called "asparagus with instant hollandaise."

Italians prefer fat white asparagus, and some people maintain that those from Bassano del Grappa or from Greve del Piave are the best. The Piedmontese, however, claim that their asparagus from Sàntena are even better. I can only vouch for those from Bassano, since the best asparagus I ever ate were those I had at the restaurant Al Sole in that town; they were warm, served with oil and lemon. But whether white, green, thin or fat, the asparagus must be fresh and young. You also need good parmesan, otherwise the cheese will kill the flavor of the asparagus instead of combining with it.

3 pounds asparagus
4 tablespoons unsalted butter
4 tablespoons freshly grated parmesan
4 to 8 eggs
freshly ground black pepper

NOTE: You can make the same dish with leeks which, after all, the French call les asperges des pauvres (poor man's asparagus).

1 First scrape the ends of the asparagus stems and snap off or cut off the hard part. Wash the asparagus thoroughly, then tie them in small bundles. Tie them in two places, at the top near the tips and at the bottom above the butts.

2 If you don't have an asparagus boiler, use a tall narrow saucepan, half full of boiling salted water. Stand the

bundles of asparagus, tips up, in the water. If necessary, put some potatoes in the saucepan to keep the bundles upright. I use the potatoes the next day for salad, or to make Potato and Tomato Pie (page 114). If the saucepan is not tall enough to put the lid on without damaging the tallest spears, make a domed lid from a sheet of foil and tie it under the rim of the saucepan.

3 When the asparagus are cooked—they can take from 7 minutes, if really fresh, to 20 minutes—lift the bundles out and place them on paper towels to drain properly before you transfer them onto individual plates.

4 Melt the butter in a nonstick frying pan and pour it over the asparagus spears. Sprinkle with cheese and keep warm.

5 Fry the eggs in the same pan and slide 1 or 2 eggs onto each plate. Grind some pepper over them and serve immediately. Break the yolk and eat the asparagus with your fingers, swirling them in the egg.

RICOTTA

Strictly speaking, ricotta is not a cheese but a by-product of cheese-making: it is made from the whey after it has been separated, by heating, from the curd. To make ricotta, the whey is heated again (ricotta means recooked) and the ricotta then forms on the surface. The curd, meanwhile, is used to make other cheeses.

Ricotta is a healthy food with a low fat content of 15 to 20 percent. It can be made from the whey from cow's, ewe's or goat's milk. The two traditional ricottas are the piemontese, made with whey from cow's milk, and the romana, made with the whey from ewe's milk. Ricotta piemontese is very creamy and is mainly eaten fresh with a little sugar and maybe a sprinkling of ground coffee or cinnamon. It is now a rare commodity that can be found only in the best delicatessens of northern Italy. If you are ever in Milan go to Peck, to Il Salumaio or to the less well known but equally excellent Salumeria Il Principe in Corso Venezia. Buy some fresh mas-carpone as well as your ricotta piemontese; eat both just as they are to enjoy their full flavor.

Ricotta romana is traditionally made with ewe's milk. When I was in Canino, a small market town near Viterbo, I went to see ricotta being made at a very small caseificio (cheese factory) nearby. It was the spring after Chernobyl and production had just started again the previous week. All cheese production had been stopped in Italy for about six weeks and the owners of the cooperative, who were the six men who worked there, were facing heavy losses. Since they had just been allowed to start work again, the atmosphere was almost festive and the casaro (cheese-maker) was only too pleased to show me the process.

He first showed me how pecorino is made. Curdled hot milk is put into cylindrical molds with perforated walls and placed on long stainless steel counters to drain. It stays there for two or three months for fresh pecorino, longer for the more mature cheese and six or seven months for the grating cheese. Next the ricotta-making took place. The whey is heated up to 175°F., at which point small blobs form on the surface. These blobs are scooped out and put in a cestello—the traditional wicker basket—to drip dry.

After seeing all this delicious cheese in the making I had no intention of leaving empty-handed, but it was equally clear that I couldn't buy the sort of quantity one would ask for in a shop. So I came away the proud owner of a 33-pound pecorino as well as of four and a half pounds of freshly made ricotta. I was worried about getting through so much ricotta before it became stale, and the prospect of having to spend my holiday making ricotta stuffings and ricotta puddings didn't appeal to me at all. I need not have worried, however, since that ultrafresh ricotta kept in perfect condition for five days, by which time we had consumed it all without difficulty. We ate it just like that—sometimes as a cheese with a little oil, salt and pepper; sometimes as a dessert with a sprinkling of sugar. It had a richer flavor than the usual ricotta, and no trace of the slight bitterness that is sometimes detectable in store-bought ricotta.

Ricotta is used extensively in Italian cooking. It is a very common ingredient in savory stuffings and fillings and in vegetable pies, as well as in desserts. It also makes an excellent spread mixed with a strong blue cheese such as gorgonzola.

HOMEMADE RICOTTA. This is not exactly the same as ricotta, but it can successfully replace it in most fillings and desserts. It is certainly better than store-bought ricotta that is no longer fresh.

To make about half a pound, bring 1 quart of milk to the simmer in a saucepan and stir in 2 tablespoons of lemon juice and ½ teaspoon salt. Simmer for 10 minutes, stirring very frequently. Line a sieve with a piece of cheesecloth and strain the liquid into a bowl until it stops dripping. Pick up the cloth, which now contains your homemade ricotta, give it a good squeeze and put the ricotta in a clean bowl.

For a richer ricotta, mix in 2 tablespoons of heavy cream after the ricotta has drained. For a pleasantly sharp edge without the added fat and calories of cream, mix in 2 tablespoons of yogurt instead.

Zucchine ripiene alla montovana
STUFFED ZUCCHINI, MANTUA STYLE • SERVES 4 AS A FIRST COURSE

Zucchini stuffed this way is characteristic of the cooking of Mantua, where some aspects of the grande cucina of the Gonzagas were incorporated into the local cooking, producing a very distinctive cuisine.

The stuffing here contains sweet elements, which not only blend beautifully with the delicacy of zucchini, but in fact enhance its flavor. There are many recipes for stuffed zucchini, but to my mind this is the most delicious. Buy Amaretti di Saronno if you can; they are less sweet than other brands.

1 Scrub and wash the zucchini very thoroughly. Drop in boiling salted water and cook for 2 to 3 minutes after the water has come back to the boil. Test by piercing each one with a skewer; they should be just tender. Drain and wipe dry. Cut off both ends and cut in half lengthwise.

2 Scoop out the inside of the zucchini, being careful not to puncture the skin. Leave a ½-inch layer of pulp all around the shell. Sprinkle the inside of the shells lightly with salt and leave upside down on a wooden board to drain off the excess water.

3 Meanwhile prepare the stuffing. Put half the butter and half the oil in a sauté pan. Add the shallot and a little salt and sauté over very low heat until soft but not at all brown. The salt helps the shallot cook without browning, since it releases the liquid inside it.

4 Finely chop the zucchini pulp and add to the shallot. Cook for 10 minutes, stirring very frequently and mashing the mixture with a wooden spoon.

5 Preheat the oven to 375°F.

6 Combine the crumbled amaretti, the ricotta, thyme, nutmeg and the egg in a bowl. Add the zucchini pulp mixture with all its cooking juices and work everything together. Add pepper, and salt if necessary.

7 Pat dry the zucchini shells inside and out with paper towels.

8 Smear the bottom of a rectangular oven dish, preferably metal, with the remaining oil and lay the zucchini shells in the dish, hollow side up.

9 Fill the shells with the stuffing. Sprinkle with some dried breadcrumbs and dot with the remaining butter.

10 Bake for about 35 minutes or until the zucchini shells are tender and a light golden crust has formed on the top. If the top is still very pale, put the pan under a hot broiler for a minute. Serve warm or at room temperature.

✸ When I have time I like to prepare a dish consisting of stuffed vegetables: these zucchini, Eggplant Stuffed with Luganega, Pine Nuts and Raisins (page 96) and Stuffed Onion Cups (page 84). They make an attractive and delicious secondo, which can be preceded by Pasta with a Garlicky Béchamel (page 202) or Choux Pastry Gnocchi (page 141).

4 medium zucchini, about 6 inches long

salt

2 tablespoons unsalted butter

2 tablespoons olive oil

1 shallot, very finely chopped

3 amaretti, finely crumbled

¾ cup very fresh ricotta

2 teaspoons chopped fresh thyme *or* 1 teaspoon dried thyme

pinch of grated nutmeg

1 egg

freshly ground black pepper

dried breadcrumbs

NOTE: The whole dish can be prepared and baked in advance and lightly reheated, if you wish, in a medium oven for 5 minutes.

Torta salata di ricotta

RICOTTA, BASIL AND OLIVE TART • SERVES 6 TO 8

If there is a dish that epitomizes Italian cooking, it is this tart. All the more remarkable, therefore, that I should have been reminded of it recently when I was served it in London, beautifully prepared by an Englishwoman. This was in Hammersmith at the delightful River Café, where Ruthie Rodgers and her partner Rose Gray serve food as authentically northern Italian as you would eat in Milan. This is their recipe.

PASTRY

- 1 **cup and 3 tablespoons unbleached flour**
- 1 **teaspoon salt**
- 10 **tablespoons chilled unsalted butter**
- 1½ **tablespoons sparkling mineral water**

FILLING

- 2 **cups fresh basil**
- 1 **cup parsley, preferably flat-leaf**
- 2½ **cups fresh ricotta**
- ¼ **cup freshly grated parmesan**
- 3 **tablespoons extra-virgin olive oil**
- 1 **egg**
- 1 **egg yolk**

salt

pepper

- 12 **pitted black olives**

1 First make the pastry in the food processor. Put the flour and salt in the workbowl, add the butter, cut into small pieces, process until the mixture is crumbly, and then add enough cold mineral water to make a ball. Wrap the ball in plastic wrap and leave in the refrigerator for at least 30 minutes.

2 Preheat the oven to 400°F.

3 Remove the pastry from the refrigerator and press down into a 10-inch tart tin. Prick it in several places with a fork. Cover the bottom of the tart with a piece of wax paper and then spread some metal pastry beads or dried beans on the paper. Bake for 20 minutes.

4 While the tart is baking, roughly chop the basil and the parsley and put them in the bowl of the food processor with the ricotta, parmesan, olive oil, whole egg, egg yolk and salt and pepper. Process until well mixed, then transfer to a bowl.

5 Cut the olives into small pieces and add to the other ingredients in the bowl. Taste and add more salt and pepper if needed. Be careful with the salt, because the ricotta is slightly salty and the parmesan somewhat more so, and the mixture might well be seasoned enough without additional salt.

6 Remove the tart shell from the oven and turn the heat down to 350°F. Fill with the ricotta mixture and put back in the oven for 30 minutes or so, until the top is set. At the River Café the tart is served at room temperature, which is certainly the right way.

Rotolo di salsa di pomodoro con acciughe e ricotta
ROLLED SOUFFLE WITH TOMATO SAUCE, ANCHOVIES AND RICOTTA •
SERVES 6 TO 8

In this dish fresh, flavored ricotta is used to counterbalance the tomato sauce, which is spiced with anchovies. The recipe was given to me by Betsy Newell, who runs a cooking school in her home in London. Betsy is a very creative cook with a particular talent for combining elements from different cuisines. She is very familiar with Italian ingredients since she spends a part of the year in her beautiful old farmhouse in Chianti, and here a French rolled soufflé is filled with a classic Italian tomato sauce.

1 Soak the anchovies in milk for 30 minutes.

2 Prepare the tomato sauce by slowly sautéing the finely chopped onion in the olive oil. When it is very soft and slightly colored add the finely chopped garlic and continue to sauté for 1 more minute. Then add the tomatoes and cook slowly for about 30 minutes or more until they are well thickened and have slightly separated from the oil.

3 Lift the anchovy fillets out of the milk, chop them and stir into the tomato sauce. Season with a generous grinding of pepper. Taste and add salt and sugar (canned tomatoes can often be a little acid).

4 Meanwhile make a roux with the butter and the flour as described on page 4. Heat the milk until small bubbles form around the edges and whisk quickly into the roux to make a béchamel sauce. Bring to the boil and place the saucepan over a larger saucepan one-third full of hot water (or use a double boiler). Cook for 20 minutes, stirring occasionally. The water should just simmer. Keep a watch on it and add boiling water if necessary.

5 Butter a 12 × 14-inch jelly roll pan and line with parchment paper.

6 Preheat the oven to 350°F.

7 When the béchamel sauce has cooked, remove from the heat and stir in a little more than half of the parmesan. Then stir in the 5 egg yolks and the nutmeg. Taste for seasoning and add salt and pepper as needed.

8 Beat the egg whites to the meringue stage—stiff but not dry—and fold into the béchamel and egg mixture. Spread carefully and evenly over the prepared pan and bake for 10 to 12 minutes, or until just firm.

9 Lay a clean kitchen towel on the table and sprinkle with the remaining parmesan and the breadcrumbs.

FILLING

3 anchovy fillets
milk
1 medium onion, finely chopped
4 tablespoons olive oil
1 or 2 garlic cloves, peeled and very finely chopped
1¼ cups chopped canned Italian tomatoes
freshly ground black pepper
salt
pinch of sugar

ROLLED SOUFFLE

2 tablespoons unsalted butter
3 tablespoons flour
1¼ cups milk *or* half milk and half light cream
⅔ cup freshly grated parmesan
5 eggs, separated
pinch of grated nutmeg
salt
pepper
5 tablespoons fine breadcrumbs

———

½ cup ricotta
5 tablespoons finely chopped fresh parsley
4 or 5 scallions, green part only, finely chopped

(continued)

NOTE: You can prepare the soufflé and sauce up to Step 11 in advance, assemble it when you are ready and heat it in a hot (375°F.) oven.

10 When the soufflé is done, turn it over immediately onto the towel, remove the paper and allow to cool.

11 When you are ready to assemble the roulade, crumble the ricotta over the soufflé, then spread the tomato sauce all over, leaving a 1-inch margin all around. Sprinkle the chopped parsley and scallions evenly over the whole surface. Roll up carefully and place in the oven for 10 minutes or until heated through. Cut into ½-inch slices. Serve at once on warm plates.

Cassata siciliana nuda

RICOTTA CAKE • SERVES 8

4 hard-boiled eggs
2 cups fresh ricotta
⅔ cup sugar
1 teaspoon ground cinnamon
1 tablespoon rose water
1 tablespoon orange water
⅔ cup chopped angelica (1½ ounces)
¼ cup chopped candied peel (¼ pound)
3 candied cherries, chopped
2 tablespoons chopped shelled and skinned pistachio nuts
grated rind of 1 orange
grated rind of 1½ lemons
2 tablespoons maraschino liqueur or Grand Marnier
1 tablespoon (1 envelope) unflavored gelatin
1 cup heavy cream

NOTE: This cake should be eaten within 2 days.

The traditional Sicilian cassata has an outer layer of madeira cake covered with almond paste or sugar icing. Once when I was making this dish I didn't have time to make the madeira cake. So when I served my version to a friend from northern Italy who is married to a dyed-in-the-wool Sicilian, I was delighted when she said "Che bellezza (how lovely)! It's cassata, but you don't have to get through the boring outside layers before you come to the good part." Una cassata nuda (a naked cassata) in fact.

I had to alter the usual cassata siciliana recipe slightly in order to be able to unmold the cake. The result is, in fact, a hybrid, being part cassata siciliana and part Russian pashka. But it is a very successful hybrid.

Buy the candied peel in large pieces, not the chopped-up kind. You can keep it, well sealed, in the freezer. The best rose water and orange water is sold in Middle Eastern shops; neither is essential to the dish, but they give the right exotic flavor. The influence of Arabic cooking in Sicily is, after all, very important.

1 Shell the eggs and cut them in half. Scoop out the yolks, and set aside the whites for another meal (you can add them to any cooked vegetable salad). Puree the yolks through a food mill or sieve into a large bowl.

2 Sieve the ricotta into the bowl.

3 Beat in the sugar, cinnamon, rose water and orange water and then add the angelica, candied peel and cherries, pistachios, grated rind and the liqueur. Mix very thoroughly.

4 Put 3 tablespoons of hot water in a small saucepan and sprinkle the gelatin over it. Dissolve over very low heat,

but do not bring the liquid to the boil. Allow to cool while you butter an 8-inch springform pan and line it with wax paper.

5 Spoon a couple of tablespoons of the ricotta mixture into the gelatin and mix very thoroughly, then transfer this mixture into the bowl with the rest of the ricotta mixture. Fold very thoroughly. By first mixing the gelatin with a small amount of the mixture, you make sure that it is evenly distributed.

6 Whip the cream until it forms very soft peaks and then fold the mixture into it, a few tablespoons at a time. When the mixture is beautifully blended, spoon it into the prepared pan. Cover with plastic wrap and chill for at least 2 hours.

7 Remove the band and the paper from the side of the cassata. Place a large round dish over it and turn upside down to unmold the cake. Remove the metal base and the paper. Serve chilled.

Ricotta alla mentuccia

RICOTTA WITH MINT • SERVES 4

I am indebted to Massimo Alberini, the food historian, for having told me about this exceedingly pleasant way of eating good fresh ricotta. If you manage to find ricotta made with ewe's milk, use it in this way. The mint must be a sweet variety such as apple mint.

For 4 people you will need about 1½ cups of the best ricotta. Put it in a square or rectangular dish or pan and leave it in the coldest part of the refrigerator for about 2 hours and then cut it into 1-inch-thick slices. Lay the slices neatly on a dish and sprinkle with 2 tablespoons of brown sugar. Put back in the refrigerator for another hour. At the end the sugar will have partly dissolved and penetrated the surface of the ricotta. Meanwhile, chop a couple of handfuls of mint leaves. Scatter the mint over the ricotta slices before bringing to the table. Pass around more sugar, which I think is needed; it also gives a pleasant contrast of texture.

Fruits and Nuts

FRUITS AND ICE CREAM

Timballini di ciliegia al latte di mandorla
CHERRY TIMBALES WITH ALMOND MILK

Macedonia invernale di frutta
WINTER FRUIT SALAD

Fagiano all'uva
PHEASANT WITH GRAPES

Ossobuchi alla milanese
OSSO BUCO, MILANESE STYLE

Faraona arrosto al limone
ROAST GUINEA HEN WITH LEMON AND
GARLIC

La fugascina
ITALIAN SHORTBREAD

Melone al sugo di mela
MELON IN APPLE SYRUP

Pollo all'arancia
CHICKEN WITH ORANGE

Fragole all'arancia
STRAWBERRIES AND ORANGES

Scaloppine alla pesca
SAUTEED VEAL SCALOPPINE WITH PEACHES

Tacchina arrosto al sugo di melagrana
ROAST TURKEY WITH POMEGRANATE SAUCE

Gelato di crema alla vaniglia
VANILLA ICE CREAM

Gelato di crema all'aceto balsamico
VANILLA ICE CREAM WITH BALSAMIC
VINEGAR

Tazzine di crema all'aceto balsamico
CUSTARD WITH BALSAMIC VINEGAR

Gelato di frutta
FRUIT ICE CREAM

Spumone di zabaglione
ZABAGLIONE ICE CREAM

Sorbetto al limone
LEMON SORBET

NUTS

Latte di mandorla
ALMOND MILK

Torta di mandorle all'arancia
ALMOND AND ORANGE CAKE

Meringhine alle mandorle
ALMOND MERINGUES

Passato di castagne
CHESTNUT SOUP

Spuma di castagne
CHESTNUT MOUSSE

Involtini di pollo ripieni di nocciole, prosciutto e formaggio
CHICKEN BUNDLES STUFFED WITH HAZELNUTS, HAM AND CHEESE

Salsa di miele, noci e pinoli
HONEY, WALNUT AND PINE NUT SAUCE

Torta di noce alla crema di mascarpone
WALNUT CAKE WITH MASCARPONE CREAM

SEE ALSO

Aspic di pesche noci
NECTARINES IN WINE JELLY

Cassata siciliana nuda
RICOTTA CAKE

Filetto di maiale alla Cavalcanti
PORK TENDERLOIN WITH BERRIES, ALMONDS AND BALSAMIC VINEGAR

Finocchi del Corrado
FENNEL WITH PISTACHIO AND ANCHOVY SAUCE

Insalata di finocchio ed arancie
FENNEL AND ORANGE SALAD

Lattuga imbottita alla napoletana
STUFFED BIBB LETTUCE

Melanzane al limone
LEMON-FLAVORED EGGPLANT

Melanzane ripiene alla pugliese
EGGPLANT STUFFED WITH LUGANEGA, PINE NUTS AND RAISINS

Pizza alle sette sfoglie
PASTA CAKE

Prugne sciroppate al rosmarino
PLUMS IN WINE WITH ROSEMARY AND SPICES

Scaloppine al basilico e limone
VEAL SCALOPPINE WITH BASIL AND LEMON

Fruit

It is a great pleasure these days to drive around Romagna, a region which seems to be almost entirely devoted to the growing of fruit. At most times of the year one or another of the trees is either flowering or bearing fruit. Cherries, apricots, peaches, plums, apples and pears hang from loaded branches waiting to be gathered, inspected, put in boxes and sent all over Europe. Although so many different fruits grow in this orchard of Europe, other crops—some of them new—tend to be concentrated in particular areas. I was surprised recently to see plantations of persimmons, a fruit that was rare before the war, growing near Nocera, to the south of Naples. The fashionable explosion of the kiwi has resulted in acres of land in Venezia Giulia and Apulia being given over to the cultivation of this fruit, which was totally unknown in Italy until a decade or so ago. Citrus fruits and almonds thrive best in the south, while the cultivation of raspberries, currants and other soft fruits takes place mainly in the north. Grapes, of course, are grown everywhere. "Even the rocks were mantled with vines" was one of William Beckford's first impressions on arriving at Bolzano in the eighteenth century. In Venice he loved to look out his window on the Grand Canal at dawn to see the barges carrying loads of grapes, peaches and melons to the Rialto market, a sight still enjoyed by today's early riser.

It was also Beckford who remarked that in Italy, "all meals finish with several dishes of fruit," and this, too, has not changed in two hundred years. A meal nearly always ends with a bowl of seasonal fruit set in the middle of the table. Only on special occasions is fruit used to provide a different ending to the meal, usually as the flavoring for an ice cream or sorbet, or occasionally to flavor savory dishes. This was a practice much in use in the past and it is now being resuscitated by the chefs of the nuova cucina, who are turning to the past for new ideas.

In this chapter I have kept to the fruits that I connect particularly with Italy, fruits that I love for their taste and their looks and that are strongly redolent of the Mediterranean. There is one fruit, however, that I did not include even though it is one of my favorites—the fig. I think figs should be eaten where they grow, popped straight from the tree into the mouth, still warm from the sun. This is the best way to eat them, without any cream or anything else. The other acceptable thing to do with figs is to serve them with salami, prosciutto or coppa (cured pork shoulder), or a mixture of all three.

TIMBALES

Fruit timbales (timballini) are very easy to prepare, especially if you have the puree ready in the freezer. When a fruit is in season I poach quite a few pounds of it in red wine and then freeze it. You can make timballini with cherries, as in the recipe that follows, or with other fruit purees or with chestnuts. The flavoring liqueur can vary: amaretto is good with cherries and apricots. I use kirsch with plums, dark rum with chestnuts, these timballini being surrounded then with a rich chocolate sauce.

Another good combination is raspberry puree flavored with orange and lemon juice. For those timballini I make a sauce by pureeing two kiwis in a food processor together with about half a cup of unsweetened apple juice, one and a half tablespoons kirsch and three tablespoons confectioners' sugar.

Timballini di ciliegia al latte di mandorla
CHERRY TIMBALES WITH ALMOND MILK • MAKES 6 TIMBALLINI

1 Make the almond milk and set aside.

2 Prepare the cherry puree as described on page 186, put in a bowl and check sweetness, bearing in mind that you will add unsweetened cream later on. If the puree is not sweet enough, make a sugar syrup and add as much as you need.

3 Heat ½ cup of water. Sprinkle over the gelatin in a small bowl and set aside to dissolve.

4 Add 2 or 3 tablespoons of the fruit puree to the gelatin and mix very thoroughly. Spoon this mixture into the rest of the puree and mix until well incorporated. Add the amaretto and then chill until beginning to set.

5 Remove from the refrigerator and very thoroughly fold in the cream. Wet six ½-cup ramekins with cold water and fill with the mixture. Cover with plastic wrap and place in the refrigerator until set.

6 Unmold the timballini onto individual dessert plates by running a metal spatula around the sides and tapping the bottom. Spoon 2 or 3 tablespoons of almond milk around each one. Decorate with a cherry, if you have some whole ones, or with a peeled almond.

✖ This very attractive dessert can be served with some almond biscuits or amaretti.

1 cup almond milk (page 190)
2 cups sweetened coarse cherry puree (page 186)
1 tablespoon (1 envelope) unflavored gelatin
4 teaspoons amaretto
⅔ cup light cream
6 cherries *or* peeled almonds

Macedonia invernale di frutta
WINTER FRUIT SALAD • SERVES 4

In the depths of winter I sometimes long for a dessert made with fresh fruit. The only good fruit in season then is citrus fruit, which makes a delicious fruit salad. For this recipe you will also need one mango.

The use of pureed mango to dress the fruit salad takes its cue from the way orange juice is often used as a dressing for peaches. Mangoes and peaches, in fact, have strong similarities, a ripe mango being just as rich and fragrant as a peach, with an extra spicy taste which goes very well with the sharpness of citrus fruit.

(*continued*)

You can vary your choice of citrus fruits, but I find that kumquats and lemons are essential. Buy a ripe mango; it must be very soft to the touch.

3 oranges, preferably blood
   oranges
2 tangerines or clementines
12 kumquats (about ¼ pound)
1 pink grapefruit
2 lemons
4 tablespoons sugar
2 tablespoons Grand Marnier
1 mango

1 Peel the oranges to the flesh and then slice into thin rounds. Choose 6 of the best rounds and set aside. Cut the other slices into halves or quarters, according to their size, and put in a large bowl.

2 Peel the tangerines, divide into segments and remove all the pith. If you have the time (and the patience) remove the transparent skin as well. Set aside a few of the best segments and add the rest to the oranges in the bowl.

3 Scrub and wash the kumquats. Dry with paper towels and cut into thin rounds. Add to the bowl.

4 Peel the grapefruit, remove all pith and then skin the segments. Cut each segment in thirds and add to the bowl.

5 Scrub one of the lemons thoroughly and cut into very thin slices. Cut each slice into small triangles. Set aside a few of the best pieces and add the rest to the fruits in the bowl.

6 Squeeze the other lemon into a small bowl, add the sugar and the liqueur and mix well.

7 Peel the mango, cut it into chunks and put them into a blender or food processor. Add the lemon juice mixture and process at full speed until the mango is completely mashed.

8 Spoon the sauce over the fruit, cover the bowl with plastic and chill for at least 2 hours.

9 Pile the fruit salad up in a deep round dish, preferably a glass one. Decorate the border with the fruit you set aside. If your tangerines had leaves, wash the leaves and use a few here and there for decorations; they are very pretty. Or you might use a few sweet geranium leaves or lemon balm, if you still have some in the garden. Anything green looks good. If you are in a hurry, put the salad in a glass bowl and just lay the reserved fruit on top.

GRAPES

Grapes are one of Italy's principal crops. They are mostly used for wine making, but when they are in season a large bunch of table grapes will always top the fruit bowl, to be eaten as they are at the end of the meal.

In Abruzzi grapes are used with walnuts to make jam, while further south, in Apulia, vino cotto—literally, cooked wine—is made from grape juice that is boiled for a long time until it acquires the texture of thin honey. I also know of quite a few old recipes in which grapes are used in meat and fish dishes, and the following is one of the most successful of these.

Fagiano all' uva
PHEASANT WITH GRAPES • SERVES 3 TO 4

For years I cooked pheasant à la Milanaise, that is, en cocotte with a rich sauce of cream and spices. An excellent recipe, but one that makes a pheasant heavier than it would naturally be. Last year I was introduced to an interesting new way to prepare pheasant. New to me, I should say, since I ate this delicious pheasant in my cousins' home in Milan, and they told me that the recipe comes from the family's ricettario (recipe book) which had been kept by their grandmother who died during the war, aged nearly 85. An old Lombard recipe, therefore.

The combination of pheasant with grapes is a natural. Pheasants love grapes. I remember in Chianti, where we had a house for many years, the farmers used to shoo the pheasants away from the vines into the bushes. But the pheasants were so tame that after a few minutes they were back among the vines, pecking at the grapes.

It is such a natural combination that Bartolomeo Stefani, chef to the Gonzagas in the second half of the seventeenth century, prepared a fantastic dish based on this theme for the banquet Ottavio Gonzaga gave in honor of Queen Christina of Sweden. The roast pheasant, covered with marzipan, was laid with its head on the edge of the dish, where two putti made of butter were sitting. One was holding the pheasant's head while the other put grapes into its beak. But I must return to my nineteenth-century recipe.

The characteristic of this dish is a pronounced taste of grapes, sharpened by the cognac marinade. The pheasant, which finishes cooking cut up in the sauce, absorbs the grape flavor.

I prefer a plump hen pheasant to a cock pheasant; it is tastier and more tender, but being smaller it is not really enough for four people. Two hens make a perfect course for six.

(continued)

PHEASANT WITH GRAPES (continued)

½ pound muscat grapes
4 tablespoons cognac
1 pheasant with its giblets
4 tablespoons unsalted butter
salt
½ cup good meat stock
    (page 3)
pepper

NOTE: The grape I use is muscat, but any kind of full-flavored grape could be substituted.

NOTE: This dish can be prepared in advance up to Step 7.

1 Wash and dry the grapes and then peel them. A rather boring job, but quite easy if you buy ripe golden muscat grapes. Remove the seeds. (I have found that every cook has a special way of doing this. I remember that one of the most accomplished hostesses and cooks I know swore that the best tool, and the one that caused least damage to the grapes, was a hairpin. "Washed, of course," she hastened to add. I still prefer the point of a small knife.) Put the grapes in a bowl and sprinkle with 1 tablespoon of the cognac. Leave to marinate for 2 hours.

2 Preheat the oven to 400°F.

3 Cut the wing tips off the pheasant. Wipe inside and out with paper towels and singe off any stubborn feather shafts. Put the liver, heart and gizzard inside the bird together with a knob of butter and 2 pinches of salt. Truss the bird with string. Set aside half of the rest of the butter and rub the remainder all over the bird. Sprinkle with salt.

4 Choose a roasting pan with a heavy base that you can put on direct heat. Lay the bird in the pan, breast down. This will prevent the breast from becoming dry since the juices will flow downward. Cook in the oven for 10 minutes and then turn the bird over and cook for another 10 to 15 minutes, by which time the breast will be brown.

5 Melt the remaining butter in a small saucepan. Pour a little of the melted butter over the pheasant and sprinkle with a little of the cognac at intervals during the cooking. I use a bulb baster.

6 Remove the pheasant from the oven and cut into small pieces at the joints. Don't worry if the pheasant is still bloody, as it is going to have a second cooking. Discard the liver, heart and gizzard.

7 Put the pieces back into a cooler oven (350°F.) for 10 minutes, or until the pheasant is cooked to your taste, turning once during the cooking. Remove them from the pan, set aside and cover it.

8 Drain the grapes. Put the pan on the heat and deglaze the cooking juices with the stock and the grape marinade. Add the pepper. Reduce over high heat while scraping the pan with a metal spoon, until the gravy is rich and syrupy. Taste and check salt and pepper.

10 Turn the heat to low and return the pheasant to the pan.

11 Heat the remaining cognac in a ladle. Set fire to it and pour it, flaming, over the pheasant.

12 When the flames have died transfer the pheasant to a

warm dish, arranging it in its original shape. Scatter the grapes on top and serve.

I have always served polenta with game. This dish, like Roast Turkey with Pomegranate Sauce (page 181), needs fried or grilled polenta, rather than polenta that has just been made, since the juice is fruity and light. If you do not like polenta, put some large croutons around. The best accompanying vegetables are either a puree of celery root, some braised Belgian endive or braised celery. I also like grated carrots, which I cook in butter and stock and finish off with a little cream and a pinch of grated nutmeg or ground coriander. A good soup to precede this dish is Chestnut Soup (page 193). Chestnuts are in season just when pheasant is plentiful. If you prefer a more solid beginning, try Tagliatelle with Mascarpone (page 146) or Stuffed Reginette (page 21).

LEMONS

I feel totally lost when I discover I haven't got a single lemon in the house. Like onions and garlic, lemons are essential to my cooking, as they are for all Italians.

Lemons play a larger part in Italian cooking than any other fruit. Grated lemon rind is added to many meat dishes, to poultry and vegetable stuffings, to most cakes and cookies, to fruit compotes, custards and creams. The juice is used as a condiment in salads and in sweet and savory sauces, and it is added to fish and meat dishes. One of the most succulent ways to cook a chicken is to rub it hard with lemon and then put another lemon, cut in half, perhaps with some garlic, into the cavity. And I always rub a rabbit with half a lemon before I cook it. When I heat mussels or clams to take them out of their shells, I put one or two lemons, cut in wedges, at the bottom of the pan; the lemon imparts flavor to the shellfish. Two recipes with lemons that have recently become fashionable are for tagliatelle and risotto. You will find the recipe for risotto on page 27. The tagliatelle is easily made, then simply dressed with a little sauce made with butter, cream and lemon juice.

I always splash raspberries, strawberries and all other soft fruit with lemon juice to emphasize their flavor (except when I am feeling extravagant and use balsamic vinegar). The same flavor-enhancing effect is produced by adding a tablespoon or two of lemon juice to a fruit puree or juice prepared for ice creams and sorbets. The lemon juice also helps to prevent crystals from forming. Any fruit salad is improved by being splashed with lemon juice an hour or so before serving, while tropical fruits and pomegranates need it even more to compensate for the lack of flavor of the ones you can buy.

When you slice apples and pears, when you prepare artichokes or Jerusalem artichokes or cardoons, rub the cut parts with half a lemon to prevent discoloration. Rub your hands, too, to prevent them being blackened before you start preparing these or any other vegetables. Never throw away halves of lemon; keep them at the sink to whiten your hands, to strengthen your nails and to cleanse them of any unpleasant smell.

You will be able to squeeze more juice out of a lemon if, before you cut it in half, you pour boiling water over it and leave it for a couple of minutes. It will also help to roll it backwards and forwards on the work surface to soften it. If, however, you only want a few drops of juice, do not cut the lemon in half, but pierce it with a toothpick in two or three places and squeeze. Enough juice will come out.

The list of domestic virtues of lemons, apart from the culinary ones, seems endless. In Italy we use them to remove spots from silver and marble, to shine patent leather shoes and to clean bronze and copper. Girls still make packs soaked with lemon juice to clear their complexions; middle-aged women cover their faces with lemon slices to rejuvenate the skin. I still remember once before a party, a friend and I squeezed a drop of lemon juice into our eyes in the mistaken belief that it would make them sparkle! Instead, we arrived late at the party, after lying down with absorbent cotton soaked in boric acid over our stinging eyes. Even longer is the list of things a lemon is said to do for your health, from eradicating corns to relieving the pain of wasp stings. When we had hiccups as children, we were given a tablespoon of lemon juice to drink, which was worse than the hiccups. The shock usually did the trick.

When you buy lemons choose the largest you can find. Go for the softer, yet full ones with a smooth skin.

My final word is one of warning about the use of the rind of most lemons available nowadays. Lemons, like all other citrus fruits, are heavily sprayed with fungicides and pesticides, which penetrate their skin. They are also waxed. Whenever you want to use the rind, even if you only want to put a little slice into a drink, you must scrub the fruit thoroughly. I use baking soda and water. Other people use salt, or vinegar and water, or household soap and water. Organically grown lemons should be all right, but I still scrub them.

- -

Ossobuchi alla milanese
OSSO BUCO, MILANESE STYLE • SERVES 4

Two important characteristics distinguish a Milanese osso buco from other versions of this dish. First, it is flavored with lemon rind, which is incorporated in a sauce called a gremolada, and second, it is cooked in bianco, without tomato. To some extent one explains the other, since the flavor of the gremolada would be swamped by a tomato-based sauce. Another good reason for excluding tomatoes is that ossobuchi alla milanese is eaten with risotto alla milanese, and this delicate saffron-flavored risotto could not survive alongside an osso buco with a strong tomato flavor. As a loyal Milanese who strives to defend our highly sophisticated cuisine from the intrusion of foreign flavors, I can do no better than quote from the great nineteenth-century food writer, Artusi: "This is a dish that should be left to the Milanese, since it is a specialty of the Lombard cuisine."

When you eat osso buco, don't forget to scoop out the marrow inside the bone. Nowadays, alas, very few households have that irreplaceable tool of days gone by, the marrow spoon, but an effective, if less gracious, substitute is the handle of a demitasse spoon. All too often I see people in restaurants leaving the marrow in the bone, which seems such a waste of the best part.

Osso buco should be cut from the middle of the shin where the bone is surrounded by meat.

1 Tie each piece of osso buco around and across as you would a little package. Choose a heavy sauté pan, with a tight-fitting lid, large enough to hold the pieces in a single layer. Heat the oil, and meanwhile lightly coat the pieces with some flour in which you have mixed some salt.

2 Brown the pieces on both sides and then remove to a side dish.

3 Add 2 tablespoons butter to the sauté pan together with the onion and the celery. Sprinkle with a little salt, which will help the onion get soft without browning.

4 When the vegetables are soft, return the meat to the pan along with the juices that have accumulated.

5 Heat the wine and pour over the meat. Turn the heat up and reduce by half.

6 Heat the stock in the pan you used to heat the wine and pour about three-quarters of it over the osso buco. Turn the heat down to very low and cover the pan. Cook for 1½ to 2 hours, until the meat begins to come away from the bone. Carefully turn the pieces every 20 minutes or so, taking care not to damage the marrow in the bone. If necessary add more stock during the cooking. If by the time the meat is cooked the sauce is too thin, remove the meat from the pan and reduce the liquid by boiling briskly.

7 Transfer the osso buco to a heated dish and remove the strings. Keep warm in a warm oven (200°F).

8 Cut the remaining butter into 3 or 4 pieces and add gradually to the sauce. As soon as the butter is melted, remove from the heat, as the sauce should not boil.

9 Mix the grated lemon rind, chopped garlic and parsley together for the gremolada and stir into the sauce. Spoon the sauce over the osso buco and serve at once.

✄ The traditional accompaniment is risotto alla milanese, often called risotto giallo (yellow risotto). Osso buco needs no other accompaniment. A salad would be nice, and if you want a first course, a vegetable dish such as Fennel Timbale (page 101) or Baked Zucchini in Tomato Sauce (page 47).

3 pounds meaty veal shanks, sawed into pieces 1½ inches thick
2 tablespoons olive oil
flour for dusting
salt
3 tablespoons butter
1 small onion, finely chopped
½ celery stalk, finely chopped
⅔ cup dry white wine
1¼ cups meat stock (page 3)
freshly ground black pepper

GREMOLADA

1 teaspoon grated lemon rind
½ garlic clove, peeled and very finely chopped
1 tablespoon chopped fresh parsley, preferably flat-leaf

NOTE: You can prepare the dish in advance through Step 6 and then re-heat it later.

Faraona arrosto al limone
ROAST GUINEA HEN WITH LEMON AND GARLIC • SERVES 4

The Sicilian origins of this recipe can be seen in the liberal use of that island's most plentiful fruit, the lemon. It is certainly one of the most delicious ways I know to prepare a guinea hen.

The guinea hen is roasted in foil, and then it is cut up and lightly sautéed in olive oil, lemon juice and lots of garlic. The sharp taste of the lemon is counterbalanced by the richness of the oil and the piquancy of the garlic. The result is a beautifully clean and fragrant taste.

1 guinea hen, about
  2¾ pounds
2 tablespoons unsalted butter
salt, preferably coarse salt
6 tablespoons olive oil
8 garlic cloves, peeled and
  bruised
⅔ cup lemon juice
grated rind of 1 lemon
freshly ground black pepper

NOTE: Scrub the lemon thoroughly with water and vinegar or baking soda before you grate the rind.

1 Preheat the oven to 400°F.

2 Wash the bird thoroughly in cold water, inside and out. Put it on a tilted board and allow to drain for about 10 minutes. Dry well inside and out with paper towels.

3 Push the butter between the skin and the flesh of the breast and drumsticks of the bird. Make small incisions in the thighs of the bird and push small knobs of butter into the cuts. Rub a liberal amount of salt all over the guinea hen, pressing it into the flesh with your hands. Also put some salt in the cavity and rub it in.

4 Wrap the guinea hen in foil. Place the wrapped bird in a roasting pan and roast for 1 hour.

5 Remove the pan from the oven and cut open the foil. Allow to cool a little and then cut the guinea hen into small pieces and collect all the juices in a bowl.

6 Heat the oil with the garlic cloves and then add the guinea hen pieces. Fry them for 5 minutes on both sides. Splash with the lemon juice and add the lemon rind. Season with salt and lots of pepper and cook for another 3 minutes, turning over once or twice.

7 Transfer to a serving dish and keep warm. Remove and discard the garlic.

8 Pour the cooking juices into the pan and bring to the boil. Cook briskly for about 1 minute and then taste and check seasoning. Spoon the sauce all over the hen.

✄ This dish is excellent served surrounded by a pile of tagliolini dressed with fresh unsalted butter and plenty of black pepper. A good beginning to the meal would be Stuffed Bibb Lettuce (page 86) or Spaghettini with Olive Puree, Anchovies and Capers (page 232).

La fugascina
ITALIAN SHORTBREAD • MAKES 40 COOKIES

Fugascina is a dialect name for small focaccia, the dialect being that of the province of Novara. This recipe was given to me by a friend, Grazia Lucchese, who makes fugascina and torta di mele (apple cake) for the saint's day of her village, Germagno, high above Lake Orta. When I asked her when the saint's day was, she answered, "Oh, c'é n'è uno al mese. Se non c'è, lo si inventa." (There's one a month. And if there isn't one, we invent it.) The children carry all the offerings of food in procession to the church, where, after the mass, the food is auctioned for the church charities. Grazia was very proud that her fugascina was recently knocked down for 40,000 lire, about $30. A stratospheric price, you will agree, when you read the recipe.

Fugascina is traditionally flavored with grated lemon rind, which is the most common flavoring in cakes all over Italy. I sometimes substitute a tablespoon of vinsanto or marsala for the lemon rind, for instance when I serve these cookies with Chestnut Mousse (page 194).

3 cups all-purpose flour
10 tablespoons unsalted butter, cut into small pieces
pinch of salt
¾ cup sugar
2 egg yolks
grated rind of 1 lemon, very thoroughly scrubbed
oil for greasing

1 Combine the flour, butter, salt, sugar, egg yolks and lemon rind and make the pastry, either by hand or in the food processor.

2 Lightly oil the *underside* of a large cookie sheet. I use peanut oil because it has a high burning point. The reason for oiling the underside will be apparent when you read on.

3 Put the ball of pastry on the oiled side of the tray and spread it out with the palm of your hand. Then, to spread it more evenly and more thinly, roll it with a small bottle filled with hot water. It should be rolled to a thickness of ⅛ inch. Make lines with the blunt edge of a knife to mark the shape of the cookies; traditionally they are made into 2-inch squares. Chill the tray for 30 minutes.

4 Heat the oven to 375°F.

5 Bake the fugascina in the preheated oven for about 15 minutes until dark gold.

6 Now comes the reason for using the underside of the tray. Stretch a thick cotton thread to the width of the tray, place it between the tray and the fugascina and, keeping it taught, pull it along the length of the tray, thus separating the fugascina from the tray. Had you used the top of the tray, the raised lip would have made this operation impossible.

7 Cut through the marked lines, and when the shortbread has cooled just a little, put it on a wire rack.

(continued)

ITALIAN SHORTBREAD
(*continued*)

✂ In Italy these cookies, often dunked in vin santo, in tea or in caffè latte, are eaten when one feels a little hungry. I find that, with their buttery taste, they are also perfect as a little accompaniment to any mousse.

MELON

"Three things in life are difficult: picking a good wife, choosing a good horse and buying a good melon." Thus wrote Franceso Sforza, Duke of Milan, in the fifteenth century. And to buy a good melon is just as difficult in the twentieth century. To look at a melon tells you nothing. If it has a scent, that is a good sign, although there are some delicious melons with no smell at all until they are opened. A good melon should be heavy; when you buy a melon, take two equal sized ones, put one in each hand and go for the heavier.

The melons of Italy are the napoletano, a yellow green melon, oval in shape with bright orange flesh, and the well-known cantaloupe. In Italy, melons are usually eaten with prosciutto or with a lovely dish of cured meats (page 70). It is probably the best marriage for a good melon. Melons "should always be eaten at the beginning of the meal followed by a glass of good wine," wrote Platina in the fifteenth century. But I find that when good and sweet they also go well at the end of a meal, as in the following recipe.

Melone al sugo di mela
MELON IN APPLE SYRUP • SERVES 4

I had this dish at dinner with our friend Mary Trevelyan. Mary is a natural cook, almost as creative with her pots and pans as she is with her paint brushes. She "invented" this melon salad just before we arrived, and brought it to the table in one of her beautiful pottery bowls. There is nothing particularly Italian about the recipe except that for me good melons, full of flavor, bring back such strong memories of blue skies, hot sun and heady Mediterranean smells. But this recipe is not here just to indulge my nostalgia, it is also one of the finest ways to end a meal.

For 4 people you will need 1 large fragrant ripe melon, or 2 smaller ones. Discard the skin and seeds and cut the melon into small cubes. Make a syrup with 1 cup of unsweetened apple juice and some sugar. The quantity of sugar needed depends on the sweetness of the melon, the sharpness of the apple juice and, of course, your personal taste. Heat the syrup until the sugar has dissolved. I add a little lemon juice to give the salad a slight edge. Pour the syrup, slightly cooled, over the melon no more than 1 hour before serving; serve well chilled. You will love it.

ORANGES

Once some years ago, I was in an orange grove in Sicily, and it struck me how much less attractive a place it must have been before the Saracens invaded the island over a thousand years ago. The air in the groves was still and heavy with the scent of the white blossoms, while every now and then there was a tree still spangled with bright oranges hanging among the dark green leaves. The Saracens first brought the orange tree to Sicily; it was the Citrus aurantium or bitter orange, grown for use as a flavoring rather than for eating as a fruit.

The orange soon became the symbol of riches and opulence, so much so that the Medicis incorporated it in their coat of arms: the five golden balls are oranges. John McPhee, in his book *Oranges,* describes a banquet given by the Archbishop of Milan in 1529. ". . . a sixteen-course dinner that included caviar and oranges fried with sugar and cinnamon, brill and sardines with slices of orange and lemon, one thousand oysters with pepper and oranges, lobster salad with citrons, sturgeon in aspic covered with orange juice, fried sparrows with oranges, individual salads containing citrons into which the coat of arms of the diner had been carved, orange fritters, a soufflé full of raisins and pine nuts and covered with sugar and orange juice, five hundred fried oysters with lemon slices, and candied peels of citrons and oranges."

Nowadays the bitter orange is not cultivated for culinary use—Italians do not make marmalade (a great failing). It is grown as a dec-orative tree, or for the extraction of oil. If you are in Rome in winter, go to the Giardino degli Aranci, the orange-tree garden on the Avellino hill. You will enjoy an hour of utter peace while admiring Rome at your feet and gathering windfall oranges for your marmalade.

The Citrus sinensis, the sweet orange, arrived much later. It was introduced to Europe, via India, by the Portuguese. It began to appear in eighteenth-century books under the name of arancia del Portogallo and continued to be referred to by that name as late as the nineteenth century. At first, sweet oranges were only used for making drinks; these were very expensive, and only wealthy people could quench their thirst with a glass of orange juice. By the beginning of the nineteenth century, however, sweet oranges were widely grown in Sicily and southern Italy, and the orange became the popular fruit it is today.

HOW TO BUY AND PREPARE OR-ANGES. Today oranges are the world's most widely cultivated fruit. There is a vast number of varieties, among which the Sicilian Tarocco and Sanguinello are the most highly regarded in Europe. These are certainly my favorites, sweet yet with just enough acidity to make your tongue tingle. Another of my favorites is the late-season Spanish blood orange, small and juicy and brimming with the perfect orange flavor. Your favorite variety might also be from Spain, or it might be from Jaffa, this orange being one of the largest and best-looking oranges, although I find its flavor rather uninteresting. More likely, though, it will come from California or Florida.

When you buy oranges, look for bright, unbruised and shiny ones, not so shiny, though, that they have obviously been heavily waxed for preservation. The best oranges are barely soft to the touch, yet full and heavy, all characteristics that mean they are juicy. To get more juice out of an orange, pour boiling water over it; it will also help if you roll it backwards and forwards on a hard surface.

Gone, alas, are the days when you could use the skin of an orange without first washing it. You must scrub it with a stiff brush to get rid of the pesticides and fungicides that are sprayed on citrus fruits. Some people scrub them with soap (use household soap), others use a vinegar and water solution. I use bicarbonate of soda and water to make an abrasive yet tasteless paste. Whenever I can, I buy untreated oranges to make candied orange peel.

HOW TO MAKE CANDIED PEEL. Candied peel is easy enough to make and is so much nicer than any you can buy. It is a necessary ingredient in many traditional Italian sweets. Cassata siciliana, zuccotto from Florence, Sienese panforte, panettone from Milan . . . none would be what they are without citron, orange and lemon peel cut into juicy pieces.

Remove the peel of the oranges—lemons and grapefruits are excellent too—in neat segments (the white pith should be left on; it is deliciously bitter and it contains riboflavin, which is good for you.) Plunge into boiling water and boil until tender. Drain and refresh under cold running water, then boil again in fresh water for another 15 minutes or so to get rid of all the bitterness. Make a syrup of 2 parts sugar and 1 part water. Add the peel and simmer until all the syrup has been absorbed. Spread the peel on oiled trays, or trays lined with parchment paper, and dry in a very low oven with the door ajar, turning the pieces over every now and then. When the peel is dry, sprinkle it with sugar and store in an airtight jar.

Pollo all'arancia

CHICKEN WITH ORANGE • SERVES 4

Although I cannot remember exactly how, when or where this dish came into my repertoire, I am sure it resulted from my wish to be able to enjoy the taste of poultry and orange more often. Duck is something of a special treat, but chicken puts little strain on the purse.

Orange and celery, although so different, have highly complementary flavors. Scrub the orange thoroughly before you grate it.

4 chicken breasts, boned and skinned and cut in half (1¼ to 1½ pounds)

1 Put the chicken breasts in a dish, add the orange juice, celery leaves, scallion pieces, peppercorns and ½ teaspoon of salt and leave for at least 1 hour, turning the breasts over once or twice.

2 Chop the celery and the white parts of the scallions and put in a nonstick frying pan with the butter. Turn the heat up slowly, and as soon as the butter has melted, add a pinch of salt. Stir well and cover the vegetables with a piece of buttered parchment paper and a lid. Cook over low heat for 10 minutes, keeping a watch on the pan and stirring occasionally. If the vegetables are turning golden, which they shouldn't for this dish, add a couple of tablespoons of vegetable stock or water.

3 Lift the chicken from the marinade and add to the pan. Cook gently for about 2 minutes on each side.

4 Strain the marinade and pour over the chicken. Cover the pan and cook, over gentle heat, until the breasts are done, about 15 minutes. Transfer to a plate and keep warm.

5 Add the fruit juices and grated orange rind to the pan and boil for 1 minute. Add the cream, stirring the whole time, and a few grindings of pepper. Scoop into the pan all the juices from the chicken breasts, mix well and then return the chicken to the pan for a final cooking of 2 or 3 minutes, to blend all the flavors. Taste the sauce and adjust seasonings. Place the chicken on a heated dish and spoon the sauce over it.

✄ As an accompaniment, my choice would be spinach sautéed in butter, which goes so well with the orange flavor of the sauce, or the Sautéed Potato and Zucchini Sticks (page 211), steamed, though, rather than sautéed. This delicate yet tasty dish can be preceded by Stuffed Reginette (page 21), Baked Polenta with Porcini (page 36) or a creamy vegetable risotto (pages 30 and 90).

MARINADE

juice of 1 orange
a few celery leaves
4 scallions, green parts only, cut into short pieces
4 peppercorns, bruised
salt

___

4 or 5 small tender celery stalks, from the heart
4 scallions, white parts only
3 tablespoons unsalted butter
salt
juice of ½ lemon
juice of 1 orange
grated rind of 1 orange
½ cup heavy cream
freshly ground black pepper

NOTE: The dish can be prepared in advance up to Step 5. Keep the chicken in the pan and reheat before you finish the dish.

Fragole all'arancia

STRAWBERRIES AND ORANGES • SERVES 6

In this recipe the fragrance of the strawberries is intensified by the sharpness of the citrus fruits and the wine. With its clean fresh taste, this is the perfect finale to a meal when strawberries are in season.

2 **large oranges**
1 **pint strawberries (1 pound)**
4 **tablespoons sugar**
juice of 1 **lemon**
⅓ **cup sweet white wine, such as moscato**
1 or 2 **sprigs of fresh mint or lemon balm**

NOTE: If moscato wine is not available, use a French Sauternes or Barsac instead.

1 Peel the oranges to the quick and cut into thin slices. Put aside a few of the best slices for decoration, and cut the other slices in half, or quarters if very large. Put these slices in a glass bowl.

2 Rinse the strawberries very quickly under cold water and then hull them. Cut large strawberries in two, or in quarters, and add to the orange slices in the bowl.

3 Put the sugar and ½ cup water in a small saucepan and heat slowly until the sugar has dissolved. Raise the heat and boil for 5 minutes. Remove from the heat and let cool.

4 Add the lemon juice and the wine to the syrup. Mix well and pour over the fruit. Cover the bowl with plastic wrap and refrigerate for about 1 hour. Do not leave in the refrigerator for much longer than an hour or the strawberries will macerate too much. Place the reserved orange slices on the top before bringing the bowl to the table and decorate with 1 or 2 sprigs of fresh mint or lemon balm.

PEACHES

The peach is a native of China, where its fruit and flowers were regarded as sacred. It reached ancient Rome via Persia, hence the botanical name prunus persica, and in due course the Romans introduced the peach tree throughout their empire. During the Renaissance, peaches, like all fruit, were often used in savory dishes. They were appreciated for their beauty as well as for their flavor, often forming part of the elaborate table decorations that were a feature of Renaissance banquets. Francesco Berni, a Tuscan poet of the sixteenth century, paid this tribute to the peach.

> Oh frutta sopra l'altre egregia, eletta,
> Utile dalla scorza infino all'osso,
> L'alma e la carne tua sia benedetta!

Which might be translated as:

> Oh noble fruit, chosen above all others,
> To be enjoyed from the skin through to the bone,
> May your soul and your flesh be blessed.

I agree. Peaches (good ones, at least) are the most beautiful and the most delicious of all fruits. The greatest delight among peaches are the small pesche da vigna, so called because, in the days before concrete posts, they grew on the trees that were used to support the vines. These small white peaches ripen late, at the same time as the grapes, and their flavor has been intensified by a full summer of hot sun. They are covered with a gray-green down and their flesh is vermilion all through to the pit. They are rare now. Another variety which became comparatively rare, but seems to be making a comeback, is the white peach, so much more succulent than the usual yellow peach.

We have to eat what the growers and distributors want us to eat, but it is often hard to enjoy these yellow peaches as a good peach should be enjoyed—eaten as it is, in its skin.

Some yellow peaches are better stewed, or macerated in wine or in lemon and orange juice and sugar, sometimes mixed with the last strawberries of the season. You can ripen them a little more by keeping them for a day or two on a sunny windowsill. Some people keep them in the fridge once they are ripe. I am against this because their flavor, instead of developing, is deadened. Nor do I like chilled fruit.

The nectarine is a variety of peach, but with smooth rather than downy skin. In Italian it is called *pesca noce* (walnut peach), perhaps because of its shape. Nectarines have become more popular in recent years, but in my view they can never compare in taste with a good peach.

Most good, ripe peaches peel easily. It is easier to peel peaches and nectarines if you first plunge them in boiling water for 20 seconds and then refresh them straightaway in cold water.

Scaloppine alla pesca
SAUTEED VEAL SCALOPPINE WITH PEACHES • SERVES 4

While I was researching *Gastronomy of Italy* I came across many recipes from the past in which fruit was added to meat or fish. In Italy this combination disappeared altogether during the nineteenth and twentieth centuries, and was even wrongly considered foreign. Now, however, it is slowly creeping back.

I was inspired by some of these old recipes, and this is one of the results. The dish is as pretty as it is delicious. I always prefer to bring a dish to the table, in the old-fashioned way, and let my guests help themselves, rather than produce beautifully arranged individual plates, restaurant-style. I arrange the peaches neatly in the middle of a round dish and surround them with the meat. If you have a pretty oval dish, you can lay the peaches along one side, fanlike, with the meat alongside.

This dish has to be made just before serving. For preparing and frying scaloppine, see the introduction to the recipe Veal Scaloppine with Basil and Lemon (page 210).

(*continued*)

SAUTEED VEAL SCALOPPINE WITH PEACHES *(continued)*

- 1 tablespoon olive oil
- 4 tablespoons unsalted butter
- 2 fresh sage leaves *or* a pinch of dried sage
- 1 pound veal scaloppine, thinly sliced and cut into neat rectangles
- flour
- salt
- pepper
- 2 large yellow peaches, peeled
- 1 teaspoon sugar
- 4 tablespoons dry white wine

1 Heat the oil and half the butter with the sage in a sauté pan large enough to contain the meat in a single layer. If necessary, use two pans, adding an extra little knob of butter to each pan.

2 As soon as the butter begins to foam, coat the scaloppine with flour and shake to shed the excess. Add the pieces of meat to the pan, but do not crowd them.

3 Brown the veal for 1 minute on each side and then remove the pan from the heat and set aside. Sprinkle with salt and pepper.

4 Heat the rest of the butter in another frying pan.

5 Cut the peaches in half and then into ½-inch slices. Add to the hot butter and sauté for 1 minute, turning them over very gently.

6 Sprinkle with sugar, splash with wine and let it bubble for 1 minute. Remove the peaches and lay them neatly on a heated serving dish.

7 Boil the cooking juices of the peaches until there are only 2 tablespoons left and then pour over the meat. Heat for 1 more minute, turning the meat over twice in the juice.

8 Taste, adjust seasoning and transfer to the serving dish. Serve at once.

One of the best vegetables to serve with this delicate dish is French beans, either steamed or boiled until just cooked (but not half raw!). An excellent alternative is grated carrots sautéed for 5 minutes in butter and flavored with a pinch of powdered cardamom. The combination of peaches and carrots was first pointed out to me by Frances Bissel, one of my favorite food writers. In a recipe which appeared in one of her first articles in *The Times* (London) as its cookery editor, 1 or 2 peaches are blended with carrots, scallions and cardamom to make a delicious and refreshing soup.

The veal could be preceded by Tagliatelle with Mascarpone (page 146) or by Risotto with Lemon (page 27).

POMEGRANATES

Although pomegranates are rarely used in Italian cooking, the fruit does appear in a few dishes from Venice because of its former trade with the Middle East. Here is one of them.

Tacchina arrosto al sugo di melagrana
ROAST TURKEY WITH POMEGRANATE SAUCE • SERVES 12

Stuffing a turkey with apples and lemon gives the meat a delicious sharp taste, emphasized by the pomegranate juice and liver sauce. This recipe works best when made with a young hen turkey, no more than 10 pounds.

1 Preheat the oven to 375°F.

2 Wash the turkey inside and out and dry very well.

3 Sprinkle the bird generously inside and out with salt and pepper. Pierce 1 lemon with a skewer in many places, stick it with the cloves and place inside the bird. Also put the apples and 3 tablespoons of the butter in the cavity.

4 Rub 2 tablespoons of the remaining butter all over the turkey. Cover the breast with the pancetta, tie it in place and truss the turkey. Put it in a roasting pan, breast down, add the stock and roast in the oven for about 3½ hours, basting every 20 minutes or so.

5 While the turkey is cooking, prepare the sauce. Cut the pomegranates in half and squeeze them. Strain through a metal sieve and press the seeds with a metal spoon to extract all the juice. Squeeze the remaining lemon and strain the juice into the pomegranate juice.

6 Pour half the fruit juices over the turkey halfway through the cooking.

7 Clean the turkey liver and heart, wash and dry thoroughly and chop or cut into tiny pieces.

8 A quarter of an hour before the turkey is cooked, remove the pancetta and the string. Put the turkey back in the hot oven to brown the breast.

9 When the bird is ready, transfer to a heated dish and place it back in the oven with the heat turned off and the

1 fresh turkey, 10 pounds or less if possible, with giblets

salt

freshly ground black pepper

2 lemons

3 cloves

4 apples, peeled and cut into small pieces

8 tablespoons (1 stick) unsalted butter

½ pound pancetta or unsmoked streaky bacon, sliced thin (about 1/16 inch)

½ cup meat stock (page 3)

3 large pomegranates or 4 small ones

2 tablespoons brandy

(continued)

ROAST TURKEY WITH POMEGRANATE SAUCE (*continued*)

oven door slightly open. The turkey must cool a little, so that the juices penetrate the meat.

10 Heat 2 tablespoons of the butter in a small saucepan, add the liver and the heart and sauté gently for 1 minute, stirring constantly. Heat the brandy in a soup ladle until it is nearly boiling. Pour the brandy into the pan and put a flame to it. Let the brandy burn away and when the flame has subsided, add the rest of the fruit juices.

11 Skim all the fat off the turkey cooking liquid and then add to the liver sauce. Boil to concentrate the flavor until rich and syrupy. Add the remaining butter a little at a time, while swirling the pan. When all the butter has been incorporated, taste and adjust the seasonings. Pour the sauce into a heated sauceboat and serve separately (if you do not like bits in your sauce, pour it through a strainer).

12 Bring the turkey to the table for all to admire and carve. When you serve the turkey don't forget to put a small amount of the apple stuffing on each plate. It is a perfect accompaniment to the turkey and complements the sauce.

I serve this turkey with grilled or toasted polenta. Vegetables served with it must be delicate and unobtrusive: steamed snow peas or braised carrots are ideal, otherwise serve a bowl of green salad on side plates or afterwards.

A light soup such as Passatelli (page 50) would be a perfect primo, as would Stuffed Zucchini Mantua Style, (page 156), which you could prepare in advance and serve at room temperature.

ICE CREAM

The best end-use for the fruits I have been writing about, apart from eating them on their own, is to convert them into ice cream or sorbet, something at which the Italians excel.

It seems that the very first sorbets were made by the Saracens, and that after they invaded Sicily in the ninth century A.D. the Sicilians improved on the techniques they learned from their Arab masters. Little is known about how these early sorbets developed in the succeeding centuries, and it is not until 1595 that we come across the next milestone in the history of ice cream. In that year Bernardo Buontalenti, architect, sculptor, painter, poet and inventor, is said to have created an ice cream dish for the dinner given by the Grand Duke Ferdinand I on the inauguration of the Belvedere Fortress in Florence.

Buontalenti was the first to add milk and egg white to fruit juice, the mixture to be beaten at length in a machine it is thought he invented, a machine that remained more or less the same for the next two hundred years. It was much the same machine as the one I remember in our kitchen in Via Gesù in Milan, a wooden bucket containing a cylinder into which the mixture was poured. Snow or ice mixed with a lot of salt was packed around the cylinder. My brother and I took turns cranking the handle. It took ages, or so it seemed, and was a boring job made bearable only by the prospect of our reward.

The oft-repeated, but never proved, story Caterina de' Medici's cooks served it at her wedding feast seems most unlikely, the more so when one considers that Buontalenti—supposedly the inventor of modern ice cream—was only three in 1533 when Caterina married the future Henry II. There is, in fact, no certain indication that ice cream spread to the rest of Europe until 1660, when the Sicilian Francesco Procopio Coltelli opened his Café Procope in Paris, where it still stands on the same site. Meanwhile another Italian chef had introduced ice cream to London or, more precisely, to the court of Charles I.

By the end of the seventeenth century ice cream and sorbet were well established in all the noble and wealthy households of Europe. And in 1747 Hannah Glasse published her book, *The Art of Cookery,* containing the earliest known recipe for ice cream in the English language. It was an ice cream made with cream, not with custard as the Italian ices were. It was this ice cream that became popular in the United States, so popular in fact that many Americans believe it was invented there.

What was invented in America was the cone, the most immediate and natural way to enjoy a gelato (ice cream). This and the parigina —two wafers containing a slice of ice cream— were the containers used by the gelataio of my childhood. He pedaled around on his tricycle, the front of which was like a ship's prow with a figurehead in the shape of a swan. I still remember the night I was taken to *Lohengrin* at La Scala. To my utter amazement the hero arrived in what seemed to me to be the guise of the ice cream man, since he was riding what I took for il carrettino dei gelati—his beautiful white swan!

Gelato was, and is, food to be enjoyed in the streets, just like pizza: it is part of the social life of every Italian town. An essential difference, however, is that gelato and sorbetto are often made at home, but pizza seldom is.

Gelato di crema alla vaniglia
VANILLA ICE CREAM • SERVES 4

Italian ice creams are usually made with egg custard, rather than cream, to which various flavors are added. The custard base makes for a smoother, more velvety texture. This is my basic recipe for ice cream. You can add fruit puree, coffee, chocolate, almond praline or pounded hazelnuts to the custard, or, for a real treat, marrons glacés. Another typical Italian gelato di crema is flavored with the grated rind of a lemon instead of the vanilla pod. Lemon-flavored ice cream is an ideal accompaniment to fresh fruit; try it with sliced peaches, nectarines, strawberries or pineapple.

2 cups milk
1 vanilla bean
4 egg yolks
½ cup sugar

1 Heat the milk with the vanilla bean in a heavy-based saucepan until just simmering.

2 Beat the egg yolks with the sugar until pale and mousse-like. I use an electric beater. Pour the milk over very gradually, beating the whole time. Pour back into the pan, and put the pan on the heat. At this stage it is best to use a wooden spoon rather than the electric beater or wire whisk, as it helps you to judge the temperature of the custard. Continue stirring until the custard is very hot, but not boiling, or the eggs will scramble. When the custard is ready, the sound of the spoon going round will change to a deeper thud and you will feel the custard thicken. Remove from the heat immediately.

3 Immediately put the saucepan into a basin of cold water and continue stirring for about 3 minutes, otherwise the custard will curdle at the bottom of the pan.

4 When the custard is cold, remove the vanilla bean. Wash and dry it and keep it for one or two more uses.

5 Freeze the custard in an ice-cream machine according to the manufacturer's instructions. If you have not got a machine, place in the freezer. This is a well-behaved ice cream which does not make ice crystals.

Gelato di crema all'aceto balsamico
VANILLA ICE CREAM WITH BALSAMIC VINEGAR • SERVES 4

This combination of vanilla ice cream and sweet vinegar is a rare specialty of Reggio Emilia and Modena, the towns in Emilia where balsamic vinegar is made. The rich dark flavor of the balsamic vinegar cuts into the delicate sweetness of the ice cream and achieves a perfect balance of flavors.

Make the vanilla ice cream as described on page 184. Divide it into 4 individual bowls and dribble 1 teaspoon of balsamic vinegar over each portion.

Tazzine di crema all'aceto balsamico
CUSTARD WITH BALSAMIC VINEGAR

Here is an even easier recipe, the creation of which was one of those lucky accidents that occasionally lead to a discovery. One evening when we had friends to dinner, I had prepared the usual egg custard for Vanilla Ice Cream (page 184). But when I went to take the ice cream machine's freezing bowl from the freezer, it wasn't there! I had forgotten to put it in after washing it. Panic struck . . . there was no time to make another dessert. So I decided to put a brave face on the situation and proceed as if nothing had gone wrong. I poured the custard into petits pots and handed around a pretty bottle containing my most precious, 100-year-old balsamic vinegar. One teaspoon added to each cup created my crema all'aceto balsamico, which was delicious—and a great success!

Gelato di frutta

FRUIT ICE CREAM • MAKES 3 CUPS

This recipe makes the smoothest ice cream I have ever tasted. I make it with peaches, apricots, or plums. You can make the puree two or three days in advance but, if you can, make the ice cream on the day you want to eat it, as ice cream loses flavor and freshness, and begins to make little crystals after 24 hours.

FRUIT PUREE

2 pounds fruit, weighed after pitting and peeling if necessary
about 1 cup sugar, depending on the sweetness of the fruit
flavoring, such as lemon or orange rind, cloves or cinnamon

ICE CREAM

1/4 cup sugar
1/2 cup water
2 egg yolks
3 cups fruit puree
3 tablespoons lemon juice
2/3 cup heavy cream
confectioners' sugar

NOTE: This ice cream turns out very well even if you do not have an ice cream machine. You simply have to put it in the freezer and freeze it. Transfer it from the freezer to the fridge about 1 hour before you want to serve it.

1 Cut the fruit into suitable segments and put in a heavy saucepan. Add the sugar and the flavoring and cook very gently until tender. Lift the fruit out of the pan and reduce the liquid until rich and syrupy. If you are using plums, the liquid will need longer reduction than the other fruits.

2 Puree the fruit with its liquid in a food processor or a blender, or through a sieve or food mill.

3 Boil the sugar in the water until the sugar makes a ribbon when pulled between thumb and forefinger (300°F. on a candy thermometer).

4 While the syrup is boiling, whisk the egg yolks until pale.

5 When the syrup is ready pour it over the yolks, whisking constantly. Fold into the fruit puree and add enough lemon juice to enhance the flavor of the fruit.

6 Whip the cream until beginning to form ribbons and fold gently but thoroughly into the fruit puree. Taste and if necessary add a couple of tablespoons of confectioners' sugar. Remember that iced food needs stronger flavoring, and that sugar helps the ice cream to achieve the right consistency.

7 Freeze in an ice cream machine according to the manufacturer's instructions.

You can also make a sorbet with this fruit puree. Add the juice of 1 lemon and 3 tablespoons confectioners' sugar to 3 cups of puree. Take care to get the right degree of sweetness, which depends on the type of fruit and how ripe it is. Freeze in an ice cream machine according to the manufacturer's instructions. If you do not have a machine and are simply freezing the sorbet in the freezer, you must whisk the half-frozen sorbet twice during the freezing with a metal whisk, or preferably, an electric beater, to break down the crystals.

SPUMONE

Spumone is a frozen concoction of Neapolitan origin. The name, meaning very airy froth, describes the ice cream, which is made with egg custard, cream and other flavorings.

- -

Spumone di zabaglione
ZABAGLIONE ICE CREAM • SERVES 6

1 Separate the eggs and put the yolks in a bowl or in the top of a double boiler. Put 3 of the whites in another bowl.

2 Add the sugar and the cinnamon to the egg yolks and beat off the heat until the custard becomes pale yellow and forms ribbons. Add the marsala and the rum, while beating constantly. Put the bowl over a saucepan ⅓ full of hot water, or onto the bottom half of the double boiler. Bring the water to the simmer while you whisk constantly—a hand-held electric beater is ideal for the job. The mixture will become foamy and will nearly double in volume. Remove from the heat and put the bowl in cold water. Leave to cool, beating very frequently.

3 Whip the cream until it forms soft peaks, then incorporate the egg custard into the cream.

4 Whip the 3 egg whites until they form stiff peaks. Add the whipped egg white by the spoonful to the egg and cream mixture, folding it in gently.

5 If you have an ice cream machine, follow the manufacturer's instructions. If not, transfer the zabaglione mixture to a large glass dish and place in the freezer. About 3 hours later remove from the freezer and beat the zabaglione with a metal whisk or electric beater. This stirring will break up any crystals that might have formed. Return to the freezer and leave for at least 4 hours.

✘ You can decorate the spumone with amarettini (small amaretti) or sprinkle chopped hazelnuts over the top. Serve with Almond Meringues (page 192).

5 eggs
½ cup sugar
pinch of ground cinnamon
½ cup marsala
2 tablespoons rum
1¼ cups heavy cream

NOTE: You can make the spumone 1 day in advance, but no more than that. I find that ice cream loses its flavor and freshness if left too long in the freezer.

- -

SORBET

Today's preoccupation with the effects of food on health is not new. In 1784 a Neapolitan doctor, Filippo Baldini, wrote, "Because of the sugar, the salt and the cold, sorbets give rise to a great number of beneficial effects in our bodies by helping with the digestion of food."

Sorbets, more than ice cream, exemplify the Italian taste for pure, basic flavors. These are often enhanced by a touch of another flavor that complements the main ingredient. You can add a tablespoon or two of Grand Marnier to your orange sorbet, the juice of half an orange to a strawberry one or a little kirsch to a plum sorbet. The thing to keep in mind is that the fruit juice must be full of flavor. Make sorbets with ripe fruits in full season, and always add some orange or lemon juice to bring out the flavor.

Now that ice cream machines have become a common kitchen accessory, the problem of crystallization need no longer be a worry. I am not a gadget-minded cook, but I cannot now think how I lived for so many years without my ice cream machine. It forms a happy trinity with my food processor and the hand-cranked pasta machine. My ice cream maker is a small one, and I keep the inside container in the freezer ready for making the ice cream, since gelati are the only desserts I serve in the summer. I am convinced that an ice cream or a sorbet is the perfect finale to any meal.

Sorbetto al limone
LEMON SORBET • SERVES 4

4 lemons
1⅓ cups sugar
sprig of lemon balm (optional)
1 egg white

NOTE: To make in the freezer, freeze the lemon syrup until it becomes firm round the edges. Whisk the egg white until stiff and whisk into the partially frozen mixture. Use an electric beater if you have one, but put the bowl in the sink and use a low speed to start off or you will have sorbet flying all over the kitchen. Freeze again and then whisk once more with a metal whisk. Return the bowl to the freezer until the sorbet is really firm.

This sorbet can also be made with oranges or tangerines to which some lemon juice is added.

1 Scrub the lemons with a vegetable brush and some bicarbonate of soda (baking soda) as described on page 170. Peel 2 of the lemons.

2 Put the sugar and 2 cups of water in a heavy saucepan. Add the lemon rind, without any white pith, and the lemon balm if you have it in the garden. Bring slowly to the boil, stirring frequently to dissolve the sugar, then simmer for 5 minutes. Allow to cool.

3 Squeeze the lemons and add the juice to the syrup. Strain the lemon syrup.

4 If you have an ice cream machine, lightly whisk the egg white until firm but still wet-looking. Fold into the syrup. Freeze following the manufacturer's instructions.

Nuts

The chestnuts of Valle d'Aosta, the hazelnuts of Avellino, the walnuts of Sorrento, the pine nuts of Versiglia and the almonds of Sicily are among the best in the world. The Italians use them freely and eat them in plenty, by themselves or in combination with meat, fish and vegetables. They are also very usual ingredients in desserts and cookies. I have always felt that there are degrees of nobility among nuts. Almonds, with their exotic flavor, are for grand tables; almond paste has lent itself to artistic decorations as well as to delicate sweetmeats, and it has flavored rich desserts of Arabic origin. Chestnuts, however, seem to belong to more humble surroundings, eaten roasted around the kitchen fire or in the street straight from the hot brazier.

ALMONDS

Almonds are the fruit of the tree that delights us with the first spring flowers. Sweet almonds only grow where there is no frost, in the same regions as oranges and lemons. They have many uses in cooking, since they are a flavoring for both sweet and savory dishes. They are also used, ground, as a thickener. Almonds are delicious by themselves, salted to nibble with drinks or coated with sugar as sweets.

Almonds keep only for a year. When the new crop arrives in the shops in late summer, ideally the old almonds should be thrown away; their flavor will have evaporated and their oil might have begun to go rancid. Almonds are sold in their shells at Christmastime to eat at the table, or in their skins all year round, peeled or ground, to use in cooking. I always buy unpeeled almonds, since it is easy to tell how old they are by looking at the skin. If their skin is wrinkled, the almonds are old.

HOW TO PEEL ALMONDS. To peel almonds, put them in a saucepan of boiling water and blanch for 30 seconds. When they are cool enough to handle, squeeze them between your thumb and forefinger and they will pop out of their skins. A food processor grinds almonds well. You can stop the machine whenever the nuts are ready for your recipe, coarsely chopped, finely chopped or ground.

AMARETTO. In Italy amaretto is a liqueur with definite class connotations. I can still remember my brother Guido, when we were in our late teens, saying of a girl that she was very pretty, but "ha una mamma che beve l'amaretto" (she has a mother who drinks amaretto). What more was there to be said? I must confess that I, too, have had to overcome residual snobbish sentiments before buying a bottle of amaretto, strictly for the kitchen, of course.

In fact amaretto had a noble enough birth. It was created in the sixteenth century for the painter Bernardino Luini when he asked the beautiful wife of an innkeeper in Saronno to be his model for a painting of the Madonna in the Santuario of Santa Maria delle Grazie. She was so honored that she made him this special liqueur by macerating ground apricot kernels in eau-de-vie.

Amaretto began to be produced commercially at the beginning of the nineteenth century by the firm of Domenico Reina, which still makes the original product. Many other firms now make amaretto, and its worldwide consumption is said to be greater than that of any other liqueur. In the United States alone 10 million bottles a year are sold.

Latte di mandorle

ALMOND MILK • ABOUT 1 CUP

Almond milk was very popular in Italy in the Middle Ages, when it was usually made with water or stock rather than with milk, and used mainly as a thickener in sauces. During the Renaissance it was also served at banquets as a soup, flavored with other ingredients. I experimented with a few old recipes and came out with this variation of almond milk. This is a thin sauce, which is a lovely accompaniment to poached fruit instead of cream or crème anglaise.

It is also delicious with a bavarian cream, especially the one with cherries on page 165, or with apricots, both fruits that blend beautifully with the taste of almonds.

¾ **cup shelled almonds
 (¼ pound)**
2 **tablespoons confectioners'
 sugar**
3 or 4 **drops pure almond extract**
1¼ **cups milk**

NOTE: You can use the squeezed-out almonds in cakes or biscuits; they are still good even though part of their flavor has gone into the milk.

1 Blanch and peel the almonds as described on page 189. Chop the almonds or process them until granular. Transfer to a bowl.

2 Heat the milk until it starts to boil, stir in the sugar and the almond extract and pour over the almonds. Cover the bowl with plastic wrap and leave to infuse for at least 4 hours.

3 Set a strainer lined with cheesecloth over a bowl. Strain the almond mixture and then squeeze out all the juices into the milk.

4 Cover the bowl with plastic wrap and refrigerate. Remove from the refrigerator and bring back to room temperature before serving.

Torta di mandorle all'arancia
ALMOND AND ORANGE CAKE • SERVES 8

This cake combines two of the most characteristic Italian ingredients, oranges and almonds. The recipe is from *La Scienza in cucina e l'arte di mangiar bene* by Pellegrino Artusi, the greatest cookbook of the last century. It is still in print today, and is well past its hundredth edition. The secret here is the use of potato starch. Used instead of regular flour, it gives a softer dough; it is also ideal for anyone on a gluten-free diet. The cake pan is heavily buttered, giving a soft rich layer on the surface of the cake; if you use less butter the cake is equally delicious, though not so rich. This delicate cake, perfect on its own, is even better as an accompaniment to a fruit salad, to soft fruits or to a fruit compote.

1 Preheat the oven to 325°F.

2 Blanch and peel the almonds as described on page 189. Chop them very finely by hand, or use a food processor, but do not blend to a paste. They should be in granules, not completely ground.

3 Beat the egg yolks with the sugar until they form a ribbon and then add the almonds and the potato starch. Mix well.

4 Thoroughly scrub 1 of the oranges with a hard brush to get rid of pesticides and grate the skin. Add to the mixture together with the strained juice of both the whole and the half orange. The mixture will be very soft and sloppy.

5 Now whisk the egg whites with a pinch of salt until stiff and then fold into the mixture, lifting it high with a gentle movement, using a metal spoon.

6 Butter an 8-inch cake pan, using all the butter to give a thick layer all around. Pour the batter into the pan.

7 Bake in the preheated oven for about 50 minutes, until the cake has shrunk from the sides and feels spongy to the touch. Unmold the cake on a wire rack and cool.

1 cup shelled almonds (5 ounces)
3 eggs, separated
¾ cup sugar
4 tablespoons potato starch
1½ oranges
salt
2 tablespoons unsalted butter

NOTE: The cake looks pretty sprinkled with confectioners' sugar, or it can be iced with a soft icing flavored with 1 teaspoon of orange water.

Meringhine alle mandorle

ALMOND MERINGUES • MAKES ABOUT 25 COOKIES

The fridge or freezer often abounds in leftover egg whites, and this is one of the very best ways to use them. They result in the prettiest friandises imaginable; with their mother-of-pearl coloring and sheen they have a distinct oyster shell look to them.

You can use ready-ground almonds if you're pressed for time, but I do not recommend it. I find that ground almonds have lost some of their flavor, just like ground pepper and ready-grated parmesan cheese.

¾ cup shelled almonds
 (¼ pound)
2 egg whites
1½ cups confectioners' sugar
1 teaspoon lemon juice

1 Blanch and peel the almonds as described on page 189. Dry them thoroughly and grind them in a food processor. Do not use a coffee grinder, as the oil in the almonds will clog it.

2 Beat the egg whites with the sugar until soft peaks form. I use an electric beater and it takes about 3 or 4 minutes. Fold in the ground almonds and the lemon juice and mix until the mixture is homogeneous.

3 Heat the oven to 300°F.

4 Line 2 baking sheets with parchment paper and place small blobs of meringue on the paper about 1½ inches apart. You can pipe the mixture from a pastry bag or use 2 teaspoons. The baked meringues look prettiest if no larger than 1½ inches in diameter, so keep them small.

5 Bake until set to the touch and very lightly colored, about 40 minutes. Leave to cool on the paper.

CHESTNUTS

Chestnuts came originally from around the town of Castanis in Thessalia, hence their botanical name of *Castanea sativa,* in Italian castagne. In Italy chestnuts grow on the Alps, and all down the Apennines as far south as Calabria. They have a short season, from October to Christmas, after which they become wrinkled and lose their flavor.

HOW TO PEEL CHESTNUTS. Peeling chestnuts, although it is a boring job, is not too difficult. It is even easier if your hands can stand a certain amount of heat; the more heat you can bear, the quicker the job. First wash the chestnuts. Then, using a small pointed knife, slit the shell of the chestnuts across the whole of the rounded side, being careful not to cut into the actual nut. Put the chestnuts in a saucepan, cover with plenty of cold water and bring to the boil. Cook until ready, which can vary between ten and twenty minutes, depending on how fresh they are. To find out, take a chestnut between your thumb and index finger and press gently: it should be just soft. Remove a few chestnuts, leaving the rest in the hot water to make peeling easier. Using a small knife, remove the outer shell, as well as all the inner skin, which has an unpleasant bitter taste. You will notice any bad nuts as soon as you begin to peel them by the acrid smell they give off; the whole nut should be discarded. The chestnuts are now ready to be cooked in stock or milk, according to the recipe. You can freeze peeled chestnuts very successfully, and you can even freeze unpeeled ones, although they are then difficult to peel.

Dried chestnuts are sold when the fresh ones are out of season. They have to be reconstituted by soaking in water for at least eight hours before cooking.

Passato di castagne
CHESTNUT SOUP • SERVES 4

I have had many chestnut soups in my time, many of them stodgy, some good and a few excellent. Although this soup had long been one of the best, it became the ne plus ultra as a result of reading Eliza Acton's *Modern Cookery for Private Families*. In that book there is a recipe that is very similar to the one I had known, but with one important extra: Eliza Acton adds cream. It transforms a pleasant but homely northern Italian soup into one that is utterly delectable.

1 Wash, boil and peel the chestnuts as described on page 192.

2 Put the peeled chestnuts in a clean saucepan, add the stock and cook very gently, covered, until the chestnuts are very soft, about 30 minutes. Puree the soup in a food processor, or through a food mill or sieve, and return to the heat.

3 Add the seasonings and then carefully stir in the cream. Do not add too much of the seasonings or the flavor of the chestnuts will be swamped instead of being enhanced. Ladle the soup into soup bowls and serve.

1 pound fresh chestnuts
4 cups light homemade vegetable *or* chicken stock (pages 3–4)
salt
freshly ground black pepper
generous pinch of grated nutmeg
2/3 cup heavy cream

Spuma di castagne
CHESTNUT MOUSSE • SERVES 6 TO 8

You can serve this dessert in white petits pots and sprinkle some grated chocolate on top, or in a lovely large glass bowl and hand around your favorite hot chocolate sauce with it. When I perfected this recipe I was lucky enough to have a bottle of 14-year-old rum in the house, and I used this in the mousse. If you don't feel inclined to rush out and buy a bottle, use any kind of dark rum. I am sure you will be quite happy with the result!

1 pound fresh chestnuts
salt
1 bay leaf
2-inch piece of vanilla bean
2-inch piece of cinnamon stick
1 cup sugar
1⅓ cups milk
3 egg yolks
4 tablespoons dark rum
⅔ cup heavy cream

NOTE: I like to hand around some plain biscuits with this mousse; try the Italian Shortbread (page 173), flavored with marsala instead of lemon.

1 Wash, boil and peel the chestnuts as described on page 192.

2 Cut the chestnuts into pieces and put them in a clean pan with a pinch of salt, the bay leaf, vanilla bean, cinnamon stick and half the sugar. Pour over enough milk to cover and bring slowly to the boil. Put a lid on the pan and adjust the heat so that the milk simmers without boiling over. Cook until nearly all the milk has been absorbed and the chestnuts are soft, about 40 minutes.

3 Remove the vanilla bean and cinnamon stick and puree the chestnuts through a food mill. If you do not have this invaluable tool (or so I find it) use a food processor and process until the chestnuts are reduced to a smooth puree. Scrape down the bits on the side of the bowl and process again.

4 Beat the egg yolks with the remaining sugar until pale and forming soft peaks. Incorporate gradually into the chestnut puree together with the rum.

5 Whip the cream and then fold the chestnut puree into the cream. It is easier and quicker to fold the mixture into the whipped cream than the other way round.

6 Spoon the mixture into petits pots or into a large bowl and cover with plastic wrap. Chill until you want to serve it.

HAZELNUTS

Hazelnuts, like all other nuts, should be eaten before the end of the year in which they are harvested.

HOW TO PEEL HAZELNUTS. To peel hazelnuts, either put them in a cast-iron frying pan and toast them for a few minutes, shaking the pan, or place them on a baking sheet in a hot oven (400°F.) for five minutes. As soon as you can handle them, rub them against each other, or in a rough towel, and blow away the papery thin skin. Blow into the sink or out of doors, otherwise you will find bits of skin flying everywhere. Discard any hazelnuts that are partly dark in color and look oily and thick in texture.

- -

Involtini di pollo ripieni di nocciole, prosciutto e formaggio
CHICKEN BUNDLES STUFFED WITH HAZELNUTS, HAM AND CHEESE •
SERVES 4

Of all nuts, hazelnuts have a flavor that goes best with white meat. In this dish their nutty taste, reinforced by the gruyère, is toned down by the white wine, which must be dry, yet full and fruity. Pinot Bianco or Pinot Grigio would be good.

1 Peel the hazelnuts as described on page 195.

2 Put the cheese in the food processor with the ham and hazelnuts. Process until chopped but not reduced to a paste. Scoop the mixture into a bowl and add the nutmeg, a very little salt and some pepper. Mix well.

3 Lay the chicken pieces flat on a work surface.

4 Melt 3 tablespoons of the butter in a sauté pan large enough to hold all the chicken. As soon as the butter has melted, turn the heat off. Dip a pastry brush into the butter and moisten the inside of each chicken piece. Season with a sprinkling of salt and pepper.

5 Pick up about 1 tablespoon of the stuffing and press it between your hands into an oblong shape. Lay it on the chicken and then roll up the meat and secure with a toothpick.

6 Add the oil to the butter in the pan and heat. When the foam begins to subside, slide the bundles into the pan and fry on all sides to a lovely deep gold.

7 Splash with the wine and boil briskly until it has nearly all evaporated. Add the stock and bring to the boil.

¼ cup hazelnuts (1 ounce)
1 cup roughly diced gruyère (about 2 ounces)
1 cup roughly diced ham (about 2 ounces)
pinch of grated nutmeg
salt
pepper
8 boned chicken thighs
4 tablespoons unsalted butter
1 tablespoon oil, preferably peanut
5 tablespoons dry white wine
½ cup meat stock (page 3)

NOTE: You can prepare the dish in advance through Step 7. Reheat the chicken bundles before you add the butter.

(*continued*)

CHICKEN BUNDLES STUFFED WITH HAZELNUTS, HAM AND CHEESE
(*continued*)

Turn the heat down to the minimum and cover the pan with a lid. Cook gently for about 15 minutes, until the chicken thighs are cooked through, turning them once during the cooking.

8 Transfer the bundles to a heated dish. Add the remaining tablespoon of butter to the pan, a little at a time, and cook gently until it has been incorporated. Taste and check seasoning. Return the bundles to the pan together with the juices from the dish. Cook very gently for 1 or 2 minutes so as to allow all the flavors to combine, and then place back on the dish and cover with the sauce.

✖ Many vegetables go well with this dish, particularly sautéed or steamed zucchini or buttered spinach. I have served these bundles, in a very non-Italian manner, surrounding a mound of tagliatelle, dressed with butter and parmesan. It is a very pretty dish, and it is excellent.

If you serve the bundles with tagliatelle, start with Passatelli (page 50) or Fennel Timbale (page 101). If you prefer to serve the bundles with vegetables, Risotto with Asparagus (page 30) would be an ideal primo.

WALNUTS

Of all the nuts walnuts are the hardest to find in good condition because of the amount of oil they contain. At Christmastime they are available in the shell, to go on the table with other nuts and dried fruits. During the year they are sold shelled, but sometimes they are too old to be any good. It's better to buy canned shelled walnuts, even though they are expensive. Or buy loose nuts from a supplier who has a quick turnover. If they are in a transparent packet, look them over: the half kernels should be large and intact. Old nuts break and as a consequence become rancid more quickly. Before you use them, discard any piece of walnut that is dark in color and compact in texture. They should be pale ivory with a light texture if they are to have that sweet taste that characterizes any dish to which they are added. When old, walnuts first develop a piquant taste that tickles your tongue unpleasantly, and later they become rancid. A single small piece of rancid walnut can ruin your dish. Keep shelled walnuts in an airtight jar in the fridge or freezer.

HOW TO PEEL WALNUTS. Some recipes call for the nuts to be peeled, as the skin is slightly bitter. To do so, blanch them in boiling water for half a minute and then remove as much skin as you can with the help of a small sharp knife. While you peel them you can easily detect any piece which should be thrown away.

Torta di noce alla crema di mascarpone
WALNUT CAKE WITH MASCARPONE CREAM • SERVES 8 TO 10

I must confess that I am not a keen cake-maker. I seldom have one in the house, and when I do I usually forget to eat it. But I do like a sweet ending to a good meal, and that is why I have a number of good desserts among my favorite recipes.

This walnut cake is always good, whether eaten by itself or with tea or coffee, with a nightcap—or at any time of the day with a glass of wine! But it is at its best filled with mascarpone cream—the same cream that I make for Tiramisù (page 148)—and served as dessert, when it makes a fine ending to the meal.

1 Beat the egg yolks with the sugar until pale yellow and forming soft peaks. Add the vanilla extract.

2 If you have time, peel the walnuts as described on page 196. Put them in a food processor and process until very coarsely ground. Add to the egg and sugar mixture and mix thoroughly.

3 Preheat the oven to 350°F.

4 Whisk the egg whites with a pinch of salt until stiff but not dry. Using a large metal spoon, fold gradually into the walnut mixture, with a gentle lifting movement, evenly and thoroughly.

5 Butter a 10-inch springform pan and sprinkle with the flour. Cover all the surface with it by rotating and tipping the pan; shake off the excess.

6 Spoon the mixture into the pan and bake until firm and set, about 50 minutes. Turn the springform over onto a wire rack. Unclip, remove the ring and allow the cake to cool.

7 While the cake is cooling, prepare the filling. Beat the egg yolks with the sugar until a ribbon forms when the beater is raised. Fold in the mascarpone, a large tablespoonful at a time.

8 Whisk the egg whites and fold into the mascarpone mixture lightly but very thoroughly. Chill.

9 About 2 hours before you want to eat the cake, cut it in half horizontally and spread a little of the mascarpone mixture over the bottom half. Replace the top half in position and spread the rest of the mascarpone cream all over the surface, using a large spatula. Decorate with the walnut halves and chill. Bring to the table straight from the refrigerator.

6 eggs, separated
1½ cups superfine sugar
3 or 4 drops pure vanilla extract
2¼ cups shelled walnuts
   (9 ounces)
salt
butter and flour for the baking
   pan

FILLING
2 eggs, separated
⅓ cup superfine sugar
2 cups mascarpone (1 pound)
walnut halves for decoration

PINE NUTS

These are the nuts of the stone pine, Pineus sativa. They are about a quarter of an inch long, of a beautiful ivory color, with a delicious taste of resin mixed with oil. They are used to thicken sauces, as in pesto, or in sweet-and-sour sauces to dress vegetables, fish or fried meats. They are also often added to cakes and biscuits. To release their special flavor, it is a good idea to heat the pine nuts in a hot oven or in a cast-iron frying pan for a few minutes.

Salsa di miele, noci e pinoli

HONEY, WALNUT AND PINE NUT SAUCE • MAKES ABOUT ¾ cup

In Piedmont there is an ancient sauce, made with honey and walnuts, that is served with il gran bui, a rich dish of mixed boiled meats. My secret here is to add a tablespoon of pine nuts which, with their slightly resinous flavor, counterbalance the sweetness of the honey.

- **1½ tablespoons pine nuts**
- **3 tablespoons shelled walnuts**
- **4 tablespoons clear honey**
- **4 tablespoons homemade meat stock (page 3)**
- **1½ tablespoons prepared English mustard**

1 Toast the pine nuts in a cast-iron pan.

2 Blanch the walnuts in boiling water for 30 seconds and then remove as much as you can of the thin skin.

3 Mix the honey and the stock.

4 Pound the walnuts and pine nuts in a mortar, adding 1 tablespoon of the honey mixture. When reduced to a paste stir in the rest of the honey mixture and the mustard. Mix thoroughly. If you have a food processor or a blender you can process the nuts with the honey mixture in it, and then add the mustard.

Serve with boiled chicken, beef or ham.

Garlic and Herbs

GARLIC

Broccoli stufati
BRAISED BROCCOLI

Gli ziti con la besciamella all'aglio
PASTA WITH A GARLICKY BECHAMEL

Arrosto di maiale all'acqua
BRAISED SHOULDER OF PORK WITH HERBS
AND GARLIC

HERBS

Pesce in bianco con salsina alle erbe aromatiche
STEAMED FISH WITH FRESH HERB SAUCE

Arrosto freddo alle erbe
COLD ROAST VEAL WITH HERBS

Pesto
PESTO

Minestrone alla genovese
MINESTRONE WITH PESTO

Scaloppine al basilico e limone
VEAL SCALOPPINE WITH BASIL AND LEMON

Bastoncini di patate e zucchine
SAUTEED POTATO AND ZUCCHINI STICKS

Prugne sciroppate al rosmarino
PLUMS IN WINE WITH ROSEMARY AND SPICES

Garlic

Garlic has played a part in many civilizations for more than two thousand years. The Egyptians worshiped garlic as a god, presumably because they were familiar with its medicinal properties. In Roman times, garlic was used mostly in plebeian cooking. In the Middle Ages, Alfonso, King of Castille, who defeated the Moors and married the daughter of Henry II of England, so hated garlic that he punished anyone who came to court smelling of it.

The fifteenth-century writer Platina, in his *De honesta voluptate et valetudine,* recommends garlic as an antidote for dog bites. It was also reputed to steady the nerves of hysterical people, to combat epidemics and infectious diseases, and to promote the passing of urine. But perhaps its most remarkable function was as a deterrent against vampires. To achieve this desirable end, beautiful young virgins, before retiring for the night, had to secure all windows and doors, place a Bible and Crucifix by their bedside and hang at least a dozen bunches of garlic around the room. Garlic is still considered beneficial to health; it is held to purify the blood, clear the skin and aid the digestive process.

Whatever its real or imagined therapeutic powers, garlic has become an indispensable ingredient of Italian cooking. It should not, however, be used indiscriminately; it must be used in keeping with the style of the dish. With some dishes you only need a suggestion of flavor, in others an assertive statement is called for. To have only a tinge of flavor, peel a clove of garlic, put it whole in the butter or oil and remove it from the pan as soon as it becomes pale gold. You can actually get just a whiff of it that point. To give a subtle yet all-pervading garlic flavor to a dish, cook the garlic in the stock, water or milk for a long time, then puree it and add it to the sauce or the dish. For more flavor, you can cut the garlic in half or in large slices, or you can chop it, the last being the method which releases the most flavor. For a full garlic flavor, sauté it in a soffritto until it is just colored and then add the other vegetables. If you want to make a soffritto with onion, garlic and other vegetables, first fry the onion by itself until translucent and then add the garlic. If you put the garlic and the onion in the pan at the same time, the garlic will burn before the onion is soft. Some cooks put a toothpick through the garlic clove so that it can be seen and removed easily whenever they think it has released enough flavor.

New garlic is sweet, tender and plump, and can be used liberally. But garlic ages quickly and becomes dried, brittle and wrinkled. Its taste is sharp and it must then be used sparingly. It is best to cut these older cloves in half and then remove the bud inside, as this is by far the sharpest tasting part. I am wary about using chopped raw garlic, or extracting its juice with a garlic press. The flavor is so pungent that it can kill any other taste. If you want a soupçon of garlic in a salad, rub the bowl with a peeled and slightly squashed clove or squash a clove in a spoon and then add the oil to it. Remove the garlic and dress the salad. To give vinegar a faint garlic flavor I often put two or three cloves in a jar and fill it with vinegar. But remember to remove the garlic cloves and put fresh ones in before you refill the jar.

Broccoli stufati
BRAISED BROCCOLI • SERVES 4

This is a dish I had recently at a friend's house in Milan. I would be surprised if her excellent cook, Pierina, from Marche, has heard of nouvelle cuisine; if she has, it is just something she has read about. Her broccoli brought back nostalgic memories of all the vegetables cooked the way they used to be in Italy. Nowadays quick cooking without any dressing is so often thought to be healthier. When cooked Pierina's way, the flavor of the broccoli is fully developed, with the result that—both in looks and in taste—it is a different dish from the broccoli spears we are used to today. Don't be put off by the quantity of garlic. Its flavor fades with the long cooking, and at the end the cloves themselves are removed.

1 Separate the broccoli stalks from the florets. Peel the toughest stalks and cut them into short pieces. Divide the florets into small buds. Wash the broccoli and blanch in salted boiling water for 3 minutes, then drain thoroughly.

2 Thread a toothpick through the garlic. (This will make it easier to remove the garlic at the end of the cooking.)

3 Heat the olive oil, with the garlic and the chili, in a sauté pan. Remove and discard the chili and add the broccoli. Turn the pieces over for a couple of minutes and then cook the broccoli, covered, for about 40 minutes, stirring every now and then with a fork. By the end the broccoli will be fairly mashed up, but it will taste delicious. Fish out the garlic and discard.

✗ The broccoli goes perfectly with Breaded Veal Chops in a Sweet-and-Sour Sauce (page 221). They are also an excellent accompaniment to an omelet or an Italian frittata.

1 **pound broccoli**
salt
5 **garlic cloves**
3 **tablespoons extra-virgin olive oil**
1 **dried chili**

Gli ziti con la besciamella all'aglio

PASTA WITH A GARLICKY BECHAMEL • SERVES 4

I find that in some dishes the garlic flavor comes through too strongly. Garlic that is not cooked enough can be overpowering. I discovered this recipe when I was doing the research for *Gastronomy of Italy;* it is in a book by the Duke Alberto Denti di Pirajno, called *Il Gastronomo educato,* which has since become one of my favorites. The flavor of garlic is just enough to give an edge to the béchamel. Denti di Pirajno was a Sicilian, and ziti is one of the shapes of pasta much favored in Sicily. It is ideal for this dish. It is best to make this dish in the late spring or summer, when the new, sweet garlic is in the shops.

2 heads of garlic

BECHAMEL SAUCE
2 tablespoons butter
1½ tablespoons flour
1¾ cups milk

¾ pound ziti, penne or other large tubular pasta
2 tablespoons butter
1½ tablespoons flour
salt
freshly ground pepper
⅔ cup freshly grated parmesan, plus extra grated parmesan for serving separately

1 Peel the garlic cloves and put them in a small saucepan. Add about 1 cup of water and bring to the boil. Cover the pan with a tight-fitting lid, turn the heat down to very low (I use a flame disperser) and simmer for 1½ hours. Check every now and then that the water has not evaporated and add more boiling water if necessary. By the end of the cooking time you should have about ⅓ cup of liquid still in the pan. Put the contents of the pan through a sieve—a chinois is the easiest—and mash the garlic cloves. Return this thick garlicky liquid to the pan.

2 Make a thin béchamel as directed on page 4 and cook for at least 15 minutes in a double boiler.

3 If the pasta is long, break it into 2- to 2½-inch pieces. Cook them in the usual way in plenty of boiling salted water.

4 Return the garlic liquid to the heat.

5 Blend the butter and flour together with a fork and add, a little at a time, to the garlicky liquid, while beating with a small metal whisk. Cook for 1 or 2 minutes and then add to the béchamel. Taste and add salt and pepper if necessary.

6 Drain the pasta (but do not overdrain it) and transfer immediately to a heated bowl. Toss well with the sauce and with the parmesan. Serve immediately, with more parmesan handed around separately. This pasta dish should be served on hot plates, as the sauce becomes gluey when cool.

✄ If you are serving this as a first course, your secondo should be a light dish, Steamed Fish with Fresh Herb Sauce (page 205) for instance, or Sautéed Veal Scaloppine with Peaches (page 179).

Arrosto di maiale all'acqua
BRAISED SHOULDER OF PORK WITH HERBS AND GARLIC • SERVES 6

I can heartily recommend this way to cook pork. All you need is some plump young garlic, a lovely bunch of fresh herbs and a first-quality piece of pork shoulder, plus patience at the end when you have to add the stock very gradually to brown the meat. Ask the butcher for the bone and the rind.

1 Remove the meat from the refrigerator 2 hours in advance. (All meat should be cooked at room temperature).

2 Trim the sinews and some of the fat from the pork and tie into a neat roll if the butcher has not already done so.

3 Heat the oven to 325°F.

4 Put the meat, bone, sage, rosemary, garlic, peppercorns and salt in an oval casserole. Add a piece of the rind (the rest can be frozen to add to vegetable and bean soups). Pour over just enough water to cover the meat. Place a tight lid on the pan and bring slowly to the boil. Place a sheet of aluminum foil over the meat, cover with the lid and put the casserole in the oven. Cook for about 2½ to 3 hours, until the meat is very tender when pierced with a fork. Turn the meat over 3 or 4 times during the cooking. Transfer to a large plate. Discard the bone and strain the stock into a bowl.

5 Put about ½ cup of the stock into the washed-out casserole, bring to the boil and add the meat. Let the stock evaporate over a very lively heat, while turning the meat over and over. When there is hardly any liquid left, add another ½ cup of the stock and let it bubble away in the same manner. Continue adding stock and bubbling it away while turning the meat, until you have about 1 cup of the stock left.

6 Transfer the meat, which by now should be dark brown all over, to a carving board. Deglaze the casserole with the wine. Boil for 2 minutes and then add the rest of the stock and reduce, still over high heat. When the juices have reduced to about half, add the butter, a little at a time, while stirring gently. Taste for salt and pepper.

7 Carve the meat into ½-inch slices and lay them on a heated dish. Spoon over a little sauce and serve the rest in a sauceboat.

✖ I like to serve this dish with Sautéed Peppers and Potatoes (page 107) or with Drunk Potatoes (page 216).

3 to 3½ pounds shoulder of pork, blade bone and rind removed and reserved

2 fresh or dried sage leaves

3 fresh rosemary sprigs, about 5 inches long, *or* 2 teaspoons dried rosemary

10 garlic cloves, peeled

5 or 6 peppercorns, lightly bruised

salt

¼ cup dry white wine

2 tablespoons unsalted butter

freshly ground black pepper

NOTE: Browning the meat takes longer than you might think—about 20 minutes. You can prepare the dish half an hour in advance, and then keep the meat wrapped in foil, in a low oven. Remove the meat from the oven at least 10 minutes before carving; this relaxes the meat and allows the juices to penetrate the inside of the meat.

Herbs

There are certain herbs—erbe odorose is their mellifluous name in Italian—that have always played an important role in Italian cooking.

Prezzemolo (parsley) is the most ubiquitous. The parsley used in Italy is the flat-leaf variety, which is more aromatic; it is now widely available in this country. Parsley is often sautéed in the soffritto rather than just added at the end, thus releasing more of its flavor.

The typical herb of northern Italy is salvia (sage). The flavor combines ideally with butter, the cooking fat of the northern regions, and with veal, Lombardy's most popular meat. A sprig of sage is usually added to melted butter for the dressing of many different pasta dishes.

Bushes of wild rosemary are a familiar feature of the Mediterranean landscape. It is a sweeter, more scented variety than the rosemary that grows elsewhere, thanks to the hot sun and the dry atmosphere. It is also cultivated, and is to be found in any garden, however small. No roast in Italy is cooked without the obligatory sprig. In her delightful book *Honey from a Weed,* Patience Gray writes that in the Salento peninsula, the heel of the Italian boot, rosemary is chopped when in full flower, steeped in olive oil and used in a soffritto. The rosemary there, she says, flowers three or four times a year. I must try that idea the next time my bush produces its spindly pale flowers; I think it would be very good for sautéed potatoes, too.

Oregano was used extensively in ancient Rome, where it arrived from the Orient via Greece. In Greece it was christened origano, from oros (mountain) and ganao (splendor). Oregano is still the splendor of the mountainsides of central and southern Italy, where it has always been used profusely, especially together with tomatoes. It is the herb that is sprinkled on a classic Neapolitan pizza, and the one most commonly used in a tomato sauce.

The next time you buy plum tomatoes try this simple method of preparing them. Peel them, cut them in half and remove the seeds. Sprinkle lightly with salt on the inside and leave them for about half an hour. Then dress them with your best olive oil and sprinkle lavishly with oregano. Oregano is also the best herb for flavoring zucchini; it should be added about ten minutes before the zucchini are done.

Then there is basil. It always calls to my mind luscious dishes of trenett or piccagge al pesto, eaten in a Ligurian trattoria under a canopy of vine leaves and washed down with liters of wine from the Cinqueterre. The best basil grows in Liguria, under ideal climatic conditions: hot sun and humid breezes from the sea. Basil grows successfully in northern countries, but to my mind it becomes something a little different, with a slightly pungent taste reminiscent of mint.

The uses of basil are varied, as it can be added to most foods cooked in olive oil and containing tomato. It transforms the simplest tomato salad. It is good with shellfish and with porgies and other full-flavored white fish, as well as with eggplant and peppers. Basil is also good added at the end to quickly fried steaks. Only a few leaves are needed, and they should be added at the last minute as basil tends to lose its flavor —and its bright green color—in cooking. Tear the leaves with your fingers rather than chopping them. When making pesto pound the leaves; it is better than when processed by a blade. Basil is one of those herbs that cannot successfully be dried. It can, however, be stored very successfully in jars layered with olive oil or salt, or it can be frozen, leaving the leaves whole.

Marjoram belongs to the same species as oregano and, with basil, it is used a great deal in Liguria, especially in stuffings for vegetables and in torte di verdure (vegetable pies).

Parsley, rosemary, sage and marjoram are often used, separately or together, to form the basis of a soffritto.

There are, of course, many other less familiar herbs, and a number of these are now back in fashion in Italian cooking. They were out of favor during the eighteenth and nineteenth centuries, perhaps due to a swing of fashion's pendulum after the important position they enjoyed in the cooking of the sixteenth and seventeenth centuries. In his book *L'Arte di ben cucinare*, published in 1662, the great chef Bartolomeo Stefani devoted much attention to recipes containing fresh herbs, edible weeds and flowers. He used many herbs that are now being rediscovered: bitter hyssop, rue, scented lavender, the samphire of Shakespearean fame, cucumber-flavored borage and many others.

Pesce in bianco con salsina alle erbe aromatiche
STEAMED FISH WITH FRESH HERB SAUCE • SERVES 4

This recipe could have gone in the fish chapter, but I feel it is the fresh herb sauce that gives the dish its distinctive flavor. A pesce in bianco is a boiled or steamed fish. I prefer steaming, and this is the way I steam a single fish such as sea bass, black sea bass or salmon trout. You could also use red snapper, Arctic char or a small grouper; a fish weighing two to two and a half pounds will serve four people. Cooked this way, the fish keeps all its flavor and the cooking liquid is added to the herb sauce that accompanies it. The herb sauce is lighter and healthier than the usual mayonnaise. It is particularly good with salmon.

1 Put the wine and an equal quantity of water in a fish poacher. Add the onion, carrot, celery, garlic, bay leaves and sprigs of parsley, rosemary and sage. Bring to the boil. Cover the steamer rack with lettuce leaves (I use the green outside leaves that are too old for a salad).

2 Season the fish inside and out with salt and pepper. Lay it on top of the lettuce leaves and cook for 10 minutes. Remove from the heat and let it cool in the poacher. (If you do not have a poacher, you can use a large oval pan with a tight-fitting lid or a deep roasting pan with a domed lid. Wrap the fish loosely in foil, but without leaving any opening, put it in the pan with the wine, water, and the flavoring vegetables and cook for 15 to 20 minutes.)

3 While the fish is cooling, put the parsley leaves, thyme, marjoram, fennel or dill and basil leaves in a food processor. Process, pulsing the machine; stop and push the herbs down with a spatula; process again until the herbs are coarsely chopped while adding the olive oil. Scoop out the herbs and put them in a small bowl with the dried chilies and the garlic cloves and leave to infuse.

⅔ cup dry white wine
1 onion, coarsely chopped
1 carrot, coarsely chopped
1 celery stalk, coarsely chopped
1 or 2 garlic cloves
2 bay leaves
sprig of fresh parsley
sprig of fresh rosemary
sprig of fresh sage
lettuce leaves
1 firm-fleshed fish, such as snapper or grouper, 2 to 2½ pounds
salt
pepper

FRESH HERB SAUCE

½ cup fresh parsley leaves
1 tablespoon *each* fresh thyme, marjoram and fennel or dill
12 basil leaves
4 tablespoons extra-virgin olive oil
2 dried chilies
2 garlic cloves
2 tablespoons lemon juice

(continued)

4 When the fish is cold transfer it carefully to an oval dish and remove the skin if necessary. Strain the cooking liquid, reduce by half over high heat and then add to the bowl with the herb mixture. Remove and discard the garlic and chilies and add lemon juice and salt to taste. Mix well, taste and check seasonings. Serve the fish surrounded by some steamed potatoes, which can be hot or cold. Hand the sauce around in a bowl.

Arrosto freddo alle erbe

COLD ROAST VEAL WITH HERBS • SERVES 8

This is a very easy dish. It is a normal roast, served with a sauce that adds a distinctive touch and makes it a suitable dish for a summer dinner party.

There are two things I should mention. First, the sauce must be made with fresh herbs, and second, the choice of the right piece of veal is essential to the success of the dish. I find that the best is a rolled-up shoulder or breast of veal. These cuts contain some fat, which is necessary when roasting meat such as veal, which tends to be dry. The marinating, too, helps to keep the meat moist during the cooking. The fact that the meat is carved cold prevents it from falling apart, as can all too easily happen when a roast is carved hot.

Ask your butcher to bone the veal and give you the bone. Ask him also to trim the sinews and any excess fat from the veal and to roll it and tie it up neatly. If you really want to remove all the unwanted bits, you may have to do it yourself. Then tie the roast at ½-inch intervals.

2½ pounds boned and rolled shoulder of veal, bones reserved

MARINADE

2 cups dry white wine
salt, preferably sea salt
5 or 6 peppercorns, bruised
1 bay leaf
1 garlic clove, bruised

———

6 tablespoons olive oil
salt
freshly ground black pepper
4 tablespoons chopped herbs: thyme, marjoram, parsley, rosemary, sage and 2 mint leaves

1 Put the meat in a pot, add the ingredients for the marinade and leave for 24 hours. The pot should be left, covered, in a cool place, preferably not in the refrigerator. If you have to put the meat in the fridge, cover it loosely and take it out at least 2 hours before cooking.

2 Preheat the oven to 350°F.

3 Heat 2 tablespoons of the oil in a heavy-bottomed roasting pan or in a frying pan, and brown the meat all over. Now transfer the meat to a roasting pan, if you are not already using one, and put the bones around it. Pour over 3 or 4 tablespoons of the marinade liquid, sprinkle with a little salt and some pepper and cook in the preheated oven for

about 1¼ hours. Baste every so often and add a couple of tablespoons of the marinade liquid whenever the meat gets too dry.

4 When the veal is tender, remove it from the pan onto a plate. Remove and discard the bones. Skim off most of the fat floating on the surface of the cooking juices and then deglaze with a couple of tablespoons of cold water. Boil rapidly for a minute or two and then strain into a bowl.

5 Just over an hour before you want to serve the meat, put the chopped herbs in a bowl and gradually add the remaining oil, while beating with a fork to thicken the sauce. Add about 3 tablespoons of the cooking juices to the herb mixture and then adjust the seasoning. You may like to add a little more of the juices, but remember that their strong flavor should not overpower the fresh taste of the herbs: it should only be a foil to them.

6 Carve the veal in thin slices and arrange them prettily on a large dish. Coat the slices lightly with the sauce and let stand, covered with plastic wrap, to absorb the flavor.

I like to accompany this dish with a cooked vegetable salad: potatoes and green beans, for instance, or potatoes and zucchini, simply dressed with extra-virgin olive oil and lemon juice. The herb and meat sauce will impart the extra flavoring.

To start with, my choice would be a soup, Passatelli (page 50). You can have the color green as the theme of the dinner—not for actors or people in the theater, though, who are very superstitious about this color. Start with a good watercress soup or Risotto with Nettles (page 128) and finish with gorgonzola and green grapes.

Pesto

PESTO · SERVES 4

Pesto needs little introduction: every cookbook hails it as the best sauce for pasta. This it certainly is, but it must be well made and, oddly enough for such an apparently simple sauce, it is not easy to make. The Ligurians, who invented pesto, know that; they say that it needs not only the local basil, but also the local touch.

The traditional recipes do not contain pine nuts, but modern versions always do, and I find this a successful addition. Some cooks add walnuts as well, but I prefer to use only pine nuts, to keep the emphasis on the fresh flavor of the basil. Use young basil leaves; basil that has been growing for too long acquires an unpleasantly strong taste. The pine nuts must be fresh, and the olive oil must be very good, though unassertive. If possible, use an oil from Liguria or from Lake Garda; they are less pungent than oil from Tuscany, and less heavy than that from Apulia. The oil must be added slowly, as for mayonnaise, so as to create the right emulsion. If you have time, make your pesto by hand in a mortar: more juices are released by pounding than chopping with a metal blade.

Recipes for pesto are numerous. Mine contains two special touches. One is that when I make pesto with basil grown far from the Mediterranean I add a couple of tablespoons of yogurt or heavy cream to modify the stronger taste, and the other is that I heat the pine nuts for 3 or 4 minutes to enhance their aroma.

The pasta traditionally used in Liguria is trenette (large tagliatelle) or piccagge—another homemade shape. In Liguria, a couple of potatoes and a handful of green beans are cooked with the pasta. Tagliatelle, spaghetti and potato gnocchi are all suitable. When the pasta is cooked, reserve two or three tablespoons of the cooking water, to add to the pesto before dressing the pasta.

1½ cups fresh basil leaves
2 garlic cloves, peeled
2 tablespoons pine nuts
(1 ounce)
pinch of coarse salt
4 tablespoons freshly grated parmesan
2 tablespoons freshly grated pecorino romano
½ cup extra-virgin olive oil
2 tablespoons plain yogurt

NOTE: Always taste the pecorino before you buy it; it is often old and tangy, or even slightly rancid. In this case, or if you cannot get pecorino, replace it with parmesan.

NOTE: Pesto freezes very well. Omit the garlic and cheese and add them just before using the sauce.

1 To make the pesto in a mortar, put the basil leaves, garlic, pine nuts and salt in a mortar and grind against the sides of the mortar, crushing all the ingredients with the pestle until the mixture has become a paste. Mix in the grated cheeses and pour over the oil very gradually, beating with a wooden spoon. When all the oil has been incorporated mix in the yogurt.

2 To make the pesto in a food processor or blender, put the basil, garlic, pine nuts, salt and olive oil in the workbowl or blender jar. Process at high speed and when evenly blended transfer to a small bowl. Mix in the cheeses and then blend in the yogurt.

Minestrone alla genovese

MINESTRONE WITH PESTO • SERVES 8

Adding pesto at the end gives this minestrone a particularly Mediterranean taste. Traditionally the old-fashioned pesto—without pine nuts—is added, but the modern version can be used quite successfully. The soup is made with olive oil and it is prepared *a crudo,* meaning that all the elements are put together at the same time in the pan when still raw.

The quantities given here are for eight people because minestrone is better made in a large quantity: it is even more delicious warmed up one or more days later. Minestrone keeps well in the refrigerator for up to three days, but it cannot be frozen. Add the pasta and the pesto in the right proportions, to the amount of soup you want to eat at one meal and chill the rest. You can serve the leftover minestrone with rice instead of pasta or just as it is, without the pesto, as a *zuppa di verdura* (vegetable soup).

- **4 tablespoons extra-virgin olive oil**
- **2 onions, sliced**
- **2 celery stalks with their green tops, sliced**
- **2 carrots, cut into ½-inch dice**
- **2 medium potatoes, cut into ½-inch dice**
- **½ cup shelled peas**
- **½ cup green beans, topped and tailed and cut into 1-inch pieces**
- **½ pound spinach, shredded**
- **a few outside leaves of Boston lettuce, shredded (optional)**
- **2 medium zucchini, cut into ½-inch dice**
- **½ pound ripe tomatoes, skinned and seeded, *or* 4 canned plum tomatoes, coarsely chopped, with their juice**
- **2 garlic cloves, peeled and sliced**
- **8 cups vegetable stock (page 4) *or* water**
- **salt**
- **freshly ground black pepper**
- **1 cup small tubular pasta, such as ditali (about ¼ pound)**
- **freshly grated parmesan**

PESTO

- **1 cup fresh basil leaves**
- **2 tablespoons flat-leaf parsley**
- **1 garlic clove, peeled**
- **2 tablespoons extra-virgin olive oil**

1 Put the oil, onions, celery, carrots, potatoes, peas, green beans, spinach, lettuce if using, zucchini, tomatoes, garlic and stock in a saucepan and bring slowly to the boil. Cook, uncovered, for 1½ hours or so over very low heat. The soup should just simmer, not boil.

2 Taste and add salt, if necessary, and pepper. Add the pasta and continue cooking until ready. The soup should be very thick (the Genoese say you should be able to stand a spoon up in it), but if it is too thick, add a little water before adding the pasta.

3 While the pasta is cooking, put the basil leaves, parsley and garlic in a mortar and pound with a circular movement. Add the oil and pound to a paste. If you do not have a mortar and pestle, make the pesto in a food processor or blender.

4 When the pasta is *al dente,* turn off the heat and mix in the pesto. Add pepper to taste and leave the soup to rest for about 2 minutes. Serve, handing around the parmesan in a bowl.

This is a simple but nourishing beginning to an informal family meal. My choice for the secondo would be Rabbit with Herbs and Dried Porcini (page 132) or Tuna Baked with Tomatoes, Capers, Black Olives and Chilies (page 59). Vegetarians could follow the soup with Baked Polenta with Porcini (page 36) or Potato and Tomato Pie (page 114).

Scaloppine al basilico e limone

VEAL SCALOPPINE WITH BASIL AND LEMON • SERVES 4

Basil adds a fresh fragrance to this traditional Milanese dish, *frittura piccata,* usually made with parsley. The dish is very easy to make, but there are a few pitfalls I'd like to point out. You must use white veal, sliced across the grain and pounded to a thickness of about an eighth of an inch. Slicing across the grain prevents the meat from shrinking when cooked.

The secret of good scaloppine is to have the fat at the right temperature when the meat goes in the pan. The butter and oil must be quite hot, yet not burning, before you add the meat, and the pan should not be crowded. If the fat is not hot enough, the veal will remain pale, soft and tasteless; if it is too hot, the meat will shrink and harden. If too many slices are put in, the temperature of the fat will drop suddenly, and there will be too much juice released for the meat to fry properly. You need a good heavy pan, copper being the best. If your pan is not big enough, fry the scaloppine in two batches, keeping the first batch warm and then returning it to the pan before adding the lemon juice.

1¼ **pounds veal scaloppine**
2 **tablespoons unsalted butter**
1 **tablespoon olive oil**
salt
freshly ground black pepper
2 **tablespoons lemon juice**
1 **cup torn fresh basil leaves**

1 Prepare the scaloppine by pounding them thin and cutting them into neat shapes.

2 Heat the butter and oil in a large heavy sauté pan and fry the scaloppine for no more than 1 minute on each side. Add salt and pepper to taste. Splash with lemon juice and add the torn basil leaves. Turn the scaloppine over in the sauce for half a minute or so and serve immediately.

✖ These scaloppine are delicious accompanied by tagliatelle dressed with a generous amount of unsalted butter, not a traditionally Italian acompaniment but one that even I would happily accept. Sautéed zucchini is also good. Serve Fennel Timbale (page 101) as a primo if you are having pasta with the meat; gnocchi if zucchini is your choice.

Bastoncini di patate e zucchine
SAUTEED POTATO AND ZUCCHINI STICKS • SERVES 4

On the rare occasions when I serve two vegetables with meat or fish, I find it easier to cook them partly or entirely together, as in Sautéed Peppers and Potatoes (page 10). Apart from saving time and effort, you save oil or butter, gas or electricity and some washing-up. Zucchini and potatoes make a good and pretty mixture. I like my zucchini tender and not too crunchy, and my potatoes properly cooked. If you prefer your zucchini al dente, add them to the potatoes twelve minutes later. The herbs can be varied according to what is best in the garden or in the shops, but I recommend oregano, which is the best flavoring for zucchini. The same two vegetables can also be steamed and served together, dressed with a couple of tablespoons of olive oil. This is an easier and healthier method, but somewhat less tasty.

For 4 people, cut 1½ pounds of potatoes, and the same amount of zucchini, into short sticks, about ¼ inch thick. Put 4 tablespoons of olive oil in a nonstick frying pan, add the potatoes and sauté for 7 to 8 minutes. Mix in the zucchini and continue cooking, over lively heat, stirring quite frequently. About 10 minutes before the vegetables are ready, season with salt and pepper and add some chopped herbs.

Prugne sciroppate al rosmarino
PLUMS IN WINE WITH ROSEMARY AND SPICES • SERVES 6

Like several other dishes, zabaglione and tarte Tatin among them, these poached plums owe their origin to a mistake. Many years ago I had two saucepans on the stove, one with some plums that were gently stewing away, the other with some potatoes that were sautéing briskly. The untimely and insistent ringing of the telephone took me away from the stove. I shouted to my little daughter to go and pick a sprig of rosemary from the garden and put it into the pan . . . but which pan I forgot to specify. When I got back to the stove, I found the rosemary in with the plums! To my surprise, and relief, the plums were delicious, and since then I have always added fresh rosemary to the dish.

(*continued*)

**PLUMS IN WINE WITH
ROSEMARY AND
SPICES** (*continued*)

The rosemary is hardly detectable, yet it gives the syrup a certain *je ne sais quoi* which never fails to puzzle people. When you serve the dish, try asking your guests what has gone into it. You can bet for high stakes and you will win!

If you have a glass bowl with a stem, serve the compote in it, but remember to let it cool before you put it in the bowl or the hot syrup will shatter the glass.

1½ cups good red wine

about 1 cup sugar, depending on
    the sweetness of the fruit

sprig of fresh rosemary, about
    6 inches long

strip of lemon rind, yellow part
    only

  2 cloves

2-inch cinnamon stick

  4 peppercorns, bruised

  2 pounds plums, ripe but firm

1 Put the wine, sugar, 1 cup of water, the rosemary, lemon rind, cloves, cinnamon and peppercorns in a large sauté pan. Heat gently until the sugar has dissolved, stirring frequently with a wooden spoon.

2 Wash the plums and add to the pan. Cover with a tight-fitting lid and cook very gently until the plums are soft but still whole. Transfer the plums to a bowl with a slotted spoon.

3 Strain the syrup into a clean saucepan and boil very rapidly until it is thick and syrupy. Pour over the plums and, when cold, cover with plastic wrap and refrigerate.

✖ Serve the plums as they are or with yogurt or heavy cream.

Wine and Vinegar

WINE

Spezzato di manzo al Barbera
BEEF BRAISED IN BARBERA WINE

Patate ubriache
DRUNK POTATOES

Aspic di pesche noci
NECTARINES IN WINE JELLY

VINEGAR

Giardiniera
PICKLED VEGETABLES

Pollo alla cacciatora
CHICKEN BRAISED WITH VINEGAR AND
HERBS

La cotoletta a la lavandera
BREADED VEAL CHOPS IN A SWEET-AND-SOUR
SAUCE

Brasato all'aceto
BEEF BRAISED IN WINE VINEGAR

Spezzatino di agnello in agrodolce
SWEET-AND-SOUR SHOULDER OF LAMB

Quaglie all'aceto balsamico
ROAST QUAIL WITH BALSAMIC VINEGAR

Filetto di maiale alla Cavalcanti
PORK TENDERLOIN WITH BERRIES, ALMONDS
AND BALSAMIC VINEGAR

213

Wine

It is difficult to cook an Italian meal without using some wine. For some cooks it is nearly impossible. Whether the wine is red or white, dry or sweet, it must be a decent wine, good enough that you would happily drink it at table. It is no good buying so-called cooking wine; it will ruin your beef or your fish, and your stomach in the bargain. You can get a good bottle of Chianti for a reasonable amount, and the same sum will buy you an even better bottle of Valpolicella or Soave, Italy's best-selling wines after Chianti. And, of course, there are many good local and California wines on the market. In this book I have suggested the use of a particular wine only when necessary to the final result.

Wine is necessary in many dishes to achieve perfect roundness of flavor. This does not mean that it can be added at will, discretion being one of the guiding rules of a good cook. If, for instance, you are cooking a dish that needs more liquid, yet you have already added all the wine that is recommended, add water, rather than extra wine, to provide the necessary liquid without the unwanted extra flavor. It is only in desserts and some fruit salads that the taste of wine should come through loud and clear.

In cooking, wine should always be brought to the boil and boiled fiercely for one or two minutes, depending on the quantity, to allow part of the alcohol to evaporate. If the food was browned first, some of the wine is usually added to the pan to deglaze the cooking juices, then the rest is combined with the food that is to be cooked in it. When I add wine to a dish to be baked, I first bring the wine to the boil; I do this both to evaporate part of the alcohol and to avoid lowering the temperature of the food.

Spezzato di manzo al Barbera

BEEF BRAISED IN BARBERA WINE • SERVES 6

Barbera is a robust and full-bodied red wine from Piedmont. First you deglaze the pan with a lighter white wine, then braise the meat in the Barbera. This is a rustic dish, rich and full of flavor, an ideal meat course to serve in the winter.

1 Chop together the pancetta, carrot, celery, sage leaves and rosemary needles until very fine and place with the olive oil in a heavy-bottomed casserole. Sauté gently until the vegetables are soft.

2 Heat the vegetable oil in a large frying pan and, when very hot, add the meat and brown well on all sides. If necessary, do this in 2 or more batches. Do not cut short this operation, because it is this frying that gives flavor to the meat, sealing in the juices. Remove the meat from the pan and place in the casserole on top of the vegetables.

3 Preheat the oven to 325°F.

4 Pour the white wine into the pan in which the meat has browned and boil rapidly for 30 seconds while scraping the pan with a metal spoon. Pour over the meat.

5 Place the sliced onions on top of the meat and sprinkle with sugar and salt. Cover the casserole with a tight lid and cook over low heat until the onion has wilted, about 10 to 15 minutes.

6 Pour the Barbera wine over the meat and place the covered casserole in the oven for about 2½ hours, until the meat is tender enough to be cut with a fork.

7 Mash the butter and flour together with a fork.

8 Take the casserole out of the oven. Add a generous grinding of pepper and then stir in the butter and flour mixture a little at a time, stirring constantly and waiting for the first bit to melt and be incorporated before adding the next one. Serve straightaway from the casserole or transfer to a heated deep dish.

✖ Polenta is the classic accompaniment, but I can also recommend Bread Gnocchi (page 44). Make them the size of a tangerine. You should not serve any vegetable, but a green salad afterwards might be very welcome to cleanse the palate.

- 2 ounces pancetta
- 1 carrot
- 1 celery stalk, with green top if possible
- 5 to 7 fresh sage leaves *or* 4 or 5 dried sage leaves
- sprig of fresh rosemary 2 inches long *or* ½ teaspoon dried rosemary
- 3 tablespoons olive oil
- 2 tablespoons vegetable oil
- 1½ pounds beef stew meat, cut into 1- to 1½-inch cubes, trimmed of sinews
- ½ pound lean pork, cut into 1- to 1½-inch cubes, trimmed of sinews and excess fat
- ⅔ cup dry white wine
- 4 large onions, thickly sliced
- ½ tablespoon sugar
- salt
- 2 cups Barbera wine
- 2 tablespoons butter
- 1 tablespoon flour
- freshly ground black pepper

Patate ubriache

DRUNK POTATOES • SERVES 4 OR 5

Each year we spend a few peaceful weeks at my brother's country house near Lake Bolsena, about 60 miles north of Rome. It is in a tiny village called Pianiano, which is surrounded by gently rolling hills planted with wheat, corn and vines. Annina, who looks after my brother's house, sits for hours in the village square with the other local women. They all knit incessantly, making sweaters with holes and bobbles in the most garish colors to be sold in the boutiques in nearby towns. When I am there I join them, and we chat about their knitting, my tapestry work and, mainly, their cooking, which is how I learned about these drunk potatoes.

Not only are they happy to share their recipes, they also sometimes invite us to share meals with them, meals of great simplicity, gargantuan quantity and extreme excellence. A typical spread would start with salami and prosciutto to whet the appetite, then tagliatelle with a ragù, chicken livers being a favorite, then pollastrelli al forno (roast chicken)—chickens which were still scratching about the day before—perhaps accompanied by these patate ubriache and certainly followed by an insalatina di campo (wild salad). Pecorino, and after that a tart filled with homemade jam or ricotta, finish off the meal, and, in my case, the eater.

2 pounds new potatoes, peeled and cut into ¼-inch slices
4 tablespoons unsalted butter
2 tablespoons olive oil
2 shallots *or* 1 small onion, chopped
1 garlic clove
sprig of fresh sage
1 cup dry white wine
½ cup meat stock (page 3)
salt
pepper
1 teaspoon potato starch
½ cup milk

NOTE: The dish can be prepared up to half an hour in advance. Leave the potatoes in the pan with the lid on and they will keep quite warm enough.

1 Wash the potatoes in 2 or 3 changes of cold water until the water is clear (this gets rid of the starch). Dry them thoroughly with paper towels.

2 Make a little soffritto in a large sauté pan with the butter, olive oil, shallots or onion, garlic clove, and the sage.

3 When the shallot is soft, add the potatoes, turning them over frequently so that they take up the taste of the soffritto. Remove and discard the garlic and the sage.

4 Heat the wine and stock and add to the pan. Season with salt and pepper and give the potatoes a good mix. Use a fork as it breaks the potatoes less than a spoon. Cover the pan and cook the potatoes over low heat until they are nearly done, by which time they should have absorbed nearly all the liquid. Stir occasionally and if they get too dry add a little more hot stock or water.

5 When testing this recipe I decided to add a finishing touch that gives the sauce a delicate liaison and tones down the flavor of the wine. About 5 minutes before the potatoes are ready add the starch dissolved in milk. Turn the potatoes over gently and finish cooking with the lid tightly on. Taste and check seasoning.

Aspic di pesche noci
NECTARINES IN WINE JELLY • SERVES 6

In Italy it is typical to end a meal with peaches in wine. You slice
the peaches (my father always used to do so at the table, straight
into his wine glass), sprinkle with a little sugar and pour over about
a cup of red or white wine. This dessert is an extension of the same
simple idea of peaches and wine. I use nectarines, instead of
peaches, because they slice more neatly. The taste is similar yet more
complex, and the aspic looks extremely handsome. You can also
make this aspic with ripe pears, peeled and cut into segments.

1 Scrub the orange and lemon thoroughly.

2 Put the wine, sugar, cinnamon, peppercorns, ginger,
cloves and the zest of about half the orange and half the
lemon into a saucepan. Bring slowly to the boil and when the
sugar has dissolved, turn up the heat and boil rapidly until
about half of the wine has evaporated.

3 Dissolve the gelatin in 1 scant cup hot water over very
low heat.

4 When the wine syrup is reduced, remove from the
heat and add the dissolved gelatin. Mix well and then strain
into a clean pitcher. Add lemon juice to taste: the juice of half
a medium lemon should be enough to give the right "bite."

5 Before you begin to assemble the dish, test whether
the aspic is hard enough by pouring a couple of tablespoons
of the syrup into a cup and putting it in the fridge to set. It
must set quite hard, as the nectarines will later release some
of their juices and dilute the gelatin.

6 Rinse a 1-quart loaf pan with cold water. Pour in
enough gelatin mixture to make a ¼-inch layer and
refrigerate.

7 When the aspic in the pan has set, wash and cut the
nectarines into thin wedges. Arrange a layer of wedges neatly
on the bottom of the pan and then pour enough syrup to
cover. Return the pan to the refrigerator. When the aspic has
set, add the rest of the nectarines, pour the gelatin mixture in
gently and chill until set.

8 To unmold, place the pan in a little hot water for half
a minute. Run a metal spatula along the sides of the pan and
turn it over onto an oval dish. Place the aspic back in the
refrigerator until you want to serve. Decorate it with mint or
scented geranium leaves. To serve, cut the aspic into thick
slices with a sharp knife.

1 orange
1 lemon
2 cups full-bodied red wine,
   such as Barbera or Chianti
   Riserva
1¼ cups sugar
1 cinnamon stick
4 peppercorns
¼ teaspoon ground ginger
2 cloves
1 tablespoon (1 envelope)
   unflavored gelatin
1¾ pounds firm nectarines
mint *or* scented geranium leaves

Vinegar

The traditional vinegar of Italy is plain wine vinegar. Within the last ten years, however, with the spread of the nuova cucina, more and more different vinegars are being used: raspberry, tarragon, sherry and lately cider, a delicious light vinegar with little acidity, yet a very full and developed flavor. In this book I have kept to the traditional wine vinegar, which is easy to find. Red vinegar is more commonly used than white, although to a certain extent it is a question of taste.

The main use of vinegar is in salad. Most Italian salads are very simply dressed: with oil, vinegar (or occasionally lemon juice) and salt. The proportion of vinegar to oil varies according to taste, to the acidity of the vinegar and the type of salad, but usually we add one tablespoon of vinegar and four tablespoons of oil to a bowl of salad for four people. But beets, for instance, call for more vinegar, while tomatoes need far less.

Vinegar is often used in place of wine as a flavoring in the cooking of meat and, occasionally, fish. Meat, rabbit, hare and game are often marinated in vinegar, especially in Umbria, where vinegar diluted with water replaces wine in most recipes. Vinegar is the essential ingredient in a carpione or scapece, sweet-and-sour dishes made all over Italy. Some cooks add a tablespoon or so of vinegar to pears or plums in the poaching liquid. This may seem odd, but I can recommend it because the vinegar cuts into the sweetness of the syrup.

The most important use of vinegar is as a preservative. The Romans developed the art of preserving food in vinegar and passed their knowledge on to their subjects all over their Empire. Writing in the first century A.D., Apicius gave these recipes for preserving turnips: "First clean them and put them in a vessel and then pour on myrtle berries mixed with honey and vinegar. Another method: mix mustard and honey, vinegar and salt and pour over the turnips put together in a vessel."

The quality of vinegar is important. Choose a good French or Italian vinegar which is strong but without the sharp unpleasant acidity of some inferior brands. I put a clove or two of garlic in my bottle of vinegar; other people add rosemary or other herbs. Tarragon is a classic for the French.

HOW TO MAKE VINEGAR. You can make your own vinegar in the special acetaia, a little barrel with a tap at the bottom, or, indeed, in a bottle. I use dregs from bottles of wine to top up the vinegar. To start, put some wine in a bottle and add some "mother" of vinegar, or four tablespoons of vinegar. Keep the bottle open in the kitchen and top it up until nearly full. Leave it for some weeks, but keep a watch on it and remove the top layer of the mother from the surface. If the mother is too thick it can block the air which helps the vinegar to develop. When ready, filter the vinegar into a clean bottle and cork the bottle. You can start another batch with the same mother. Some country people stick two strands of spaghetti into the bottle in which the vinegar is being made. The semolina helps the fermentation.

Giardiniera

PICKLED VEGETABLES • FILLS A 1-QUART PRESERVING JAR

Also called sottaceti, these pickles can be bought in many Italian delicatessens. However, they are so easy to make that you might like to prepare them yourself. The selection of vegetables can vary, but it is nice to have a good variety. There are some vegetables that should always be used, others are added according to taste and availability.

1 Cut the carrots and celery stalks into ½-inch cubes. If you are using a large pepper and a piece of a large cucumber, cut into the same size cubes. Peel the onions, remove the stalks from the mushrooms and divide the cauliflower or broccoli into very small florets. Peel and julienne the celery root, cut the beans into 1-inch pieces, and the turnip into ½-inch cubes.

2 Put 1 cup of vinegar and 2 cups of water in a saucepan and bring to the boil. Add the carrots, celery, peppers and, if you are using them, the green beans, turnip and celery root. Cook for 5 minutes and then add the other vegetables. Cook for 10 minutes or so, until the vegetables are cooked al dente. Drain and dry the vegetables with paper towels.

3 Put the rest of the vinegar in the same saucepan and add the oil, sugar, salt, bay leaves, garlic and peppercorns. Bring to the boil, stirring occasionally, and boil for 2 minutes.

4 Wash the preserving jar or jars thoroughly. Rinse with boiling water and let drain.

5 Pour a ladleful of the vinegar mixture into the jar and then transfer all the vegetables using a slotted spoon. Pour in the rest of the vinegar mixture so that the vegetables are well covered. When the giardiniera is cold, seal it and give the jar a good shake.

6 Put the jar in your pantry and forget about it for at least one month. I think you will enjoy it.

1½ **pounds vegetables, including carrots, celery stalks, peppers, tiny cucumbers or a piece of a large cucumber, pearl onions, button mushrooms and cauliflower or broccoli florets, with a piece of celery root, a few topped and tailed green beans or a small turnip (optional)**

3 **cups white wine vinegar**

4 **tablespoons olive oil**

2 **tablespoons sugar**

2 **teaspoons salt**

2 **bay leaves**

2 **garlic cloves, peeled**

12 **black peppercorns**

Pollo alla cacciatora

CHICKEN BRAISED WITH VINEGAR AND HERBS • SERVES 4

Vinegar is often used in cooking instead of wine, especially in central Italy, where wine is considered too rich for stews. You can make this dish with rabbit, which is now available from many butchers.

1 chicken, 3 to 3½ pounds, cut into 8 pieces

1½ ounces pancetta, in a single slice, *or* bacon, blanched for 3 minutes

½ tablespoon fresh rosemary needles

6 fresh sage leaves

3 sprigs of fresh thyme

1 bay leaf

4 tablespoons olive oil

3 garlic cloves, peeled and bruised

1 chili

½ cup red wine vinegar

salt

pepper

1 teaspoon sugar, if necessary

1 tablespoon butter (optional)

1 Wash and dry the chicken pieces very thoroughly. Remove the skin, if you prefer.

2 Chop up the pancetta with the rosemary, sage, thyme and bay leaf to make a very fine battuto (pounded mixture).

3 Choose a large sauté pan. Heat the oil with the battuto, the garlic and the chili over gentle heat for a few minutes, until the garlic releases its aroma and begins to color. Remove and discard the garlic and the chili.

4 Add the chicken. If your pan is not large enough to hold the pieces in a single layer, brown them in 2 batches. The chicken must be nicely browned all over, which will take 10 to 15 minutes: be patient about doing this.

5 Raise the heat and splash the chicken with vinegar. Let the vinegar bubble away for 1 minute and then pour over ⅔ cup hot water. Season with salt and pepper, cover the pan and cook until tender, about 30 minutes. If the chicken becomes too dry you may have to add a couple of tablespoons of hot water during the cooking.

6 When the chicken is tender, remove to a heated dish and keep warm. Skim off the fat that floats on the surface of the cooking liquid. Check the cooking liquid. If too watery, reduce over high heat until rich and syrupy; if too dense, add a little water; if too sharp sweeten it with a little sugar. It all depends on the amount of water the chicken contained and on the sharpness of your vinegar. Also check the seasoning, then add the butter, if using, in small pieces, to give the sauce a more mellow flavor and a beautiful sheen. Spoon the sauce over the chicken and serve at once.

✖ Boiled rice dressed with a little olive oil goes well with the chicken. If you prefer to have some vegetables, I suggest Drunk Potatoes (page 216). Minestrone with Pesto (page 209) or Bread Soup (page 43) would be a good first course for hearty eaters; people with a more modest appetite might prefer Baked Mushrooms with Anchovies and Capers (page 134) or Panzanella (page 121).

La cotoletta a la lavandera

BREADED VEAL CHOPS IN A SWEET-AND-SOUR SAUCE • SERVES 4

This recipe is from a book written by Giuseppe Fontana, who was chef at the famous Savini Restaurant in Milan from 1905 to 1929. The book, called *La Cusinna de Milan* (The Cooking of Milan), is a collection of recipes, all written in verse and for the most part in Milanese dialect. Being Milanese I am lucky to be able to enjoy them from both the literary and the gastronomic point of view.

No explanation is given as to why this recipe for breaded chops is dubbed *a la lavandera*, meaning cooked the washerwoman's way, nor can I think of one. If you like balsamic vinegar, as I do, you can use it instead of the plain vinegar and leave out the sugar, since the balsamic vinegar provides sufficient sweetness.

"Puccia dent ben la cotoletta e a coeur seren gustala se la pias," wrote Fontana in broad Milanese: douse the chop well and, with a light heart, taste it to see if you like it. I am sure you will.

You can use pork or veal chops for this dish. Cook the chops as described in the recipe for Veal Chops, Milanese Style (page 50), but do not add salt to the beaten eggs. When the meat is cooked, transfer to a heated dish, leaving the cooking juices in the pan. Add 1 tablespoon of sugar to the pan and cook for 1 to 2 minutes, stirring constantly. Deglaze with 4 tablespoons of your best wine vinegar and the same quantity of hot water, then add 2 tablespoons *each* of golden raisins and pine nuts and salt to taste. Turn the heat down to low and cook for 1 minute. After this, return the chops to the pan for another couple of minutes, turning them over once. No pepper was used by Fontana, but I think 5 or 6 grindings added with the salt give the right amount of piquancy to the meat. Place the chops on the serving dish and pour the sauce over.

✄ Serve with buttered spinach and creamed potatoes or with Braised Broccoli (page 201). The chops are also delicious cold, accompanied by a potato salad or Wine-dressed Green Bean and Tomato Salad (page 120).

Brasato all'aceto
BEEF BRAISED IN WINE VINEGAR • SERVES 8

LARDING

2 ounces pancetta *or* unsmoked bacon, in a single slice

8 fresh sage leaves, chopped, *or* 1 tablespoon dried sage

salt, preferably coarse salt

freshly ground black pepper

MARINADE

2 tablespoons olive oil

juice of 1 large lemon

⅔ cup red wine vinegar

5 or 6 black peppercorns

---

3 to 3½ pounds chuck *or* rump roast

2 tablespoons vegetable oil

1 onion, very finely chopped

3 garlic cloves, peeled and finely chopped

2 anchovy fillets, chopped

2 tablespoons chopped fresh parsley

1 tablespoon chopped fresh sage leaves *or* ½ tablespoon dried sage

2 tablespoons finely chopped celery leaves

2 tablespoons olive oil

salt

2 teaspoons brown sugar

3 tablespoons heavy cream

1 tablespoon unsalted butter

freshly ground black pepper

In this old Lombard recipe a pot roast, brasato, is cooked in red wine vinegar instead of the more usual red wine. In northern Italian homes, brasato is one of the most popular dishes for serving on Sundays or at dinner parties. It is not the sort of dish you will be able to sample at a restaurant because it requires time, patience and the use of a large piece of meat. But it is ideal at home. It is a generous dish, and it has the advantage that it will not be spoiled if your guests, or your children, are late. Brasato is so well behaved that it can even be prepared in advance and slowly reheated in a low oven.

1 Cut the pancetta into pieces about 4 inches long and ½ inch thick. If you are using bacon, parboil for 3 minutes and drain on paper towels before cutting.

2 Mix together the sage leaves, salt and pepper and coat the pancetta pieces with the mixture.

3 Lard the meat by cutting deep slits in it, following the grain of the meat, and pushing the pieces of pancetta into the slits. If you don't have a larding needle, use a chopstick or the end of a clean round pencil.

4 For the marinade, beat together the olive oil, lemon juice, vinegar and peppercorns in an earthenware pot or a bowl and place the meat in it. Cover the bowl and leave to marinate for 24 hours, turning the meat over as often as you can. Unless the weather is hot, do not put the bowl in the refrigerator. The vinegar in the marinade will help to preserve the meat, and the beef will become more tender out of the fridge.

5 Preheat the oven to 325°F. Take the meat out of the marinade, reserving the liquid dry it very thoroughly and tie it into a neat oblong shape.

6 Put the vegetable oil in a heavy frying pan and, when the oil is hot, slip in the meat and brown very well on all sides over high heat. Transfer the meat to a side plate.

7 Strain the marinade and add to the frying pan. Deglaze for 1 minute, scraping the bottom of the pan with a metal spoon. Measure the liquid and add enough boiling water to make 1 cup.

8 Put the onion, garlic, anchovies, parsley, sage, celery and olive oil into an oval casserole, large enough to hold the

meat comfortably but snugly. Put on the heat and cook for a minute, stirring frequently.

9 Place the meat on the bed of herbs, then add the marinade and a little salt. Bring slowly to the boil. Cover the pan with a lid and transfer to the oven. Cook for 1½ hours. Keep a watch on the meat: it should cook at a very low but steady simmer. Turn the meat over 3 or 4 times.

10 Sprinkle with sugar and continue cooking, always tightly covered, for another 1½ hours, until the meat is very tender indeed.

11 Transfer the meat to a cutting board and allow to cool a little, while you make the sauce.

12 Skim the fat from the juices in the casserole. If the liquid is too thin, boil briskly to reduce until the juices are rich and syrupy. Add the cream, stir well and cook for a couple of minutes. Remove the pan from the heat and add the butter, cut into 3 or 4 small pieces, a little at a time. Shake the pan gently and allow the butter to melt properly. This butter added at the last minute gives the sauce a beautiful sheen. Taste and check salt and pepper.

13 Carve the meat into ⅜-inch slices and lay them, slightly overlapping, on a heated oval dish. Spoon over the sauce and serve.

✄ I love brasato with polenta, the traditional accompaniment. Alternatively try a puree of potatoes and celeriac, or grated carrots sautéed in butter and then cooked with a little stock for 5 minutes with a final addition of two tablespoons of cream.

- -

Spezzatino di agnello in agrodolce
SWEET-AND-SOUR SHOULDER OF LAMB • SERVES 4

Few dishes are more satisfying than a good stew. Shoulder of lamb is an ideal stewing cut because it has enough fat to keep the meat moist and tasty during the lengthy cooking.

In this recipe from Apulia, the heel of the Italian boot, the milk and sugar added to the sauce counterbalance the vinegary marinade, while the basil lifts and refreshes the flavor.

(continued)

MARINADE

⅔ cup red wine vinegar
6 juniper berries, bruised
3 garlic cloves, squashed
2 bay leaves
4 or 5 peppercorns, lightly crushed
salt

———

1¾ pounds shoulder of lamb, cut into 1-inch cubes
3 tablespoons olive oil
1 large onion, very finely sliced
salt
1 tablespoon vegetable oil
1 tablespoon tomato paste dissolved in ½ cup warm milk
3 tablespoons sugar
freshly ground black pepper
10 fresh basil leaves, torn, *or* 2 teaspoons dried oregano

NOTE: The dish can be prepared in advance. It is actually better made the day before and then slowly reheated, either in the oven or on top.

1 Combine the vinegar, juniper berries, garlic, bay leaves, peppercorns and a generous pinch of salt in a bowl for the marinade. Add the meat, cover the bowl and put it in a cool place and leave for at least 4 hours. Drain and dry the meat, reserving the marinade.

2 Gently heat the olive oil with the onion in a heavy pot, preferably a flameproof earthenware one, and add a little salt (this helps soften the onion without browning it).

3. Meanwhile, sear the meat in a nonstick frying pan with the vegetable oil. If necessary, do this in 2 batches, because the meat will brown only in a single layer. Sauté on all sides for about 10 minutes, stirring very frequently. Then transfer all the meat to the pot containing the onion. Mix well and let the meat take the flavor for 2 or 3 minutes.

4 Add the dissolved tomato paste and stir well. Turn the heat down to very low and cover the pan, placing the lid slightly askew. Some of the steam will escape, thus concentrating the flavor of the tomato and of the meat juices.

5 Cook for about 30 minutes, keeping a watch on the meat. Should it get too dry, add a couple of tablespoons of hot water. Add the strained marinade and the sugar, and salt and pepper to taste. Cook for another 20 minutes, still with the lid askew, turning the meat occasionally. The lamb is ready when it is very tender; the exact cooking time depends entirely on the age of the lamb. Remove the fat from the surface. When the lamb is done, add the basil leaves, taste and adjust seasoning.

✕ I like to accompany this dish with a buttery potato puree or with some medium pasta such as lumache or shells. Nothing more is needed other than a lovely salad afterwards. If you want a primo, choose Grilled Peppers (page 105) or Tomatoes Filled with Rice and Black Olives (page 231).

BALSAMIC VINEGAR

This very special vinegar, made from the cooked and concentrated must of the white grapes of the Trebbiano vine, exists in two forms, one of which can be bought without too much diffi-culty, while the other is almost a collector's item. The first is labeled, simply, aceto balsamico (balsamic vinegar) and it is given its characteristic flavor by the addition of a little caramelized sugar. It has a sweet yet vinegary fragrance, and a beautiful dark brown color glinting with gold. This is the balsamic vinegar found in this country in Italian shops and good supermarkets. It is a good product that can be used without qualms in all the recipes I give here.

The other, more rarified version is called aceto balsamico tradizionale, and by law it can only be given this name when it has been aged for at least ten years. This balsamic vinegar is similar in color to the first, but its flavor is full and velvety, a perfect balance between sweet and sour, with a more subtle—a more elegant—fragrance. Made on a very small scale in and around Reggio Emilia and, above all, Modena, aceto balsamico tradizionale is the object of a gastronomic cult, not to say obsession. Pages have been written about it and societies formed to foster it. "It can be sipped in small glasses, like a very rare liqueur, served on a silver platter so as to give it due honor." Thus wrote Paolo Monelli in his *Giro gastronomico d'Italia*, published in 1939, and this is exactly what I did recently when I went to Emilia to study the mystique at first hand.

The setting for my initiation into the mysteries of this cult was a charming house in the countryside not far from Reggio Emilia. It is the country house of Maria Carla Terrachini Sidoli and her husband, Gigi, and apart from the charm of its owners, not to mention the aceto balsamico tradizionale made in its attic, it is remarkable for the fact that it remains today exactly as it was when Baron Franchetti built it as a hunting lodge in 1889, and had all the furniture and fittings made expressly for the house. As a result the house, and everything in it, is a perfect example of art nouveau.

We were asked for five o'clock and, naturally enough, looked forward to a refreshing cup of tea. But as we sat in the garden on that sunny afternoon, with the fertile expanse of the Po valley curling away into the distance. Maria Carla produced a silver tray bearing not cups and saucers, but tiny glasses, a plate of white bread and a small vial—rather like those used in church for sacramental wine—containing the precious liquid. This was the cue for Gigi, who is a chemist specializing in medicine as well as a large-scale pig-farmer, to launch into a discourse about the favorite of his three occupations, making aceto balsamico tradizionale in the attic.

First the grape must is brought to the boil and reduced. It is then poured into large wooden vessels called sogli and any excess acidity is neutralized by the addition of a small amount of marble powder or ash. The must then separates and the clear, pale liquid that will become balsamic vinegar begins its years of aging in different barrels. Various woods may be used for the barrels—oak, chestnut, mulberry, birch, or juniper—and the liquid is transferred from one barrel to another about every 12 months. Typical of the attention paid to detail is the fact that the barrels must be plugged with a stone that comes from a river. The reason that vinegar-making takes place in Gigi's attic, as it does in the attics of many old palazzi in Modena and Reggio Emilia, is that the space under the roof provides the necessary heat yet can be arranged to give plenty of ventilation. In some of these attics there is balsamic vinegar over a hundred years old, to be enjoyed only by family and friends. It is used with great reverence.

So it was that sunny afternoon. A few drops were poured out of the little vial into each glass, and, on tasting it, I began to understand why this vinegar is treated as an elixir. That balsamic vinegar had been started in the nineteenth century and had been aged only in barrels made of juniper wood. Its nose was incredibly rich and all-pervading, and I could realize why Lucrezia Borgia was said to have kept on sniffing it—in the manner of smelling salts—while giving birth to her first son. Therapeutic properties were also attributed to balsamic vinegar by Rossini, who wrote to a friend, "a little vinegar from Modena, with its well-known soothing and refreshing effect, succeeded in restoring me to a degree of health and serenity."

The earliest mention of balsamic vinegar is found in a chronicle of 1046 written by a Benedictine monk who wrote about the life of Matilda of Canossa. Her father, Bonifacio, heard that the

Emperor Henry II wished to taste this famous preparation. "As soon as he heard of the Emperor's wish, he ordered there to be made a casket and a silver cart with two oxen, and had it brought to the Emperor, who was amazed and full of admiration."

I felt equally moved and grateful when the Sidolis presented me with a vial of this nectar, which I am now using, counting the drops, in my favorite dishes. Not surprisingly, aceto balsamico tradizionale is far from cheap at $140 a quart or more! It has to be used very sparingly, not only because of its cost but also because a few drops are all that is needed.

The recipes I have chosen are made with the ordinary balsamic vinegar. I never use it to dress a simple salad, nor indeed does any Italian I know, but you can use it for a special salad. I like it, for instance, on cauliflower florets, boiled or steamed, mixed with four parts oil, flavored with a little garlic and two anchovy fillets pounded together to a paste. Another treat is to use balsamic vinegar in a vinaigrette for avocados. Mix two tablespoons of balsamic vinegar with four tablespoons of extra-virgin olive oil, some salt and pepper, fill four avocado halves and snip four or five chives over them.

Quaglie all'aceto balsamico
ROAST QUAIL WITH BALSAMIC VINEGAR • SERVES 4

During our last visit to Italy we explored the cooking of Emilia-Romagna in some depth. The best meal we had was at a restaurant called Al Portone in Scandiano, a small town to the south of Reggio Emilia. You reach the restaurant through a medieval courtyard which, on this April evening, was beautifully floodlit. The restaurant itself is in an eighteenth-century building attached to the twelfth-century rocca, the castle that belonged to Count Matteo Maria Boiardo, lord of the provinces of Reggio Emilia and Modena and famous for his epic poem L'Orlando innamorato.

We had a delightful meal, and the evening ended in a long and stimulating conversation with the owners, Paola and Luigi La Carruba. Paola, who does most of the cooking, learned her métier from her mother-in-law, who comes from Parma but is married to a Sicilian. A better gastronomic match would be hard to find. One of the best dishes that evening was a roast guinea hen flavored with balsamic vinegar. Paola told me that she cooked pheasant and quail in the same way. She feels that balsamic vinegar gives the perfect touch of sweet-and-sour to a sauce for game, especially the smaller feathered game, even farm-raised.

Back in London I tried her creation with both guinea hen and quail—pheasants were no longer in season. I prefer the quail, partly because the guinea hens are less moist than the ones in Emilia. Quail are juicier, and because of their size they cook very quickly.

1 Heat the oven to 400°F.

2 Clean and wipe the quail and rub each with salt and pepper inside and out.

3 Heat the oil in a heavy-based pan and fry the quail over moderately high heat, turning them over on all sides. This will take no longer than 5 minutes. Add a couple of tablespoons of the stock and place the pan in the oven. Bake for 10 to 15 minutes, basting twice. Halfway through the cooking dribble 1 tablespoon of balsamic vinegar over the birds. When they are cooked, transfer to a heated dish and keep warm.

4 Deglaze the pan with the remaining vinegar and then add a couple of tablespoons of stock. Bring slowly to the boil and boil for 1 or 2 minutes.

5 Cut up the butter and add it little by little to the sauce, stirring constantly. Taste and check salt and pepper. As soon as the butter has melted spoon a little over the quail and serve the rest in a heated bowl.

✖ Serve with a little timbale of risotto (page 26), or with sautéed carrots or a puree of celery root and potato.

4 quail, fresh or defrosted (about 8 ounces each)

salt

pepper

3 tablespoons olive oil

½ cup strong homemade meat stock (page 3)

3 tablespoons balsamic vinegar

2 tablespoons unsalted butter

Filetto di maiale alla Cavalcanti

PORK TENDERLOIN WITH BERRIES, ALMONDS AND BALSAMIC VINEGAR •
SERVES 4

Ippolito Cavalcanti, Duca di Buonvicino, was not only a fashionable aristocrat and a great gourmet, he also wrote a very remarkable cookbook. Called *Cucina teorico-practica,* the book is a mine of information and a collection of excellent recipes, all in the spirit of the time and place—Naples at the beginning of the nineteenth century, where artists, philosophers, musicians and archeologists gathered, often over sumptuous meals. Cavalcanti stresses the importance of best-quality ingredients and the right use of spices, salt, stock, alcohol and wine. His recipes are light and inspired, and extraordinarily modern.

The following recipe is my adaptation of one of Cavalcanti's; in his recipes quantities and timings are not given. The pork is

(*continued*)

PORK TENDERLOIN WITH BERRIES, ALMONDS AND BALSAMIC VINEGAR
(*continued*)

2 **pork tenderloins (about 1¼ pounds)**
3 **tablespoons olive oil**
3 **tablespoons unsalted butter**
½ **cup red wine**
salt
pepper
4 **teaspoons sugar**
pinch of cinnamon
2½ **tablespoons balsamic vinegar**
2 **tablespoons very finely ground almonds**
4 **tablespoons elderberries *or* wild blueberries**
2 **tablespoons capers**

cooked first and then flavored with elderberries or wild blueberries, capers and almonds. The capers are the liaison in taste between the vinegar and the elderberries, while the ground almonds serve as a thickener, as they did in most antique recipes. I use balsamic vinegar because I find it has the perfect balance between sweet and sour necessary for this dish.

1 Trim the pork tenderloins of fat, then cut them across in half, if necessary, so that they will fit in a large sauté pan.

2 Heat the olive oil and half the butter in the pan and add the pork. Sauté until brown on all sides.

3 Bring the wine to the boil in a separate small pan and pour over the meat with 2 tablespoons of hot water. When the liquid has come back to the boil, add salt and pepper. Turn the heat down so that the liquid will just simmer, cover the pan tightly and cook for 20 to 30 minutes until the pork is done. Remove the meat from the pan and keep warm.

4 Add the sugar, cinnamon, vinegar, almonds, berries and capers to the pan and cook, stirring constantly, for 2 minutes. Break the remaining butter in small pieces and add gradually to the sauce while gently swirling the pan.

5 Slice the meat, not too thinly, and return to the pan for 2 minutes to absorb the flavor of the sauce. Transfer the contents of the pan to a heated oval dish and serve at once.

✖ This is a dish that needs the minimum of accompanying vegetables. I like buttered spinach, which goes very well with the sweetness and sharpness of the meat sauce. A few steamed potatoes are good too, although I prefer to serve grilled polenta, especially if I have planned the meal well in advance and have had polenta and meat stew the previous day!

✖ A lot of alternative first courses can precede this dish, as long as you remember that this is a dish of a certain style and should be announced by a primo of comparable elegance. What about Choux Pastry Gnocchi (page 141) or molded risotto (page 26)? The risotto can be prepared before you start on the meat, and the gnocchi (the dough can be made well in advance) can be boiled while the pork is cooking. If you want something you do not need to think about at the last minute, I recommend Lemon-flavored Eggplant (page 94) or any primo that you can serve cold.

Olives and Olive Oil

OLIVES

Puré di olive nere
BLACK OLIVE PUREE

Crema di mascarpone e olive verdi
MASCARPONE, OLIVE AND GRUYERE SPREAD

Pomodori ripieni di riso e olive nere
TOMATOES FILLED WITH RICE AND BLACK OLIVES

Spaghettini alla puré di olive
SPAGHETTINI WITH OLIVE PUREE, ANCHOVIES AND CAPERS

OLIVE OIL

Torta di mele
APPLE CAKE

Pizza alle sette sfoglie
PASTA CAKE

SEE ALSO

Cavolfiore strascinato con la mollica
CAULIFLOWER AND BREADCRUMBS WITH ANCHOVIES, CAPERS AND OLIVES

Fagioli all'uccelletto
DRIED BEANS WITH SAGE

Insalata di finocchio ed arancie
FENNEL AND ORANGE SALAD

Pasta e peperoni al forno
BAKED PASTA AND GRILLED PEPPERS

Peperoni alla siciliana
GRILLED PEPPERS WITH ANCHOVIES, OLIVES AND CAPERS

Peperoni e patate in padella
SAUTEED PEPPERS AND POTATOES

Tonno alla calabrese
TUNA BAKED WITH TOMATOES, CAPERS, BLACK OLIVES AND CHILIES

Torta salata di ricotta
RICOTTA, BASIL AND OLIVE TART

Olives

Olives, green, black or purple, are a quintessential part of the Italian scene. Although a great proportion of them finish up in the frantoio—the press where they are crushed to make oil—there are many recipes that make use of olives, whether in sauces or in salads, stuffed, or even stuffed and coated with egg and breadcrumbs and fried.

The Ligurians are so fond of their very small, purply black olives that they eat them fresh, before being cured, even though they are very bitter. Usually, however, olives are eaten preserved. The earliest known recipe for preserving olives was written by Colunella, a botanist who lived in the first century A.D. He said, "Scald and drain olives and then place them in a layer in an amphora, covered with a layer of dry salt and a final layer of herbs." Today, methods of preserving vary widely, from those of the large industrial concern to those of the family, which often remain a secret. These latter are the olives with the faintly bitter yet very refreshing taste that appear in trattorias in the countryside. They are preserved in brine containing wild fennel, oregano, other local herbs, chili and garlic. In Umbria, orange peel and bay leaves are added too.

Broadly speaking, I would say that the green olive, with its young, exciting taste is better with rabbit, chicken and lamb, while the darker and richer flavor of the black olive combines better with vegetables or fish. I like to buy olives by the pound from Greek or Italian shops. I keep them in jars layered with slivered garlic, chili and oregano and covered with oil. They are handy to serve with drinks or to nibble while cooking.

Puré di olive nere

BLACK OLIVE PUREE • MAKES 1½ CUPS

This puree is excellent spread on crostini—squares of bread moistened with a little olive oil and toasted in a hot oven for about eight minutes. It is very easy to make. The only thing you need besides olives is extra-virgin olive oil. It is much nicer than the store-bought puree which, like tapenade, contains other ingredients. If you make your own puree you can add capers, anchovies, garlic, herbs and so on later, according to the way in which you want to use the puree.

The proportion I use is 5 tablespoons of olive oil to 1 pound of loose black olives. Pit the olives and put them in the food processor. Process the olives while pouring the oil through the funnel. I prefer a coarse puree, but this is a matter of taste.

Crema di mascarpone e olive verdi

MASCARPONE, OLIVE AND GRUYERE SPREAD • MAKES 1½ CUPS

Green olives give this spread a characteristic Mediterranean flavor, while the gruyère adds a touch of nuttiness. The friend who gave me the recipe serves this cream spread on canapés with drinks. I have also used it for dressing tagliatelle by diluting the mixture with a cupful of the cooking water. I like to serve tagliatelle dressed with this sauce together with Tagliatelle with Mascarpone (page 146) at the same meal. The two complement each other very successfully. If you use this crema as a sauce for pasta, bring a bowl of parmesan to the table and a little pitcher with more of the pasta cooking water (see the last paragraph of the recipe for Tagliatelle with Mascarpone on page 146).

You can buy green olives already pitted. They are sometimes flavored with garlic and oregano, which go well with the other flavors in the spread. Do not buy stuffed green olives or the ones that are canned or vacuum-packed.

Put ¼ pound pitted sweet green olives (⅔ cup) and ¼ pound gruyère, cut into pieces, in a food processor and process until smooth. Add ⅔ cup of mascarpone and process until the spread is homogenized. Transfer to a bowl and add cayenne pepper to taste. Be careful, not too much, or it will kill the other flavors.

Pomodori ripieni di riso e olive nere

TOMATOES FILLED WITH RICE AND BLACK OLIVES • SERVES 4

In these stuffed tomatoes, the sweet black olives give a fruity taste to plain boiled rice. The rice and olives should be mixed at least six hours in advance, so that the rice has time to absorb the flavor of the olives.

⅔ cup long-grain rice
salt
1 cup black olives
freshly ground black pepper
3 tablespoons extra-virgin olive oil
4 beefsteak tomatoes
12 fresh basil leaves *or* ½ cup fresh parsley

1 Steam or boil the rice in salted water, keeping it very *al dente:* cold rice is better this way. Drain if necessary and rinse under cold water. Spread the rice out to dry thoroughly on a dish or tray lined with paper towels.

2 Meanwhile pit and chop the olives. Put them in a bowl and add the rice, the pepper and the oil. Mix well and leave for at least 6 hours. Do not refrigerate.

(continued)

TOMATOES FILLED WITH RICE AND BLACK OLIVES (*continued*)

3 Wash the tomatoes and cut them in half. Remove and discard the seeds with a pointed teaspoon and squeeze out the juice. Scoop out the pulp using the same spoon. Chop the pulp and add to the rice.

4 Sprinkle the insides of the tomatoes with a little salt and place them upside down on a board to drain for at least 30 minutes.

5 Dry the inside of the tomatoes with paper towels. Check the seasoning of the rice mixture and then fill each tomato half with some.

6 Tear the basil leaves into small pieces, or chop the parsley, and sprinkle on top. Serve at once.

This is a perfect primo to any summer lunch. It would also be an attractive side dish for a buffet party, but for such an occasion it would be better to buy small cherry tomatoes, so that your guests can eat them without using a knife. Cherry tomatoes stuffed in this way are also suitable for serving with drinks.

Spaghettini alla puré di olive

SPAGHETTINI WITH OLIVE PUREE, ANCHOVIES AND CAPERS • SERVES 4

We had this pasta at the delightful O'Parrucchiano restaurant in Sorrento. This restaurant is one of the few remaining delights in a town that has been taken over by mass tourism. The sauce takes no longer to prepare than the pasta takes to cook.

- 1 tablespoon capers
- salt
- 3/4 pound spaghettini
- 1/2 cup dry white wine
- 5 tablespoons extra-virgin olive oil
- 4 garlic cloves, peeled
- 2 dried chilies
- 6 anchovy fillets
- 1 cup chopped fresh parsley
- 2 tablespoons Black Olive Puree (page 230)

1 Put the capers in a bowl of warm water and let stand, to get rid of the vinegar.

2 Heat a large pot of water with 1½ tablespoons of salt and, when boiling, cook the spaghettini in the usual way, or follow the Agnesi method described on page 8.

3 Bring the wine to the boil and simmer while you prepare the rest of the sauce.

4 Heat the oil in a large frying pan. Bruise the garlic and add to the oil together with the chilies.

5 Chop the anchovy fillets and the parsley and add to the frying pan. Cook over very gentle heat while mashing the anchovies to a paste.

6 Drain and dry the capers and add with the olive puree and the wine. Continue cooking very gently until the pasta is ready. Remove and discard the garlic and chilies.

7 When the pasta is cooked, add 3 or 4 tablespoons of the pasta water to the sauce. Drain the pasta either through a colander, or by lifting it out with a spaghetti lifter or with two wooden forks. Add the spaghettini to the sauce and stir-fry for 1 minute or so. Serve immediately from the pan.

✗ This highly appetizing dish is definitely a primo. It could be followed by a number of different secondi, but they should be robust, with a touch of earthiness. Red Mullet en Papillote (page 60) or Grilled Pepper and Monkfish Bundles (page 108) would be my choice. If you do not want to serve fish, choose Rabbit with Herbs and Dried Porcini (page 132) or, for a meatless meal, Crespelle with Mozzarella and Tomato Sauce (page 115).

Olive Oil

The olive is the fruit of the Olea europaea, also known as the cultivated olive tree; it is a descendant of the Olea oleaster, the prickly wild bush that grows around the Mediterranean. Olive trees have been cultivated in the Mediterranean basin since the third millennium before Christ, and in the sixth and fifth centuries B.C. the Greeks found olive wood so beautiful that they used it for carving statues of their gods and goddesses. To any Christian the graceful and silvery beauty of the olive tree brings to mind the sorrow of Christ in the garden of Gethsemane, a scene depicted by so many of the greatest painters.

The fruit of this ancient tree produces the oil that has always played such a large part in the lives of Mediterranean people. Kings and priests have been anointed with olive oil; Roman athletes oiled themselves with it to make their muscles supple; and noble ladies used it to keep their skin soft and fresh. Above all, however, olive oil was used extensively in cooking and as a dressing on food. The Romans even poured olive oil on their breakfast cereal, which was a kind of polenta.

Today, for those who love the Mediterranean, olive trees are often a reminder of Italian holidays, of walking in the Ligurian hills, of driving along the winding roads of Chianti or past the groves of huge olive trees in Apulia. And these are, indeed, the three regions whose olive oil is the most generally acclaimed. Generally, but not universally, since olive trees grow in all the regions of Italy except Piedmont and Valle d'Aosta, and many regions have their champions who will insist that their oil is the best. In fact there is excellent oil from around Viterbo in Latium, from Umbria and from Lake Garda, the latter being the most northerly area where olive trees grow.

As the fruit must be ripe before it is crushed, there is a considerable variation in the harvesting time between the north and the south. When I was in the Cilento, south of Naples, in late September 1987, the nets were already laid out on the ground ready to collect the olives when the trees were shaken, but in Chianti the olives are harvested in late October. The best oil is made within one week of the harvest, and the process takes place without any use of heat or chemicals. Olive oil is pure olive juice.

There are six grades of olive oil: first cold-pressed extra-virgin olive oil, with a maximum acidity of one percent; superfine virgin olive oil, with acidity up to one and a half percent; fine virgin olive oil, with acidity up to three percent; virgin olive oil, with acidity up to three and a half percent and pure olive oil, which is a blend of virgin olive oil and refined residue. Three of these grades are widely available in the United States, pure olive oil, virgin olive oil and extra-virgin olive oil. My advice is to buy extra-virgin olive oil; it costs a little more, but you are sure of a reliable product. In specialty stores you can also sometimes buy bottles of estate oil. This is oil that comes entirely from the olives of a single estate, olives that are usually picked by hand and pressed within two days. The price of a bottle of an estate oil is high, yet not excessive when compared to a bottle of wine that is finished at one sitting.

THE USES OF OLIVE OIL. The main use of olive oil is in salads. In Italy the word insalata (salad) implies raw or cooked vegetables, always dressed and mostly with olive oil, wine vinegar or lemon juice and salt. The other oils are never used in traditional Italian salads. Walnut oil sometimes makes brief appearances in some nuova cucina salads, but I doubt if the chauvinistic Italians will ever take to it, even in a special dish.

It is interesting to note that in the past walnut oil was used in northern Italy by the poor who could not afford the more expensive olive oil. Manzoni mentions this in *I Promessi sposi*, his novel set in seventeenth-century Lombardy. There were many walnut trees of majestic beauty in Lombardy, and walnut oil was cheap. With the economic miracle of the late 1940s walnut trees came to be seen in a new light, not as a source of cheap and rather poorly regarded oil, but as the provider of a most valuable and highly regarded timber; the wood was ideal for the manufacture of massive pieces of furniture in the factories of Brianza. So the walnut trees were felled, and now walnut oil has become very expensive and is seen as an exotic product.

Olive oil is also widely used as a cooking fat. It has always been the condiment and cooking fat of central and southern Italy, but it is only since the last war that it has broken through the so-called butter line, which ran across Italy between Emilia-Romagna and Tuscany. The final victory of olive oil over butter came with the drive for healthy eating. Olive oil contains mono-unsaturated fatty acids, and an adequate proportion of polyunsaturated fatty acids. It is also a fat with a high critical, or smoking, point, above which toxic substances are formed. Contrary to what is sometimes said, this characteristic of olive oil makes it a good frying oil. The ideal temperature of the oil or fat for deep-frying is 350°F. and the smoking point of olive oil is 410°F.; only peanut oil has a higher smoking point. The only snag about using olive oil for deep-frying is its cost, but the extra price is worth paying. Indeed, the secret of the excellence of the best Italian fritti is that the oil used is olive oil. Moreover it is olive oil that has not been used before; it is thrown away after each use, and not recycled.

I must finally mention one of the best uses of olive oil, which the Tuscans have taught us, the battesimo dell'olio—christening with oil. One, two or more tablespoons of the best olive oil are added to some dishes after they have been cooked, usually at the table. The Tuscans add oil in this way to la ribollita (a bean and cabbage soup), and to their Dried Beans with Sage (page 40), to name but two. I add it also to my Bread Soup (page 43) and to most zuppe of chickpeas or beans.

Torta di mele

APPLE CAKE • SERVES 8 TO 10

This is an apple cake with a difference: the fat used is olive oil. It is good either for tea or as a dessert, with a bowl of softly whipped cream. The cake is better eaten the day after being cooked, when the flavors have had time to combine and develop. Scrub the lemon thoroughly before you grate it to get rid of the pesticides.

1 Soak the raisins in warm water for 20 minutes or so.

2 Preheat the oven to 350°F.

3 Pour the oil into a bowl, add the sugar and beat until the sugar and oil become homogenized. Add the eggs, one at a time and beat until the mixture has grown in volume and looks like a thin mayonnaise.

4 Sift together the flour, cinnamon, baking soda, cream of tartar and salt. Add gradually to the oil and sugar mixture, folding in with a metal spoon. Mix thoroughly and then add the apples and the lemon rind.

5 Drain and dry the raisins and add to the mixture. Mix very thoroughly. The mixture will be stiff, with the appearance of pieces of apple and raisins coated with cake mixture.

6 Butter and flour an 8-inch springform pan. Spoon the mixture into the pan and bake for at least 1 hour, until a toothpick inserted in the middle of the cake comes out dry.

7 Remove the cake from the pan and cool on a wire rack.

¾ cup golden raisins

⅔ cup olive oil

1 cup sugar

2 eggs

2⅓ cups all-purpose flour

1 teaspoon cinnamon

1½ teaspoons baking soda

½ teaspoon cream of tartar

½ teaspoon salt

1 pound tart and firm apples, such as Granny Smiths, peeled and cut into small cubes

grated rind of 1 lemon

✄ A similar cake can be made using pears instead of apples, in which case you must substitute almonds for the raisins. If you like chocolate with pears, replace 2 tablespoons of the flour with 2 tablespoons unsweetened cocoa powder, and add an extra 2 tablespoons of sugar to compensate for the bitterness of the cocoa. It too is a good cake, although since chocolate is not one of my favorite flavorings, I prefer the apple version.

Pizza alle sette sfoglie

PASTA CAKE • SERVES 10 TO 12

I first made this oil-based cake from the province of Foggia, in Apulia, under the strict supervision of Angela, my mother's cleaning woman. Like all southerners, Angela is very generous with her recipes and tips, and with things she has made, but also like all southerners she has a deep distrust of other people's food and recipes, especially if they are new to her. She often brings me dried tomatoes, homemade *orecchiette* (pasta made with durum flour), grape preserves, and all sorts of other goodies, but she has never asked me for one of my recipes, nor ever tasted any of the things I make. She comes into the kitchen and asks, "Signora Anna, what are you making?" She watches me with a mixture of interest and suspicion, declares "Noi non lo facciamo cosi" (we don't make it like that) and off she goes.

Angela's cake has a mixture of unexpected and exotic flavors that conjure up an image of huge dining halls with monks sitting round refectory tables enjoying the delicious puddings, cakes and cookies sent by the nuns in the nearby convent. I think that of all the preparations I have made, it is the nearest to medieval cooking. This in spite of the use of sugar! I have tried to replace it with honey in the pasta, but it did not work. I expect that in the days before sugar, the pasta was unsweetened and the sugar in the filling replaced by honey.

This cake is called a pizza because in southern Italy the word is applied to old-fashioned cakes or tarts, whether savory or sweet. The sette sfoglie refers to the seven layers of sfoglia (strips of pasta) on which the cake is based. In Apulia this is the traditional Christmas cake, which is made two or three months in advance so that it can mature, just like an English Christmas cake or fruit cake. Here is Angela's recipe.

2 ounces unsweetened chocolate
¼ cup raisins
¼ cup currants
2 cups candied peel (about ½ pound)
2 pieces of preserved ginger
1 tablespoon orange flower water
1 tablespoon rose water

PASTA

2 cups all-purpose flour
salt
⅓ cup sugar
2 eggs
2 tablespoons dry marsala *or* sherry

———

1 cup olive oil
1 cup damson plum jam *or* other sharp homemade jam

1 Soak the apricots and the golden raisins in the rum.

2 Plunge the almonds and the walnuts into boiling water and boil for 30 seconds. Drain and peel. The almond skin will come away easily, but the walnuts are fiddly to peel and will take time and patience. The skin is very bitter, so remove as much of it as you can. If, when you remove the skin, you notice any walnuts with a darker color and a thick, oily texture, discard them—they are old and rancid. .

3 Put the hazelnuts in a heavy frying pan (a cast-iron pan is ideal) and toast them over high heat, shaking the pan frequently. Remove the nuts from the pan and, if you are using unpeeled nuts, rub them in your hands as soon as they

are cool enough to handle. Blow off the paper-thin skin, a job best done over the sink or in the yard.

4 Toast the almonds in the same way until pale gold.

5 Put all the nuts in the workbowl of a food processor and chop finely. Transfer to a bowl and add the cloves, pepper, ginger and cinnamon.

6 Grate the chocolate and add to the nut mixture. Mix thoroughly and set aside.

7 Cut the soaked apricots into strips and put in a second bowl with all the raisins, the rum and the currants.

8 Cut the candied peel and the preserved ginger into small pieces and add to the second bowl. Mix in the orange flower water and the rose water and stir everything together. Set aside.

9 You are now ready to make the pasta. Put the flour, a pinch of salt and the sugar in the food processor. Turn the machine on and drop the eggs through the funnel one by one. Pour the marsala through the funnel and process until the dough has formed a ball. As always when giving instructions for making pasta (or pastry, for that matter), it is difficult to give the precise quantities of flour and liquid. If the dough does not form a ball, add a little cold water. If, on the other hand, you find the dough too sticky, transfer it to a work surface and add a little flour.

10 Roll out the dough through the pasta machine, stopping at the next-to-the-last notch, as directed on page 9. Alternatively, roll it out by hand as thin as you can.

11 Preheat the oven to 325°F.

12 Line a 9 x 7-inch metal lasagne dish with foil. Brush the foil all over with olive oil and cover with a layer of pasta. Do not let it overlap. (It is much easier to cut it with scissors than with a knife.) Drizzle with some olive oil. Sprinkle on a tablespoon or so of the spice and nut mixture, and then dot here and there with some of the dried fruit mixture and blobs of jam. Cover with another layer of pasta strips, dribble with olive oil, sprinkle with spices and nuts and dot with fruits and jam. These are the layers that you build up, finishing with pasta strips. Brush all the surface well with olive oil. You may only get 6 layers of pasta, it all depends on how successful you are at using the cut-up pieces. Don't worry, the cake is also very good with 6 layers. Cover with a piece of foil and tuck the foil under the rim of the dish. Bake for 1½ hours. (This is one of the very few dishes I know in which the pasta is baked without being boiled first). Test if it is ready by inserting the point of a knife in the middle of the cake: the

FILLING

- 12 unsulfured dried apricots
- ⅓ cup golden raisins
- 6 tablespoons rum
- scant ½ cup almonds
- heaping ⅓ cup walnuts
- heaping ⅓ cup hazelnuts
- ½ teaspoon ground cloves
- ¼ teaspoon ground white pepper
- ½ teaspoon ground ginger
- 1 teaspoon powdered cinnamon

NOTE: Although this cake can be eaten after 2 or 3 days, it is better to leave it to mature for at least a month, wrapped in foil in a cake tin, like fruit cake or Christmas pudding.

pasta should not offer any resistance.

13 Leave the cake to cool. Remove the foil from the top. Place a large piece of foil on a wooden board, place the board over the pan and turn the pan upside down. The cake will fall onto the board. Remove the old foil and wrap the cake in the new sheet of foil to store.

· ·

INDEX